I0792906

California Dreaming

INTERSECTIONS

Asian and Pacific American Transcultural Studies

RUSSELL C. LEONG
DAVID K. YOO
Series Editors

California Dreaming

Movement and Place in the Asian American Imaginary

Edited by

Christine Bacareza Balance
Lucy Mae San Pablo Burns

University of Hawai‘i Press
HONOLULU
In association with
UCLA Asian American Studies Center
LOS ANGELES

Paperback edition 2021

Printed in the United States of America

26 25 24 23 22 21 6 5 4 3 2 1

Library of Congress Cataloging-in-Publication Data

Names: Balance, Christine Bacareza, editor. | Burns, Lucy Mae San Pablo, editor.
Title: California dreaming : movement and place in the Asian American imaginary / edited by Christine Bacareza Balance, Lucy Mae San Pablo Burns.
Other titles: Intersections (Honolulu, Hawaii)
Description: Honolulu : University of Hawai'i Press ; Los Angeles : in association with UCLA Asian American Studies Center, 2020. | Series: Intersections: Asian and Pacific American transcultural studies | Includes bibliographical references.
Identifiers: LCCN 2020022874 | ISBN 9780824872069 (cloth) | ISBN 9780824883546 (pdf) | ISBN 9780824883553 (epub) | ISBN 9780824883560 (kindle edition)
Subjects: LCSH: American literature—Asian American authors. | American literature—21st century. | California—In literature.
Classification: LCC PS508.A8 C35 2020 | DDC 810.9/895073—dc2 3
LC record available at https://lccn.loc.gov/2020022874

ISBN 978-0-8248-8976-0 (pbk.)

Partial support provided by the Arthur C. and Molly Phelps Bean Faculty Fellowship in Performing & Media Arts (Cornell University).

Cover art: *Rapture* by Gina Osterloh from *Somewhere Tropical* series (2006). Courtesy of the artist.

University of Hawai'i Press books are printed on acid-free paper and meet the guidelines for permanence and durability of the Council on Library Resources.

Contents

1. *California Dreaming*: An Introduction 1
Christine Bacareza Balance

2. Sensual Labor of Claiming Place 17
Nayan Shah

3. Bohulano Family *Binangkal* 29
Dawn Bohulano Mabalon

4. 100 Tiki Notes 35
Dan Taulapapa McMullin

5. Cambodian Classical Dance: Unsettlement, Authenticity, Affect, and Exclusion 45
Tiffany Lytle

6. Lao Fighters/*Refugee Nation* 54
Leilani Chan and Ova Saopeng (TeAda Productions)

7. 21 Reasons Why This Movie Sucks 68
Prince Gomolvilas

8. From the Island of Berkeley: Hawaiian Belonging in California 74
Kevin Fellezs

9. Somewhere Tropical 87
Gina Osterloh

10. Dreamers: A Dialogue on Education Rights and the Movement for Undocumented Migrants 93
Raymundo M. Hernandez-Lopez and Tracy Lachica Buenavista

11. Claiming Malibu: Indian Diasporic Dancing Bodies Aligning Geographies across Time and Space 101
Priya Srinivasan

12. Oh, Angelita Garcia! 110
Jason Magabo Perez

13. Moving Tradition: Alleluia Panis and Kularts 124
Joyce Lu

14. Tips for Bus Riding in Los Angeles (excerpted from *Going Green the Wong Way*) 134
Kristina Wong

15. Reels 142
Larry Padua

16. Vacuuming Dreams 150
Lucy MSP Burns

17. L.A. Dreaming in Taipei 155
SanSan Kwan

18. Poems 166
Mai Der Vang

19. "Parents' Fairytale": *Excerpt from* Self (The Remix) 170
Robert Farid Karimi

20. Traveling Subjects and the Subject of Travel in Vietnamese Diasporic Films 187
Lan Duong

21. Photographs from Live and Online Performances 200
Philip Huang

22. Abstraction 2: Television Sitcom from *DentalOptics* 205
Karen Tei Yamashita

23. Generations Within: Los Angeles 1992 and South Korean 8008 220
Yong Soon Min

24. Golden States of Mind: Cambodian and Vietnamese Artistic Organizing in Southern California and Southeast Asia 236
Việt Lê

25. Excerpts from *D'FunQT* 252
D'Lo

26. Of Railroads, Camps, and Strip Malls: Symbolic Landscapes of the San Gabriel Valley 261
Wendy Cheng

27. Where You've Been: An Epilogue 280
Lucy MSP Burns

Bibliography 293
Contributors 303

Chapter 1

California Dreaming

An Introduction

Christine Bacareza Balance

Since 1893, the "frontier mentality" has overwhelmingly figured our visions of the American West. In his canonical essay "The Significance of the Frontier in American History," Frederick Jackson Turner argued that the frontier was a place where an essential American character was forged. This character, the rugged individual who conquers the elements of an unforgiving landscape and an otherwise lawless society, was predicated upon and helped further a mindset of human superiority. Turner argued that, rather than being affected by the presence and actions of humans, nature simply functioned as provider of unlimited resources. Rather than regard Native peoples, already living in the West, as equals, the frontier individual viewed them as another aspect of the natural landscape to be tamed.

Yet, the frontier mentality also informed much of the U.S. exceptionalist discourse that fueled the nation's empire-building project overseas—the moral and ethical need to civilize and tame the wilderness and its primitive inhabitants, vis-à-vis an "Edenic discourse," the desire of U.S. business and government to tap natural resources in systemic ways otherwise unrealized by locals and/or previous settlers. Military and colonial tactics used in seizing and settling Native lands in the western United States were also used in the seizure and settling of lands in the Pacific and Caribbean. Frontier states, like California, provided the training grounds for U.S. war and empire overseas. Many parts of the Golden State, most notably Fort Mason in San Francisco, served as the training grounds and last points of departure for soldiers shipped off to war in the Philippines and other parts of Asia.

At the end of the twentieth century, almost one hundred years after Turner's writing, Asian American studies scholars tuned into these intertwined local and global histories. By doing so, they recalled the origins of Asian American Studies as operating within both a domestic context *and* a transnational imaginary.[1] In turn, they argued for undoing the notion of the U.S. as the sole driver of historical change. Such critical attention to the field's broader internationalist dimensions, as Oscar Campomanes has argued, "disallows the domestication of Asian American Studies in the double sense of having it parochialized and, to borrow Robert Lee's word, 'defanged.'"[2]

Within the frontier imaginary, California promised a land of opportunity for all people. But the length and extent of that opportunity depended much upon one's legal status, ability to own property, and capability of laying claim to the fruits of one's labor. As it operates within Asian American studies scholarship, the frontier mentality also calls to mind histories of those first waves of male migrant laborers—Chinese railroad workers, Filipino stoop laborers, and Sikh farm workers. As much as the untouched land was there for humans to toil upon, it was capital and companies who hired the men to do such work.

For an Asian American studies that "subsists on a particular narrative of immigration and assimilation," Campomanes argues, "California looms large as a mythical destination and a congeries of settlements." Which "particular narrative" we reference, however, is crucial, for one particular narrative of immigration and assimilation actually depends upon a type of disassociation from or counter-identification with such "congeries of 'settlements.'"[3] That is to say, an assimilated Asian American would not necessarily seek out sites of Asian/Asian American dominance or hypervisibility. Other narratives of Asian American assimilation—especially ones predicated upon melting-pot multiculturalism—actually turn and return to places such as California and Hawai'i as ostensible meccas for Asian American-ness, an identity category coded as somehow already politically resistant and identity affirming. As Stephen Aron writes, frontier mentality was figured by Turner as "the meeting point between (Indian) savagery and (European) civilization" (Turner, 1994a), while more recent scholarship has recast frontier in more neutral terms as the meeting point between indigenous and intrusive societies."[4] Within this logic, even Asian Americans can function as settler colonists.

For certain scholars, frontierism also invokes a field logic of California's dominance, one predicated upon the notion that, "fundamentally, where the communities are, Asian American studies ought to bloom."[5] With its overwhelming number of Asian Americans, a fact somehow signifying various forms of diversity (ethnic, generational, economic) simply by demographic presence, California has been figured as the frontier (or perhaps more fittingly the "haven") of Asian American culture and, by extension, of Asian American studies. In this logic, California serves as a place of possibility and site of opportunity as well as an upper limit of achievement. This frontierist logic of California's dominance has also depended upon certain historical and institutional claims—the ways in which it has functioned as the fount of the field's origin stories, people, and places; the longevity and spread of established Asian American studies departments and programs within higher education (and even at the secondary and elementary school levels); and these departments and programs' proximity to historical sites and contemporary communities. Due to these temporal and geographical reasons, many have argued that Asian American studies in California, unwittingly or not, has set "the terms of reference," the political and intellectual norms, for "East of California" Asian American studies and its assertions.

Operating within this same logic, some critics argue that California-based studies fail to reach or reference beyond the state's geographical boundaries and cultural particularities. According to these critics, California-based Asian American scholars and studies tend toward the local, seemingly unable to emplace themselves within larger frameworks of understanding—the regional, the national, and the transnational, for example—and therefore continuing hegemony through provincialism. If this were perhaps true, they would not be the only ones, as the emerging field of place-based Asian American scholarship and anthologies reveals. I would argue, however, that, acutely aware of the state's intellectual and historical place within the field, California-based Asian American scholars and artists often work hard to imagine and sense their state differently. In turn, these tropes and models of "California dominance" have not only stifled our ways of thinking about the field of Asian American studies and the places of Asian American California. They have also desensitized us from the work of emplacement done by California-based Asian American scholars and artists. These two concerns drive this current anthology and what it intends to address.

This introduction starts by outlining three different scalar models for approaching cultural production in Asian American California—the translocal, the regional, and the archipelagic. While the first two have gained much traction in both Asian/Asian American studies and California studies, the last one requires a more speculative disposition. While each of these models has found import in other academic fields, all of these analytics still have much to offer the interdisciplinary field of Asian American studies, especially in its studies of place and cultural production. From there, I move to consider a critical method of "landscaping," one offered by the field of cultural geography and that requires we reckon with a different understanding of place, not as fixed but as always becoming and in-motion. Finally, I close this introduction with a brief historical overview of the interconnected relationships between culture and knowledge production in Asian America, from its earliest instantiations as a social and cultural movement in the 1960s up until today. By focusing on when, where, and how knowledge and culture are produced, I want to set the stage for considering this anthology as an example of the many ways in which artistic and scholarly co-laboring has and will hopefully continue to take place.

Shifting the Scales of Asian American California

California Dreaming appeals to the different scalar models required by California-based Asian American arts and artists and the different approaches to culture and knowledge their work produces. A term borrowed from the fields of migration studies and media studies, the translocal offers Asian American studies a means for thinking through the local, national, and transnational simultaneously.[6] The translocal understands localities as networked nodes, sites linked to other locations through the cultural objects, people, and practices that circulate and move between them. It understands migration as a process that takes place within as well as across national borders. Within a translocal framework, assumed divisions between the local and transnational, ones that often take shape as romanticized visions of authenticity versus Westernization, are muddied, while the category of the nation/national is likewise included.

Within a translocal framework, the first waves of Asian immigrants were therefore not simply settlers moving in only one direction. These migrant laborers often experienced multiple departures and arrivals before arriving in U.S. cities or towns that they remained in for various periods of time. Many of these migrant workers developed into what historian Linda España-Maram has termed "portable communities," as they often traveled along a West Coast–based itinerary of seasonal jobs.[7] A translocal framework allows us to apprehend these multiple movements as both produced by and productive of the larger phenomena of wars, empire and colonization, and U.S. business.[8]

The translocal also attunes Asian American studies scholars to media and technology's role in building and maintaining relationships between people in geographically distant places. Through media forms such as social networking sites, film/TV, and popular music, immigrant and U.S.-born Asians/Asian Americans, within the U.S. and in other places around the globe, develop and maintain connections to the people and popular cultures of their "homelands" as well as those of other Asian countries. Their productive use of these technologies facilitates translocal and transnational kinship ties while also expanding the reach and accelerating the circulation of Asia's popular culture. Again, these uses signal multi-directional and translocal routes, the ways in which cultural objects and practices move with people and between places, and their impact upon places and industries in both the U.S. and Asian countries.[9]

The translocal moves us from a static notion of place to one that is attuned to the processual, the networked, the mobile, and the "on the go." These characteristics help us think differently about the now and then of Asian American California. Against a frontierist model of Asian American studies, contemporary ethnic enclaves—Koreatowns, Little Tokyo/Japantowns, Little Saigons, and Chinatowns—do not merely operate within the contexts of the local *or* national *or* transnational. Instead, as the work of Lan Duong and Wendy Cheng, within this anthology, shows us, translocal places operate simultaneously along all three axes, each a node that is part of a larger global network of sites.

A more common category within California studies, the analytic of the "regional" still warrants further exploration within Asian American cultural studies. As a literary genre, regionalist writing is characterized by its focus on characters, customs, topography, and dialects specific to a geographical region in the U.S. Unlike "local color" writing, which often looked down upon its characters, making them quaint and often stereotypical, regional writing "flesh(ed) out the communities that are being observed or written about."[10] "Regional writing's careful, thick descriptions of the rhythms of rural life and provincial communities," literary critic Stephanie Foote observes, "embodied a formal or technical commitment to fidelity."[11] Through its detailed descriptions, regional writing promised the "real" for its mainly urban readership, fulfilling both their nostalgia for the past and touristic desires for the pastoral. Mediated by narrators who visited rural regions, approaching locals with a sympathetic yet ironic distance, these stories and poems were also about figuring these urban guests and, by extension, their readers as tolerant of and yet superior to the regional inhabitant. Through its focus on the rural, regional writing signaled an attempt to construct a unified national past. "(R)egional writing," Foote points out, "gave strangers with accents literary recognition at exactly the same moment that accented strangers in the form of immigrants were clamoring for recognition and representation in the political arena."[12]

Yet, despite any attempt toward consolidating the nation, as a form that "works to preserve local customs, local accents, and local communities, regional writing is a form about the representation of difference."[13] "As this literary genre emerged during a period of massive industrialization and increased immigration due to the higher demand for labor, Asian American literary scholar Stephen Sohn writes, "the literary imaginary confront(ed) such immense national changes through varied spatial representations." Therefore, "rather than depicting a familiar, timeless, and shared agrarian past, regional writing *defamiliarizes* narratives about the origins of national identity in the United States" (italics in original) and, as Foote suggests, sets the stage for late twentieth-century Asian American literary writing. Asian American and other minority literatures precisely call into question one of regionalist writings' major claims—of unifying the nation through aesthetics and culture. That is to say, the overwhelming *presence* of Asian American literature and writers makes evident their absence in earlier regionalist writings, therefore "challeng(ing) the contention that regional representation could rehearse the multifocal and multilocal nature of American identity." In addition, Sohn also rightfully points out the critical possibilities that the regional has to offer Asian American and other minor literatures. "(I)n terms of Asian Americanist critique, an analytical consideration of region is also vital to re-opening and extending attention toward the incredibly rich geographies that should include different scalar models."[14] Here, we can think of scalar as operating in the sense of size, range, magnitude, and extent, and not merely direction (i.e., diaspora/homeland), as well as through systems of standard and comparative measurement.

In 1997, Caribbean studies philosopher Èdouard Glissant declared, "the entire world is becoming an archipelago."[15] Taking Glissant's contention seriously, we ask in what ways we might imagine even California as an archipelago or its own set of islands. More recently, Bay Area–based writer Rebecca Solnit has made a strong case for considering California through an island imaginary—though "places apart," "(islands) are not necessarily isolated." [16] While mid-sixteenth-century maps figured California as an island unto itself, Solnit suggests that it might be more apt to "imagine (California) as an archipelago off the coast of the continent—many 'islands' of distinct ecological and cultural presence or as degrees of islandness, of separateness from the mainstream." Distinguished by the Mexican border to the south, the Pacific Ocean to the west, high deserts and mountains to the east, and "world-famous wine country and an even larger shadow economy of marijuana" to the north, Solnit argues, California's cultural specificity (as the "world's eighth-largest economy" and the U.S.'s liberal-left majority) draws much from these geographical and ecological distinctions. Through this particular model, we recognize the diversity of ideas and images that arise when locals and visitors hear the word "California." It is a different way of recognizing some of the Golden State's various societal divides: northern California versus southern California; beach towns versus desert cities; L.A. versus the Bay; cities versus suburbs; to name a few.

Turning and returning to California, this present anthology's contributors and their work offer up to us readers various types of archipelagic thinking. Archipelagic thinking, of course, brings to mind those artists and artistic practices originating from and associated with the Pacific Islands. In this anthology, both Dan McMullin poetry/performance art and Kevin Fellezs's scholarly writing invoke the "islands" as places figured by both visitors and locals. In her contribution to this present collection, Gina Osterloh also gestures toward the diverse ways in which California has stood in for and connected viewers to "somewhere tropical." An archipelagic line of thinking also works more broadly through conceptions of California as composed of islands, seemingly individual regions that actually work in concert and require each other. In this anthology, we see these visions most clearly in Robert Karimi's selections from "Self: The Remix," a solo performance piece that spans the distance from the northern California suburb of Union City to The Mayan, a downtown Los Angeles dance club.

At the same time, archipelagic thinking requires that we "dislocate and deterritorialize static island tropes of particularity." That is to say, as Jonathan Pugh writes, "the key thrust of this (archipelagic) ontology is (therefore) island movements: not a simple gathering of islands, but an emphasis upon how islands act in concert."[17] How do the "islands" of California—their geographical and cultural meaning—work in tandem with each other as well as in comparison and contrast to the island of Manhattan, for example? As Lucy Burns reminds us in this collection's epilogue, the relationship between Los Angeles–based writers as well as San Francisco/Bay Area dancers/choreographers to the arts/culture capital of New York City mirrors more that of an "island to a continental mainland" than of an inter-island connectedness. That is to say, California (for Asian American studies and arts, in particular) is often figured as a "creative island unto itself," one set apart from the more established East Coast's cultural institutions and values. With this, we might return to and complicate further Campomanes and others' imaginings of California by understanding it as both frontier *and* island. By doing so, we recall the historical resonance between these two imaginaries and spaces while again complicating where cultural norms are produced.[18] To conceive of Asian America in this archipelagic fashion allows for a more expansive move toward encounters and affiliations, rather than simply adhering to differences between seemingly singular (read, isolated) regions and locations across our nation.[19]

Both within and outside of this anthology, various writers continue to think, write, and create in and alongside a plethora of landscapes—the city, the suburbs, the port, the desert, forests, and the coastline. *California Dreaming*'s entries help us to think about California's geopoetics, that is, of how its natural and man-made landscape impacts and is impacted by these artists' and scholars' ways of thinking and doing. These affects often occur through the modes of the sensorial, and their effects often manifest through a certain sensibility—visuality transformed by the quality of light; the sonic/musical and gestural altered by the architectural; kinesthesia and movement shaped by modern technology's temporalities; places of one's past and present evoked by redolent smells. As an anthology concerned with the translocal, the regional, and even the archipelagic, *California Dreaming* also makes sense of the diverse biomes, locales, and areas that make up the landscapes of Asian American California—national and municipal parks, suburban strip malls, urban bus routes, and freeways, to name a few.

Landscaping: A Performative Approach

At the end of his essay "Landscape, Land, and Identity: A Performative Consideration," cultural geographer David Crouch puts forth an idea of "spacing" that offers

> a way to rethink how and where landscape relates in life. . . . Spacing offers a way of thinking through how space is given meaning and how landscape may relate in this process. Meanings and relations constituted in performance and intersubjectively become mutually enmeshed in institutional closure; kept open, fluid.[20]

As both noun and verb, space/spacing connotes both an *act* of positioning and situating as well as a *sense* of expanse, also indexing the temporal in terms of "a period, span, duration, stretch." Whereas places, "archetypal in popular tourism literature"—such as "the site or monument to be visited, 'the vibrant city'—connote a sense of fixity and stagnation, space and spacing more easily allow us to conceptually link sites, locations, areas to *processes*." Spacing attunes us to "the intensities of landscape, however mundane, soft, or powerful, borne in and through representations that are imagined, felt, and observed." As Crouch points out, these representations

> can circulate feelings of belonging but also of detachment. To 'feel' landscape in the expressive poetics of spacing is a way to imagine one's place in the world. The individual can feel so connected with space that s/he no longer is aware, momentarily, of being (merely) human; we may *become* the event, become the landscape.[21]

In the artwork and in life itself, both the critic's and the artist's ability to *feel* landscape becomes a form of critical relationality, a method of ethical emplacement. Rather than depending upon familiar understandings of land, landscape, and artistic *objects* as inert, an idea solidified by depictions of art-making and performance as ephemeral and always "in-motion," Crouch's work asks us to take seriously "(T)he performative 'life' or vitality of the artwork."[22] His study of landscape argues that the triad of artistic objects, artists, and art-making practices functions as "co-laborers," working together to make meaning in and through an artistic work.

As broadly conceived by Crouch and other like-minded cultural geographers, landscape is "the assemblage of landforms, concrete shapes, fields, gutters, designed spaces, and serendipitous collection of things," including our own human bodies. "Situated in the expression and poetics of spacing," Crouch calls upon a critical method of landscape "constituted in a flirtatious mode: contingent, sensual, anxious, awkward."[23] Through this method, one approaches geography, artwork, and practices as forms of "becoming" rather than "being" and is able to deal with the representational and non-representational. By doing so, landscape, as critical method, reckons with the rhythms of movements, both ones remarkable and extraordinary as well as those habitual and mundane. Landscape is not the static scenery that just "pass(es) by and emerg(es) serially as in a movie" from one's "fleeting view from the car window."[24] Instead, it too constantly transfigures and changes. "(S)ites that were very familiar to (us) suddenly appear(ing) very different, as having been 'come across unawares' (quoted in Crouch/Toogood 1999)." In this current anthology, we see this most readily in SanSan Kwan's essay, which weaves together experiences of living in Taipei and in Los Angeles's San Gabriel Valley. With a method of landscape/landscaping, we "com(e) across unawares" those sites, locations, and representations otherwise figured as familiar and therefore known. In doing so, we extend the work of feminist thinkers such as Eve Sedgwick and Alexandra Vazquez, who remind us of the "reparative" and "surprise" as powerful methods of analysis.[25]

California Dreaming's contributions also ask us to remain open to surprise. They require us to go beyond the myths and popular cultural tropes of California—Malibu Barbie, Hollywood starlets, San Francisco hippies, San Diego military bases and militiamen—in order to take in the various other sides of the Golden State and its inhabitants. The pieces within this collection go beyond the typical and mythical sites of California—Laurel Canyon and the Hollywood Hills, the beaches and Lake Tahoe resorts, and the urban spaces of San Francisco and Los Angeles—and instead present and, maybe, even reintroduce us to the backyards and kitchens of the Central Valley, the strip malls of suburban Chinatowns, the bedrooms of Orange County through the stories of Asian immigrants and Asian Americans. In doing so, they demand a broadening of how we define and imagine Asian American California at the beginning of the twenty-first century. Beyond the ethnic enclaves and "congeries of settlement" invoked by the social movements of the 1960s and 1970s, Asian American California now accounts for the historic and unexpected locations where immigrant, refugee, and U.S.-born Asians and Asian Americans have established themselves over the past 50 years and for the ways in which they have shifted and shaped those places. By defamiliarizing the domestic, the local, and the everyday, this anthology also aims to broaden our understanding of where and how Asian American culture and knowledge are produced.

The Where and How of Knowledge Production

As a term of identity, "Asian American" emerged from the social, political, and cultural movements of the 1960s and 1970s, and from student and community activists, namely those based in California (and, more specifically, those involved in protests and organizing at UC Berkeley, San Francisco State University, and other places in the San Francisco/Bay Area region). University-level Asian American studies classes at UC Berkeley and SF State were first taught by community activists and artists.[26] Asian American politics thrived and took shape through cultural forms (poetry/writing, journals/anthologies, theater, music) and community arts organizations (Kearny Street Workshop, The International Hotel, Asian American Theater Company, etc.).[27] While more militant/leftist political groups marked their "cultural arms" as superfluous at best or counter-revolutionary at worst, throughout the broader Asian American political movement, cultural production(s) became sites of expression, contestation, and emerging voices and visibility. By the 1980s, however, sites of culture and cultural production were co-opted by the U.S. government, businesses/companies, and other mainstream institutions under the banner of multiculturalism. While opportunities for certain racialized artists and cultural producers expanded, overall, the terrain of minoritarian cultural production intensified as the culture wars raged on.[28]

During the late 1990s and at the turn of the twenty-first century, globalization impacted U.S.-based understandings of Asian American culture by introducing "the new Asian cool."[29] Thus, while some previous Asian American artists, activists, and scholars made strong claims for Asian America's "domesticity," the increase of global media technologies and the shift in post-1965 Asian demographics made apparent the links between the U.S. presence overseas in Asian countries and the presence of Asians in America. Now, at the beginning of the twenty-first century, Asian American cultural producers and audiences continue to grapple with how technologies of media, migration, and mobility expand, complicate, and extend our definition(s) of Asian America and its cultures.

As *California Dreaming*'s contributors show, knowledge production takes place not only at universities, theaters, galleries/museums, arts/film festivals, and gigs/venues, but also in cars and on buses, while cruising through Griffith Park, on family visits to mosques and hikes through Yosemite National Park, in our homes and online. Focusing on the locations where knowledge is produced directs our attention to the particularity of California's landscape and its own labor in the production of arts and culture. More specifically, the previous pieces help us consider how Asian America's artists touch upon, engage with, and work against and within California's various industries—agricultural, entertainment, transnational/global banking, military, national parks, prison industrial, transnational/global film and arts, and higher education. They continually work against what Lucy Burns has described as one of the "myths of California"—a Golden State of leisure and escapism, a dreamland of liberal consumption. These dreams of and desires for leisure, escape, and consumption require forms of physical labor to feed and fuel them. These dreams and desires have also helped produce new groups of laborers—those in the service-oriented and performative industries as well as those of what Richard Florida has termed a creative class.[30] By turning our attention to the "where" of knowledge production, we begin to expand our sense of "how" meaning is made and remain attuned to the politics of "who" labors and to potential acts of co-laboring still on the horizon.

Lucy and I co-organized *California Dreaming* both as a series of gatherings and as a publication, in the spirit of our own prior experiences as artists—actor/performer, dramaturge, musician, and writers—as well as artistic collaborators—events producers, grant writers, and, of course, teachers who help develop audiences through the critical skills necessary for viewing arts and culture. Because of these particular experiences on stage, in theaters and music venues, in funders' meetings and boardrooms, in both arts- and academic-based conferences, and, of course, in the classroom—it made perfect sense to us to bring artists and academics together in one room and to dialogue with each other about our work. These workshops and gatherings were not the first (nor will they be the last) times we have found ourselves in conversations involving artists, scholars, community developers, and other audience members.[31]

In this spirit, we organized this anthology's contributions through a loosely thematic flow rather than by genre. By doing so, the works of scholars and artists live alongside each other, between this collection's pages, as they do in our everyday lives. We hope to spark in readers' imaginations a reminder and an invitation to everyday processes of co-laboring, that is, the ways in which artists and scholars might (and already do) work with and strive alongside each other.[32] By calling our readers' attention to these processes, we want to ask: how might we further cultivate and innovate our ways of working and thinking together?

We, of course, recognize that artists and scholars, more often than not, labor under different systems of production and evaluation. Rather than upholding a certain "romance of community" narrative (as Miranda Joseph's work points out), actual artist–scholar collaborations bring to the fore issues of evaluation—different voices, styles, and modes; working across difference and disciplines—as well as different forms of access and privilege.[33] The perceived stability of a tenure-track professor is tempered by the reality that her position is precarious until tenure and by the real ways in which her work must be deemed legible and therefore "of value" by her institution and by academe at large throughout her entire career. The perceived freedom of the individual artist or arts-based organization is tempered by the realities of being bound, as well, to "making a living"—making art "after-hours" (from part- or full-time gigs, including adjunct teaching) and/or continually hoping to land major grants and fellowships, all in the hopes of being able to, one day, simply make a living off one's art. These themes and concerns are so roundly critiqued by performance artist Philip Huang's own short photo-essay within this collection.

But, as our personal backgrounds and the larger field of Asian American studies have shown us, there remains much radical possibility in our working alongside and with (rather than away from) each other, especially if we each remain attuned to the diverse conditions under which we labor. The political and life-changing potential of co-laboring is most notable at the level of knowledge production. Through the analytic of co-laboring, we begin to expand our ideas of how, where, and why knowledge is produced. We redirect our attention to collaborations that take place in both arts- and scholarly-based places and locations. We reconsider collaboration through and in processes of teaching and learning. We remain attuned to the crucial roles that creative practices, such as improvisation, kinesthesia, storytelling, and listening, play in even the most academic of endeavors. And we return to California again, but with a new sense of place, politics, and frontiers of possibility.

Notes

1. For more on the simultaneously domestic and transnational nature of the Asian American movement, see Daryl Maeda, *Chains of Babylon: The Rise of Asian America* (Minneapolis: University of Minnesota Press, 2009).
2. Oscar Campomanes, "New Formations of Asian American Studies and the Question of U.S. Imperialism," *positions: east asia cultural critique,* 5:2 (1997): 532.
3. Campomanes, "New Formations of Asian American Studies and the Question of U.S. Imperialism," 532.
4. Stephen Aron, "The Making of the First American West and the Unmaking of Other Realms," in *A Companion to the American West,* ed. William Deverell (Boston: Blackwell Publishing, 2004), 524.
5. Aron, "The Making of the First American West," 524.
6. For more on the translocal, see Deirdre McKay, "Translocal Circulation: Place and Subjectivity in an Extended Filipino Community," *The Asia Pacific Journal of Anthropology* 7, no. 3 (2006): 265–278, and *Music Scenes: Local, Translocal, and Virtual,* eds. Andy Bennett and Richard A. Peterson (Nashville: Vanderbilt University Press, 2004).
7. Linda España-Maram, *Creating Masculinity in Los Angeles' Little Manila: Working-Class Filipinos and Popular Culture, 1920s–1950s* (Columbia University Press, 2006).
8. For example, see the following book-length studies of Filipino labor, migration, and U.S.–Philippine relations: Catherine Ceniza Choy, *Empire of Care: Nursing and Migration in Filipino American History* (Duke University Press, 2003); Dorothy Fujita-Rony, *American Workers, Colonial Power: Philippine Seattle and the Transpacific West, 1919–1941* (UC Press, 2003); and Dawn Mabalon, *Little Manila Is in the Heart: The Making of the Filipina/o American Community in Stockton* (Duke University Press, 2014).
9. See *Global Asian American Popular Cultures,* eds. Shilpa Dave, Leilani Nishime, and Tasha Oren (New York: NYU Press, 2016); and Jung-Sun Park, "Korean American Youth and Transnational Flows of Popular Culture Across the Pacific," in *Transpop: Korea Vietnam Remix,* eds. Viet Le and Yong Soon Min (Seoul: Arko Arts Center/Arts Council Korea, 2008), 144–171.

10. Stephen Sohn, "These Desert Places: Tourism, the American West, and the Afterlife of Regionalism in Julie Otsuka's *When the Emperor Was Divine*," *MFS: Modern Fiction Studies* 55, no. 1 (2009): 163–188.
11. Stephanie Foote, *Regional Fictions: Culture & Identity in Nineteenth-Century American Literature* (University of Wisconsin Press, 2001), 5.
12. Foote, *Regional Fictions,* 5.
13. Foote, *Regional Fictions,* 4.
14. Sohn, "These Desert Places," 180–181.
15. Edouard Glissant, *Poetics of Relation* (University of Michigan Press, 1997).
16. Rebecca Solnit, "California as an Island," *BOOM: A journal of California studies* 14, no. 1 (spring 2014). Accessed July 20, 2018. http://www.boomcalifornia.com/2014/03/california-as-an-island/.
17. Jonathan Pugh, "Island Movements: Thinking with the Archipelago," *Island Studies Journal* 8, no. 1 (2013), 10.
18. Chris Friday, "Where to Draw the Line?: The Pacific, Place, and U.S. West," in *A Companion to the American West,* ed. William Deverell, (Boston: Blackwell Publishing, 2004): 271–285.
19. See the Global Arts Exchange and its working group on "Transpacific Art Circulations/Islands," as well as the work of Gaye Chan, Sean Connelly, and other Asian/Pacific American visual artists. See also Brian Russell Roberts and Michelle Ann Stephens, eds. *Archipelagic American Studies* (Duke University Press, 2017).
20. David Crouch, "Landscape, Land, and Identity: A Performative Consideration," *Spatial Practices* 13, (January 2012): 58.
21. Crouch, "Landscape, Land, and Identity," 60.
22. Crouch, "Landscape, Land, and Identity," 60.
23. Crouch, "Landscape, Land, and Identity," 48.
24. Crouch, "Landscape, Land, and Identity," 53.
25. See also Eve Sedgwick, "Paranoid Reading and Reparative Reading: Or, You're So Paranoid You Probably Think This Essay's About You," in *Touching Feeling: Affect, Pedagogy, Performativity* (Duke University Press, 2003); and Alexandra Vazquez, "Salon Philosophers: Ivy Queen and Surprise Guests Take Reggaeton Aside," in *Reggaeton,* Deborah Pacini-Hernandez, Wayne Marshall, and Raquel Z. Rivera, eds. (Duke University Press, 2009), 300–311.
26. *Roots: an Asian American Reader,* Amy Tachiki, Eddie Wong, Franklin Odo, and Buck Wong, eds. (UCLA: Asian American Studies Center, 1971).
27. See William Wei, *The Asian American Movement* (Temple University Press, 1993).
28. See Jeff Chang, *Who We Be: A Cultural History of Race in Post-Civil Rights America* (St. Martin's Press, 2014).

29. See Mimi Nguyen and Thuy Linh Tu, introduction to *Alien Encounters: Popular Culture in Asian America*, eds. Mimi Nguyen and Thuy Linh Tu (Durham: Duke University Press, 2007), 1–32.
30. Richard Florida, *The Rise of the Creative Class: And How It's Transforming Work, Leisure, and Everyday Life* (Perseus Book Group, 2002).
31. For example, in Spring 2005, this anthology's co-editors, along with Alleluia Panis (KulArts), Joel Barraquiel Tan (formerly of Yerba Buena Center for the Arts), Bernadette Sy (Filipino American Development Foundation/Bayanihan Center), and Olivia Malabuyo Tablante (Gerbode Foundation), co-organized "Puro Arte," a one-day gathering of San Francisco/Bay Area artists, scholars, and community development organizers.
32. For more on co-laboring and artistic collaboration, see Danielle Goldman, *I Want to Be Ready!: Improvised Dance as a Practice of Freedom* (University of Michigan, 2010).
33. Miranda Joseph, *Against the Romance of Community* (University of Minnesota Press, 2002).

Chapter 2

Sensual Labor of Claiming Place

Nayan Shah

The rugged and monumental California landscape circulates globally in popular and artistic imaginaries through photography, visual culture, and tourism. Yosemite Valley, the Monterey Coastline, and Death Valley are at once sublime wonders and approachable "wilderness." The physical and mental journey, artistic labor, and the strategies of visual aesthetics situate human presence and consciousness in the monumental landscape. The global circulation of images contributed by the reproduction of visual art and vernacular photography created new transnational icons and also made the physical landscape a marvelous and aspirational dreamscape for people around the globe.

The questions of who belongs in this landscape and to whom (collectively) this landscape belongs have erupted frequently across the years. In the twentieth century, ideologies of the settler colonial nations of the United States and Canada differentiated human interaction and attachment with the landscape in ways that heightened the belonging of Indigenous people's spiritual claims and white settlers' conquest, development, and property claims. Chicano/a legacies of spiritual and conquest claims are frequently invoked and displaced by these prioritized national claims. However, people whose origins are in Asia and Africa are often absented, recognized only as foreign and at best a misplaced curiosity in the North American western landscape. These assumptions and claims suture and displace narratives of national and sovereign claims.

To turn the question around is to ask: How do diverse people resonate and contend with a particular land and topography? What is the nature of the connection to a particular land and topography? How are claims for connection, expressive belonging, even adversarial intimacy and transcendental awe, made manifest? Do a person's history and origins impact one's aesthetic of, engagement with, and ethics of relating to rock, water, flora, and fauna? Does a capitalist understanding of "nature" that can be organized, managed, owned, and exchanged prevail over other understandings of the spiritual, the social, or the political? Does any of the value that accrues to these ideas of human difference (race, ethnicity, national identity, gender, age, class) necessarily matter? Even when there are claims of individual humanity and universal appeal, are there assumptions of human character that guide this consciousness? Are the spaces transformative of aesthetics or ethics, or do they reflect preconceived worldviews? Are these worldviews already mediated by the anticipation created by the circulation of images and meaning-making of visual representations both in photographs themselves and in the magazines, books, albums, slide shows, and postcards upon which they travel?

These questions emerge out of my reflections over the confluence of two intensive streams of engagement and creativity. The first relates to my parents' love affair with the national parks and the vernacular photography that documents their experiences and journey. The second is my experience of seeing the paintings, block prints, and photography of early twentieth-century Japanese American and Chinese American artists that have over the past two decades been collected, exhibited, and reframed in the curatorial practices of California art institutions.

Into the Western Landscape

Nearly thirty years ago, the artist and writer Shani Mootoo expressed astonishment that my parents, by then in their late fifties, took a six-week trip in a rented minivan to visit national parks in the Mountain West.[1] My mother and father removed the back seat from the van, left it in a friend's garage in Salt Lake City, and drove into the wild blue yonder. They were eager to visit Yellowstone and the Tetons and make it to every national park and monument from Glacier National Park on the Montana/British Columbia border to the Grand Canyon's northern rim in Arizona. Shani is an avid hiker in the Canadian Rockies and found kinship in my parents' desire to commune with the wilderness, or at least the wilderness framed by the National Park Service.

My parents' car camping adventure resuscitated an enthusiasm they had carried forward from decades past. Since their arrival as students at Syracuse University in the late 1950s, my parents have nurtured a passion for claiming an aesthetic and spiritual relationship to the North American landscape and have since the very beginning been awestruck by and eager to visit monumental topographies. When the Syracuse newspaper reported on my parents' wedding in the university chapel in November 1959, my father lamented that my mother's visa prohibited them from enjoying their honeymoon at Niagara Falls; instead, they had to make do with Rochester, New York.

The weekend after they bought their first car, a Rambler Classic, in 1963, they hit the road out of Washington, DC, to Niagara Falls. They drove the car to the Badlands, Yellowstone, and the Grand Tetons.

Over the decades, they have traveled the length and breadth of North America, their AAA maps marked by routes that took them to various national parks. They have ambled, hiked, photographed, and car camped across the United States and Canada. My mom will tell anyone the story of how, in 100-degree heat in August, she was trying to wrangle an eager two-year-old toddler (me) from the precipice of the Grand Canyon while holding my infant brother in her arms, while my Dad framed his perfect shot of his family. Needless to say, my parents have been infinitely happier to experience the sublime beauty without their sons, whether as infants or cantankerous teenagers. It is only as much older adults that my brother and I have appreciated the national park trekking that my parents do. Their experiences and fond memories suture their relationship to "America" and a sense of social conviviality with other park-goers. Shani Mootoo adored how my parents fearlessly ventured to remote parks, reveled in the magnificence of the landscape, and inhabited this "wild" landscape.

My parents continue to live in their split-level house in suburban Maryland. It's a lush landscape teeming with maples, cherry trees, dogwoods, rhododendron, and now herds of deer, raccoons, and squirrels that pretty much devour most of the succulent annuals my mother plants. She and my father are far from the vast monuments of rock, endless forests, and cascading waterfalls they revel in and visit in the West.

They have come to peace with their two sons' migration to California two decades ago, and try to pair every visit to San Diego and Palo Alto with a pilgrimage to a national or state park. It's their alternative to the family domestic life: travel to be with family but not in the family home. They don't car camp anymore; my brother and our families are too enamored with the creature comforts of a cheap motel to countenance my parents' fearless travel adventures.

In April 2010, my partner, Ken, and I drove with my parents to Yosemite, which my mother pronounces in such a way that one could mistake her invocation for a journey to the Himalayas. All conversation stopped when the car first breached the mountains and climbed down into Yosemite Valley. My mom gasped in awe. I knew to find the first lookout I could for my parents' communion, *darshan,* with the monumental and sublime. With a keen eye, my mom pointed out every water cascade she could find as the snowmelt trickled across the face of the valley. My father smiled, carefully framed shots through the camera lens, and snapped a dozen photos.

My father took hundreds if not thousands of photographs. In his mid-seventies in 2010, he didn't so much hike as amble. He was not very fond of inclines, but would still pursue the perfect position and angle for his shot. Instead of the old brown leather camera bag on his shoulder that I remember so vividly from my childhood, he now walked about with a 35 mm Nikon dangling around his neck and a digital camera in his shirt pocket. Once we got into the park, he would point up at the waterfalls and direct us to any trails that would bring him closer to the cascades.

On this trip, my father was content to follow the hikes that stayed on the valley floor. He spent much of the morning and afternoon taking the shuttle around the valley, stopping frequently to check out the viewpoints, pick up postcards at one stop and write short messages, and mail them around the world. He found no end of amusement in striking up conversations with the passengers and drivers.

On the other hand, my mother keeps on moving and will not be deterred from leading the way. In her baseball cap and windbreaker, she will climb and climb as far as her companions are willing to go. She is the eldest of seven, and her competitive spirit and athleticism come alive on a walk. For years, none of us could keep pace with her, and she would cajole everyone to step lively and hurry up. Her strides are long and daring. She climbed up to Vernal Falls and began moving beyond it.

She was well into foot-high piles of mushy snow and ice before Ken and I claimed fatigue. She remained undaunted but, of course, assumed responsibility for us weak desk guys to get down safely. She shared little Ziploc packets of nuts and cranberries, spicy flatbreads, and chickpea flour fried snacks that she had prepared in the week before the trip. My mother had become an expert in deploying her labor

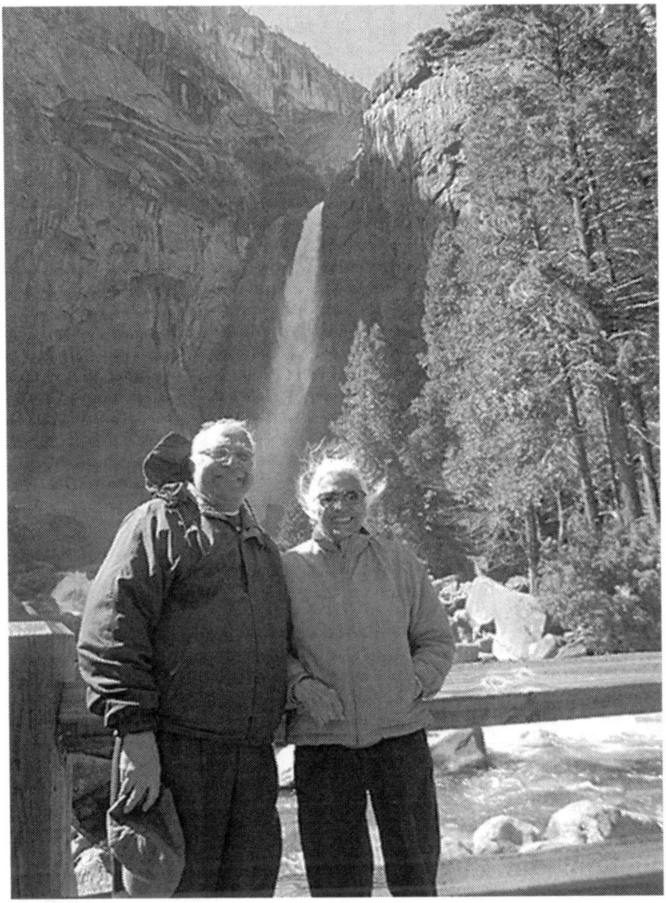

Devyani and Bhupendra Shah at Sentinel Falls, Yosemite Valley, 2010. Photo by Nayan Shah.

before the journey, all geared toward surviving the national parks' limited repertoire of fast food and mass-produced meat products. The National Park concessions have until very recently been a hostile environment for vegetarians, or, for that matter, anyone who would prefer a healthy and tasty snack to salty, mass-produced food.

Yosemite Pilgrimage

Thinking of my parents and of how they nourished, by their example, such pleasure, joy, awe, and wonderment at being in the monumental

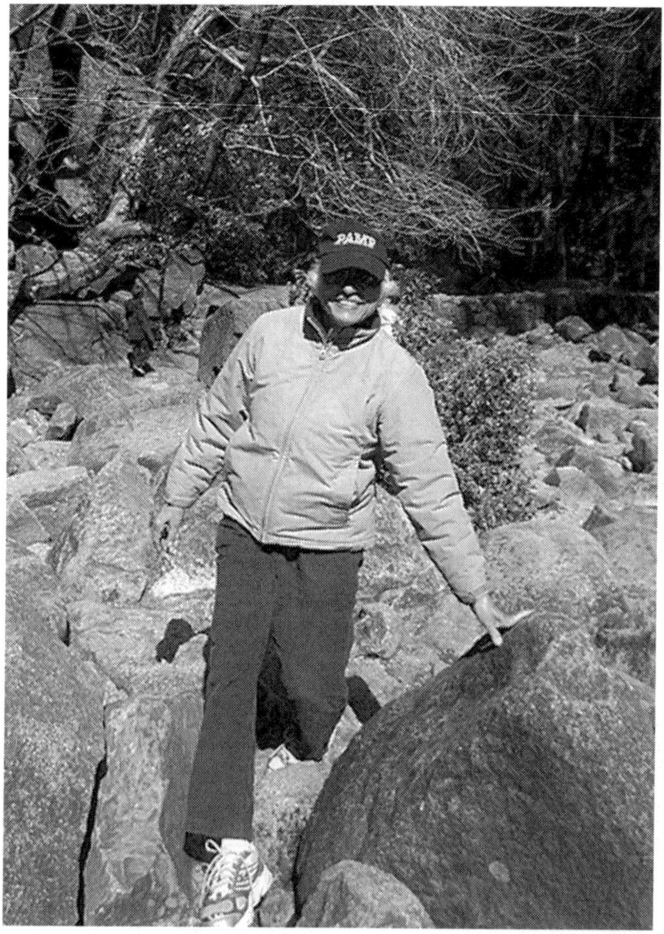

Devyani Shah in Yosemite Valley, 2010. Photo by Nayan Shah.

physical landscape makes me reflect anew on my discovery of Japanese American and Chinese American artists in the first half of the twentieth century and their creative engagement with the landscape. In the *Asian/American/Modern Art: Shifting Currents 1900–1970* exhibit, which I saw at its only venue, the de Young Museum in San Francisco, in January 2009, the curators' selections and contextualization of painting, photography, and sculpture made me consider how these artists claimed place and bodily inhabited the landscape of the western United States. The co-curators, Daniell Cornell, former curator at Fine Arts Museum of San Francisco and Palm Springs Museum of Art, and

Mark Johnson, professor of art at San Francisco State University, addressed how a range of Asian American artists reproduced the sensuality of the physical landscape in terms of both Western wilderness landscape and the bleakness of the internment camp surroundings.[2]

The legendary artist Chiura Obata, who immigrated from Japan to California in 1903 at the age of eighteen, visited Yosemite frequently in the late 1920s. Obata's exploration of Yosemite Valley began as an expedition organized by Worth Ryder, a newly appointed art professor at Berkeley and "inveterate hiker of the Sierra Nevada." They were joined by the sculptor Robert Boardman Howard, who had been commissioned to finish a mural in the lobby of the newly opened Ahwahnee Hotel.[3] Chiura Obata kept frequent contact with his family in San Francisco through letters he wrote to his wife, Haruko Obata.[4] Ryder's expertise, contacts, and resources made the camping trip feasible. Ryder drove his car, which they had packed up with "two beds, fourteen boxes of food, painting materials, fishing gear, two suitcases, a tent, a large saw, a large axe, a big shovel, [and] a big bucket of water in case of emergency" for their two-month camping trip. At the beginning of the trip, Obata remarked that the "big load" provided amusement for passersby and said, "Most people smile at us, thinking we are going to the mountains to find gold."[5]

A month later, on July 8, Obata expressed amusement at their deep suntans when they walked (naked) down the trail; he believed that many people mistook him for "an Indian" because of his brown coloring.[6] Both misperceptions were telling for Obata because they underlined iconic and romantic figures in the Sierra Nevada wilderness—the gold rush miner and the Indian. They also demonstrated how context and coloring provided the necessary masquerade to make the presence of a Japanese man on the camping trail intelligible to white observers, and perhaps, more significantly, to the recipients of his letters—his wife and friends in San Francisco.

The immense and intricate scenery absorbed Obata. His companion, Robert Boardman Howard, who joined Ryder and Obata in Yosemite, remarked, "Every pause for rest saw Chiura at work. That is almost the first impression he gives one, either working or on his way to work, never getting ready. Just somehow always ready, for at least a brief sketch." Obata explained as they sat before "the campfire in the cool silence of the High Sierra" the urgency of painting one hundred pictures in a month.[7] He wrote to his wife that "every place we go amazes and interests me, so I have been doing nothing but sketching." The atmosphere was vibrant and his senses were heightened:

> The air in the high mountains is so clean and the trees, grass, birds and flowers are fascinating beyond description. . . . Beautiful flowers bloom in a stream of icy water. I can only feel gratitude. I want to bring you and our friends here, and I will.

As much as he promised to bring his family and friends to see the sights, Obata craved the solitude of the trail and the heightened perception it created. He wrote,

> [the] speed of the universe is surprisingly fast. The uproar of Lindbergh's transatlantic flight is no comparison to nature. To the grand changes of this great nature my eyes, my ears, my hands and my feet, and my whole body and mind are reacting at a high speed. In San Francisco I was hardly reacting to the streetcars, automobiles, phones.[8]

Bodily sensations were enhanced far from the intensity, pace, and noise of the modern city. He wrote about bathing in the early morning, and how remote it was where they camped. As they hiked on the trail, they quickly encountered people. In one of his published dispatches to the Japanese-language paper *Shin Sekai,* Obata wrote, "We started down the trail at 6:30 am and soon we reached the top of Yosemite Falls." They saw people come up the trail, "including women . . . so we put on clothes. We've been naked in the camp and on the trail. [It] was good to be naked in the hot weather in the mountains."[9] Obata was eager to convey his sense of freedom from conventional life rhythms, his heighted consciousness, and his unleashed creativity in the remote wilderness to his readers.

Obata wrote repeatedly of the "music" that he wanted to bring alive in his paintings. He told Ryder and Howard at the campfire that it was the music of Yosemite Falls that he wanted to represent in his very first watercolor. The complexity of the music that Obata heard seems to have been sublimely orchestral. For his woodblock print, *Before the Thunderstorms, Tuolumne Meadows,* he inscribed,

> Like a sleeping Lion the Lembert Dome rests unconcerned in the center of Tuolumne Meadows, walled in by a train of high, surrounding rocky mountains. He sleeps in the midst of an

> approaching storm. Thunder rumbles and roars through the vast meadow, like a huge orchestra at the height of its frenzied rendition of an overture, announcing the coming of the storm.[10]

In the inscription of another woodblock print, *Silence, Last Twilight on an Unknown Lake, Johnson Peak,* Obata transposes and aligns the movement of the visual with the aural:

> After the passing of a thunderstorm, the freshly brightened colors vanish as the evening falls. As the deep blues turn to purple, one can still hear the melody of a thousand streams. In the silence that follows, Nature reveals herself.[11]

For Obata, musicality is focused on the soundscape that accompanies water's movement, on the particular tempo of weather events, and on the rotation of daylight and night. The play of sound and silence particularly evoke the sensation of waterfalls. He writes in *Shin Sekai* that "the river turns into the immense Yosemite Falls. This waterfall makes the music of heaven; it is a music more inspiring than man-made."

Transformational and Transnational Labor

Obata became famous for the process of transformation that he employed in representing this landscape in the sketches and watercolors he produced during his camping exploration; his methods were similar to the labor-intensive process of woodblock printing in Japan. Obata adopted Yosemite and the High Sierras as a significant subject in 1927, the year that the Ahwahnee Hotel opened and the High Sierra camps were inaugurated, increasing the park's profile as a tourist destination. The watercolors and sketches that Obata produced in Yosemite in 1927 served as the models for the innovative portfolio of prints that he produced in Japan between 1928 and 1930. Of Obata's *World Landscape Series,* composed of thirty-five color woodblock prints, all but one show California scenes, and twenty-seven are views of Yosemite and the High Sierra country. Art historian Susan Laundauer, who helped organize a 1993 exhibition of the prints, drawings, and paintings, describes Obata's technique and expressive style as "delicate poetry with an unerring eye for the tranquil beauty of the High Sierra," as "intense, often calligraphic expressiveness," and as "quiet lyricism." Obata himself described the trip as the "greatest harvest of my whole life and future in painting."[12]

Obata's strong personal response to the landscape he encountered is evident both in his art and in the collection of his letters and published essays from that journey, which challenged his artistic practice. His own physical exertion and sensual labor are manifest in the way he speaks of the context of creation of his watercolors and sketches, and the intensity of his pace of creation. This work process in the camps of the High Sierras was, however, a prelude to a pivotal career-defining and life-changing training in wood block printing when he returned to Japan, soon after his father's death in 1928.

His watercolors and sketches became the study he used to create the progressive woodblock prints that secured both his reputation and a position as art professor at Berkeley. The printmaking process Obata used at the time was labor-intensive and time-consuming; it demanded the labor and expertise of dozens of artisans and was tremendously expensive. For instance, in creating one print, "Lake Basin in High Sierra," Obata directed the making of 107 impressions to create the final composition. Since cherry blocks are expensive material, they were often reused for repeated applications of ink to build up color density. Japanese printers and artisan teams of woodblock carvers drew on the watercolors to meticulously carve the blocks, relying on both Obata's artistic vision and his management of the lengthy and complex artisan labor process of printing.

Obata both drew sketches and managed and approved the carvings, printings, production, and publication. He also had progressive proofs made after each printing stage, which was a very costly and unusual practice but ultimately enabled a careful study of his process by Crocker Museum Art Curator Janice Driesbach. She speculates that this may have been "motivated by his interest in offering demonstrations of the carving and printing process on his return to the United States."[13] The appearance of artisans' and woodcarvers' names on their works is rare. However, the "detailed execution [of the prints] attests to the presence of skilled block carvers; the degree of craftsmanship exhibited would have been beyond the ability of an artist, such as Obata himself, who had not received lengthy training in this specialty."[14] But in proof 99, the names of Shizuka Baba, the carver, and Majuro, the printer, appear. As Driesbach notes, "these credits fail to acknowledge the host of artisans working under their direction, [whose names] do not appear on any of the prints in the portfolio collection."[15]

Obata's work as an illustrator in Japanese-language newspapers and magazines in the 1920s financed both his travel to Japan and the woodblock printing process. The publication of the block print *World*

Landscape Series led to his full-time teaching appointment at UC Berkeley and secured his national and international reputation. In 1938, *Time Magazine* named him as one of the most accomplished artists in the West. Then, during World War II, Obata was interned. During his incarceration, he co-founded art schools at Tanforan Assembly Center and Topaz Camp. After the war, he returned to Berkeley and taught until his retirement in 1955.

Howard concluded his testimonial of his time with Chiura Obata in the Sierra Nevada thus:

> He stands for work, love, laughter; indefatigable work; a sensitive love of life, of mountains, of tiny plants and mighty trees, of fog and skies; and of laughter that comes from the heart, the joy of living and the knowing that all is right with the world because he has made it his.[16]

Obata's claim on Yosemite was made through the labor of his journey and his enthusiasm for capturing the feelings emanating from his visual and aural experience with the High Sierra landscape. The art-making process was spontaneous in his sketching and painting in the mountains and valleys. But it required transnational labor and engagement with Japanese aesthetic and artisan practices to achieve. Both Obata's collaboration with other Japanese artists and his management of the woodblock printing process were critical to his achievement.

Obata and my parents share a common practice of claiming communion and reckoning with the magnificent combination of rock, water, and sky. This sensual intimacy with place radiates through the mediums of drawing, printing, and photography.

Contemporary artist Binh Danh, a Vietnamese American refugee who grew up in San Jose, has repurposed the 150-year-old photographic practice of daguerreotypes to invest artist and viewer simultaneously within the monumental landscape of Yosemite. First, he photographs Yosemite mountain faces, made iconic by the viewpoints of nineteenth-century photographer Carleton Watkins. Then, in a labor-intensive process that he carries out in his white van, which doubles as a mobile darkroom, Danh "coats sheets of copper with silver, polishes the plates to a blinding gleam and synthesizes them with iodine to create crystals that act as pixels." This layered photographic practice produces a highly reflective, mirror-like effect that enables viewers, as he explained to a reporter, to "look at my work" and "see themselves in the picture."

The process of looking is transformed into a fusion with the landscape both spiritually and physically, enabling viewers to "become part of this land. . . . in a way, merge with the land—but they don't quite disappear into the land. . . . They still see themselves in it."[17]

Notes

1. Shani Mootoo's videography engages with the place of South Asians in the Canadian Rockies in *Wild Woman in the Woods* (1992) and *A Paddle and Compass* (1992).
2. Daniell Cornell and Mark Dean Johnson, eds., *Asian/American/Modern Art Shifting Currents, 1900–1970* (University of California Press, 2009).
3. Susan Landauer, "Obata of the Thousand Bays," in *Obata's Yosemite: The Art and Letters of Chiura Obata and His Trip to the High Sierra in 1927* (Yosemite: Yosemite Association, 1993), 25.
4. Obata's letters were written in Japanese and a selection of them were translated and published for the first time in *Obata's Yosemite: The Art and Letters of Chiura Obata and His Trip to the High Sierra in 1927* (Yosemite: Yosemite Association, 1993).
5. *Obata's Yosemite*, 78.
6. *Obata's Yosemite*, 129.
7. "Obata Gets the Spirit of California in His Prints: Sierra Trip with Obata is told by John (sic) Howard, Important Local Artist." *Art and Artists* 2 (January 1931), pp. 1, 3. Reprinted in *Obata's Yosemite*, p. 138.
8. Ibid, p. 92.
9. "Sierra Trip: Yosemite Creek Impressions. Following the Old Mountain Path from the Upper Part of Yosemite Falls down the Valley," *Shin Sekai* (1927), reprinted in *Obata's Yosemite*, 128.
10. *Obata's Yosemite*, 110.
11. *Obata's Yosemite*, 106.
12. *Obata's Yosemite*, 25 (fn16).
13. Janice T. Driesbach, "From Watercolor to Woodblock," in *Obata's Yosemite*, (Yosemite: Yosemite Association, 1993), 60.
14. Driesbach, "From Watercolor to Woodblock," 60.
15. Driesbach, "From Watercolor to Woodblock," 67.
16. "Obata Gets the Spirit of California in His Prints: Sierra Trip with Obata is told by John (sic) Howard, Important Local Artist," *Art and Artists* 2 (January 1931), pp. 1, 3. Reprinted in *Obata's Yosemite*, p. 141.
17. Neda Ulaby, "National Park Daguerreotypes Invite Viewers To 'Merge With The Land,'" July 5, 2016, http://www.npr.org/2016/07/05/484051741/national-park-daguerreotypes-invite-viewers-to-merge-with-the-land, accessed July 9, 2016. Binh Danh's photographs and artworks are available at http://www.binhdanh.com.

Chapter 3

Bohulano Family *Binangkal*

Dawn Bohulano Mabalon

During Thanksgiving week 2012, I updated my Facebook status with a list of what I was making for my family feasts: *lumpia, pansit, suman,* pumpkin cheesecake, sweet potato pie, and *binangkal*. The chef/author/food scholar Amy Besa posted a question: "What is binangkal?" So I posted a photo. Several friends, many of them second- and third-generation Filipina/o Americans with roots in the Visayas, reacted quickly and rapturously to my *binangkal* photo, thrilled that Facebook love had been given to an obscure regional treat beloved across the Visayas and wherever in the world Visayans settled.

My writer friend Rashaan Alexis Menesis posted, "My grandpa used to make these! Sob."

"My mom n dad been bringin these home after every Bohol Circle meeting since . . . forever," wrote Bay Area Boholano Anthony Caybut.

"That's my mom's specialty," wrote my old friend Carlo Bacor of Mindanao, whose family roots are in the Visayas.

"I know how to make it too lol."

"Post the recipe!" asked family friend Delvina Modesto, whose father was from Carcar, Cebu.

"My Grandma Annie used to make these and have them waiting for me when I would come over to visit," wrote my friend Christine Miculob Ainza. "I'm sad that she passed without me learning."

The outpouring of *binangkal* love and nostalgia surprised and warmed me.

Binangkal is a sesame-covered baking powder donut, deep fried until crisp and brown on the outside and pillowy on the inside. When made well, its surface is craggy, brown and caramelized from the hot oil, its insides moist and fluffy. A popular snack in Cebu and the Visayas, it has look-alikes in Chinese dim sum restaurants and bakeries, which is a clue that *binangkal* may have some Chinese influence. If flashier desserts like mango chiffon cake, *Brazo de Mercedes,* and *Sans Rival* are the O. A. beauty queens of the Filipina/o American dessert table, then regional Visayan treats like *binangkal* and the anise-scented cake called *torta* are the humble, homely, and dependable wallflowers. Pretty *turon* glistening with a caramel crust may get all the attention, but *binangkal* has *integrity.*

Affection for *binangkal* was strong among Visayan immigrants to Hawaii and the West Coast who arrived in the first decades of the twentieth century. All of the ingredients (eggs, flour, brown sugar, canned milk, oil, sesame seeds) were easily available. In *Flavors of Filipino American Kitchens,* a spiral-bound community cookbook produced in 2012 by the Central Valley (California) chapter of the Filipino American National Historical Society, no less than three *binangkal* recipes are included. Many of the pioneering Filipina/o American families in the Central Valley/San Joaquin Delta County area have roots in the Visayas, hailing from Cebu, Panay, Bohol, Negros, Leyte, Samar, and Siquijor.

In 2008, my husband Jesse (a Manila native who had never seen a *binangkal* until we began dating) and I spent a week in Cebu City. On a food culture tour led by a sweet and knowledgeable guide named Mike, I tasted *binangkal* made in Carcar City, just outside of Cebu City, a town that lays claim to hosting the biggest shoe industry in the world (sorry, Marikina). At a snack stand, he bought us a plastic package of *binangkal,* each barely bigger than a ping pong ball. I eagerly stuffed one into my mouth then proceeded to nearly break my tooth. I protested that *binangkal* should be like a soft, sweet, crispy donut. Mike laughed.

"*Binangkal* is meant to be food that you can take into the fields with you," he admonished me. "You bring a bunch of these hard little balls, which last for a long time, for your lunch. Then you drink a lot of water, and then they expand. Now you're full." It was a revelation for me, a Filipina/o American historian just beginning to make the connections between our recipes and our immigration history. *Binangkal*'s trip to America transformed them from hardy food for the fields to rich party fare. How *American* were my family's *binangkal:* sizable, pillowy balls full of abundance, enriched with large eggs, copious amounts of brown sugar, rich canned cow's milk, vanilla, and Bisquick. *Bisquick?* Yes. More on that later.

My grandmother, Cebu City native Concepcion Moreno Bohulano, a highly skilled and creative cook who loved both Philippine and American cuisine, probably learned how to make *binangkal* from the family cooks as a young girl growing up in Cebu City. Grandma Conching loved making desserts and snacks for her family. During World War II, the family left the city, like thousands of others in the Philippines, for her family's ancestral home in Palompon, Leyte. At a dance in Palompon during the waning days of World War II, she met Delfin Bohulano, a Filipino American soldier with the US Army's First Filipino Infantry Regiment who was doing mop up work in Leyte with his Philippine Civil Affairs Unit. They married, and my uncle and mother Christine were born. My grandparents used the GI Bill to finish college: Grandpa with a BA in business at Far Eastern University, and Grandma with a degree in education (which had been interrupted by the war) at San Carlos University. Grandma became an elementary school teacher and Grandpa tried to make a run at a grocery store business in Cebu.

But opportunities in America called; Grandpa had heard postwar wages were higher, and now that they had college degrees, he hoped their fortunes would be better in America. In 1952, the Bohulanos left the Philippines to settle in rural Tracy, California, near Stockton, the capital of Filipina/o America. There, racism restricted my college-educated grandparents to the only jobs available to them: Grandpa became a farm labor contractor and Grandma worked in the local peach cannery and in the fields. Two more children were born: my aunts Virginia and Adeline. Everyone in the family, including my mom and her siblings, worked in the fields at one time or another. The Bohulanos later moved to Stockton in 1956, buying a suburban-style ranch home in the city's first integrated suburban subdivision on the city's south side, Lever Village. In 1962, Grandma was hired at the local Tracy Unified School District and became one of the first Filipina public school teachers in the area, if not the state.

Somehow, Bisquick made its way into our family recipe in the 1950s. Perhaps one day my grandmother ran out of flour and baking powder, and, like many other homemakers in the 1950s, subbed in the mass-produced convenience product and liked the results. Or she might have traded notes with another wily Visayan war bride who didn't mind bucking tradition to add American ingredients to improve a traditional recipe. My uncle Delfin Bohulano, Jr., remembers that Grandma often made *binangkal* as a snack, even after a long day in the peach cannery, or, in the 1960s, after a tiring day as a public-school teacher. It was an everyday kind of snack, rarely made for special occasions, holidays, or parties. Only later, when life became busier, and time even more precious, did they only show up at parties and holidays.

By the 1970s, my mother Christine had inherited the mantle of *binangkal* maker. One afternoon at Grandma's dining room table, I listened as a handful of neighborhood aunties heaped compliments on the *binangkal*. My grandmother gave her oldest daughter the ultimate compliment. "She makes them even better than I do," she told her *comadres*. I beamed with pride for my mother, a good cook whose dishes were often overshadowed by Grandma's almost supernatural cooking prowess.

Binangkal requires time, patience, and a strong arm. When Grandma and Mom made *binangkal*, they mixed by hand. Raw *binangkal* dough is so sticky and stiff that it blows out rickety hand mixers. I can still see Mom standing in a bright caftan over a large bowl, sweating and stirring for what seemed like hours. Then she spent what seemed like an eternity rolling each ball of dough meticulously, first in egg then in sesame seeds. She always let me lick the bowl. Now, I'm the family's *binangkal* maker, and I draw on generations of wisdom (yes, I use the Bisquick, because I don't mess with a good thing), and a modern appliance, my heavy-duty Kitchen Aid 6-quart stand mixer. I can whip up a batch of *binangkal* in minutes. One Thanksgiving I showed my mom my mixer method, and her eyes widened as the mixer turned seven cups of flour into the egg and sugar mixture with ease.

"I could get rich making batches and batches of *binangkal* now, *and sell them!*" she exclaimed. At the time, she had just retired after 35 years of public-school teaching and had a bad back. I had to talk her out of going into a whole new business venture.

When the dough is turned out of the mixer, I must still do what my mother, grandmother, and all of my Visayan ancestors did before me: I roll. I sit down at the table in my tiny San Francisco kitchen, lightly dip my hands in beaten eggs, scoop up an egg-sized ball of sticky dough, roll that ball in sesame seeds, and place the ball onto waxed paper. I make rows and rows. Life slows down and my heart rate slows. I put on NPR, and after an hour, I have neat rows of glistening, sesame-flecked balls.

When I make *binangkal*, I imagine my Grandma, just home from her job canning peaches, sweating in a tiny farmhouse kitchen in Tracy, California, stirring eggs into canned milk, brown sugar, and vanilla, opening a box of Bisquick, making an after-school treat for her four children. I see my mother in her 1970s caftan, preparing for a family party, thoughtfully reducing the brown sugar in the recipe for her diabetic father-in-law, my *binangkal*-loving *Lolo* Ambo, then quietly and methodically rolling the balls, frying them over a low flame until they explode into crispy balls of love.

I recently brought six dozen to a huge family gathering on my father's side in Stockton this past summer. On a table full of *leche flan, turon,* my secret-recipe *ube* cupcakes and other treats, *binangkal* got *love:* two huge pans were gone in a flash. I was flattered. It turns out relatives and friends were eating them hand over fist, but also hiding stashes in their purses for later. I caught one cousin shoveling them by the handful into a paper bag for her *baon.*

"What!" she retorted guiltily, when I gave her an accusing look. "They're so good with coffee in the morning!"

I heard another cousin yelling that her stash had disappeared; she had been hiding the last three in a foil-wrapped red Solo cup, but an overzealous uncle on cleanup duty had thrown it away.

I don't bring *binangkal* to gatherings of mostly Tagalog or Ilocano post-1965 immigrants, or their children, because I get blank stares and questions and all my hard work seems wasted. To those parties, I bring my lush *leche flan* and pretty purple *ube* cupcakes. But every time I bring them to gatherings in my hometown of Stockton, a center of pre-1965 Visayan immigration, I get the same nostalgic sighs, like the ones on Facebook last month. "*Binangkal!*" friends and strangers exclaim, sometimes a little teary. And the stories of loving Visayan grandmothers and mothers, and even Lolos, hunched over bowls of dough and vats of oil, commence.

Bohulano Family Binangkal (recipe)

Sift together dry ingredients:

7 ½ cups all-purpose flour
3 cups Bisquick baking mix
6 tsp baking powder

Combine in a large, separate bowl, or in the bowl of a stand mixer fitted with the paddle attachment, until well blended:

6 eggs, beaten
1 can evaporated milk

½ cup whole milk
3 tbs vanilla
2 tbs dark brown sugar
2 cups sesame seeds
Vegetable oil for frying

Add the dry mixture a little at a time until you get a soft, sticky dough. Let the dough rest at least an hour, or overnight in the fridge. Dough will last at least 3–4 days in the fridge. Let it come to room temperature before rolling. Prepare your rolling station: a small bowl of 2 beaten eggs and about ¼ cup of water, a shallow dish of sesame seeds, and two waxed paper–lined cookie sheets sprayed with cooking spray.

To roll, first dip very clean fingers into the egg mixture. Scoop up a golf-ball-sized mound of dough and roll until round and smooth. Roll in the shallow dish of sesame seeds and then place on waxed paper sprayed with cooking spray or oil.

Use a large wok or wide frying pan (I like my cast iron pan for this). Heat at least 3 inches of oil to medium low (300 degrees Fahrenheit). Don't be tempted to heat the oil up to 350—you'll only burn the outside and leave the inside raw. It will take a while—up to 5 minutes or more—for the *binangkal* to begin to puff up and cook. The hot oil reacting with the baking powder will cause craggy fissures to crack open all over the *binangkal*—this is what you want. Keep turning them. The *binangkal* is done when it is a caramel brown all over and cracked. Be patient. You've already burned up a whole afternoon rolling these things, so stand there and think about Filipina/o American history.

Best on the same day, but still great the next few days with your coffee. Store them in a plastic bag. This recipe makes two half-size aluminum steam pans full. It will feed a lot of people, especially if placed on a dessert table in which *carioca/cascaron/bitsu-bitsu* steals all the attention. That's okay. More for you.

Chapter 4

100 Tiki Notes

Dan Taulapapa McMullin

1. Tiki walked into a bar . . .
2. The American bartender said, "Move over, Tiki. You are a Pacific Islander god/dess; therefore, you do not exist . . ."
3. "Your islands belong to us long time, since the first missionaries on gunboats squirted their diseased spirit over your fragrant seas . . ."
4. "Make way for tiki kitsch, and all kinds of cheap simulacra . . ."
5. "Accept your welfare check and stand down. We don't serve you anymore . . ."
6. "We serve up your image."
7. There's an avant-garde American artist in Los Angeles who makes a specialty of tiki kitsch assemblages . . .
8. He's in all the museums in Los Angeles with his version of Pacific Islander art—at museums where no contemporary Pacific Islander Americans are shown . . .
9. He grew up in a Los Angeles household with tiki kitsch. That's how he feels about it. He loves it . . .
10. A lot of connected artists in Los Angeles were saying, "Dan, you should get to know him. You both deal with the same subject . . ."
11. He saw my work in my studio while visiting a studio neighbor when I was away. I had collaged a photo of a Polynesian

wooden dildo that he had fabricated in a homoerotic collage I made of Hawaii Five-O actors and the tiki kitsch dildo. I don't know what he thought . . .

12. I sent him Facebook friend requests. He reported me to Facebook. They shut down my account for a little while.
13. There's a tiki kitsch artist in Orange County California who makes sixties cartoon like paintings of Americans going wild with tiki kitsch abandon . . .
14. I went to see his show in the Orange County California art district. Some American patrons leaving the gallery were saying to each other, "Let's go. There's all these brown people here now . . ."
15. Meaning the Mexican Americans who had taken over the neighborhood, including taking over opening nights in the art district, which was started by American artists from the universities in Orange County, California . . .
16. I realized, looking around, that the American university faculty and visiting American tiki kitsch artist and invited American patrons had all left after their own private preview at the gallery, before the people who lived in the area showed up for the public opening, before the zombies like me showed up . . .
17. As there were no other university art representatives present, I asked the university art students who were present as security for the university gallery, "Wouldn't you be insulted if this was a kitsch representation of your culture? I'm a Pacific Islander. This is my culture represented." They looked completely puzzled by my remark. Even though we all spoke zombie.
18. I did some research into the history of tiki kitsch. I found an amazing website with endless photographs of white women dressed or undressed as Pacific Islander savages looking intoxicated while worshipping giant Tikis, and I realized tiki kitsch originated at the intersection of two commodities: pornography and alcohol . . .
19. When American soldiers came back from World War II, they brought memories of the South Pacific with them. To them the South Pacific represented women's breasts and getting drunk . . .

20. My father was an underage Samoan American ship electrician during World War II in Pago Pago, American Samoa. He told me that it was common for young Samoan women in American Samoa to be bare-breasted in the village, up to the 1940s and despite the missionaries, due to the tropical heat. Samoan men respected this aspect of women's lives in Samoa, but American men took the Samoan women's mode of dress in public as a sexual invitation and kept touching them. The American Samoan government banned traditional Samoan women's mode of dress in regards to breasts because of American soldiers' touchy feelings . . .
21. Tiki kitsch begins with notions of paradise and ends with pornography; pornography is about covering up the body, not about revealing it . . .
22. Tiki porn begins with the Western patriarchal notion that females are savages and ruin paradise . . .
23. Tiki porn begins with Eve, and her line never ends. It continues with someone else: same name, no relation . . .
24. Tiki porn is a snake, is a pagan god, is a graven image, is a bar stool.
25. After World War II, the first tiki kitsch bars opened in Los Angeles. Also, the mass-production porn industry began in earnest in Los Angeles, and to a great extent tiki kitsch was associated with sexual liberation for Americans. In that sense, notions of the savage were renewed within commodities of American privilege. Now Pacific Islanders perform it. Yay.
26. Tiki porn is anti-blackness—the notion that the devil is black and graven images are devilish.
27. Tiki porn is the notion that native people are sick and must be cured, but cannot be cured.
28. Tiki kitsch is a kind of mockingbird. Tiki kitsch is a doppelgänger of a doppelgänger of a doppelgänger of a dildo.
29. Tiki porn is the notion that the devil is everywhere, especially in black holes. The devil is a woman, a savage, a Polynesian, a very naughty.
30. Tiki porn is not just the fact that Queen Elizabeth claims to be a direct descendent of Adam, but that Adam and Eve claim to be our ancestors.

31. Tiki porn is any romanticized story of the kidnapping and rape of native girls by explorers and soldiers and missionaries, those lovely hula hands, those silhouettes at sunset.
32. David Zwirner said of Jeff Koons, "He says if you're critical, you're already out of the game." This is the dilemma of colored people and women and queers in art: we do not have the viewpoint of straight white men who cannot be critical no matter how hard they try. But we do some of us want to play the game. After all, why not? "Change the game" is just easy to say.
33. The question might well be, "Is the critical viewpoint imposed on the subject by the game?" That is to say, is my criticism of colonialism and appropriation part of my colonization? Can the truly critical viewpoint be to have none? How would this be possible? Yet, how is it possible to change the game unless I first discard my critique?
34. But is my work critical? It is not critical of itself. Art truly is not critical of itself; that's not its nature. The question, then, would be, "What does critique do but address the difference between?" The difference between Tiki and tiki kitsch, for instance.
35. One can explain things forever, and one can volunteer one's life away. Explaining is a form of volunteerism. Let me volunteer to explain.
36. Tiki is native memory in the hills and among the trees and far out to sea, endless songs. Tiki was the first one of us. Tiki is the last one of us. Is was. Was is. If so, then Tiki truly no longer exists, and Adam and Eve sometimes use Tiki's name. Tiki tacky, whacky. Tick tock.
37. Tiki is Sina falling in love with a strange white seabird that comes unknown, then goes forever. This is from an old song that explains how someone felt about it.
38. Tiki is her brothers disappearing on the horizon in pursuit, to hunt it down and kill it for her. That is how it goes when we all turned into seabirds and left. Tiki is a lonely statue.
39. Tiki is a way of counting time. From then to now.
40. Tiki porn in Shakespeare is the character Caliban, who has bad breath; he is the anti-lover, the tiki, the voyeur, the child of an evil witch. Caliban is the recipient of porn, the lover of his

own imagination, the 'other' that Shakespeare inhabits and shuns, a creature of nature, the body of the author, unseemly, all-seeing, naked to his own flood of perception.

41. Tiki pornography was popular after World War II. Tiki pornography consists of an American woman writhing in ecstasy, dressed in leopard skin or nothing, beneath a giant or small, fat or skinny, lumpy or elegant wooden tiki, in a backyard in Los Angeles, by a swimming pool, in a stripper bar, against a tropical background. It represented the end of the colonization of North America and the beginning of the colonization of the world.
42. Tiki kitsch is missionaries throughout the world burning wooden gods and saving some for sale.
43. Tiki porn was missionaries in Aotearoa-New Zealand cutting off the wooden penises of the gods.
44. Tiki porn is a NZ Maori curator telling me of an archived box of these penises in a museum in Aotearoa.
45. Tiki porn is the banning of native language and texts by missionaries, a million pagan poems. Tiki porn is a woman without language. Tiki porn is never having sex.
46. Tiki porn was the old missionary law that short-haired pagan Polynesian women grow long Christian hair.
47. Tiki porn was the old missionary law that long-haired pagan Polynesian men get short Christian haircuts.
48. Tiki is the dance. As Gertrude Stein wrote in *Three Lives,* "You look ridiculous if you dance. You look ridiculous if you don't dance. So you might as well dance." So dance, betch!
49. Tiki is Melville sleeping with Polynesian men in search of the ultimate harpooning. Tiki kitsch is Moby Dick; tiki porn is Moby Dick's dick and a coffin, and the sea, pages and pages of it.
50. Tiki porn is Hollywood; tiki kitsch is the Department of the Interior.
51. Tiki is Gauguin sleeping with Polynesian youth and turning into the red stray village dog. Tiki is the conversation we have with him still. Tiki kitsch is the museum and parking.
52. Tiki kitsch is the notion that hybridity is new and natives are cows of knowledge to be sucked.

53. Tiki is Gauguin fishing up bottles of absinthe from the coolness of a well by running a fishing line on a pole from the window of his second-floor studio in the islands of Polynesia, and ultimately dying from drink while painting.
54. Tiki porn is only fucking in the missionary position.
55. Tiki kitsch is when Polynesians and other Pacific Islanders only make art that looks and sounds Polynesian and Pacific Islander and and and and. End.
56. Tiki porn is hating our bodies because they are bar stools for our souls.
57. Tiki porn is the reason American Samoa per capita weighs more than independent Samoa.
58. Tiki kitsch is native art as scientific discovery, as tired lame tourist airport commodity, without *mana* and *aga,* without relationship and spirit, labeled nameless, a trophy, roadkill.
59. Tiki kitsch is the notion within mimicry that the originals exist without stories, without breath, without relatives, without ownership, without family, like orphans, and sex slaves.
60. Tiki kitsch found its modern form in Picasso's first cubist painting, *Les Demoiselles d'Avignon*. The resemblance between *Les Demoiselles d'Avignon* and any plastic tiki beer mug being sold online is astonishing and unsurprising. This is a good thing. It means we influenced the world. Doesn't it? Or just the image of. Roadkill.
61. Picasso is a Pacific Islander, a beachcomber. We adopted him. All the savages did. We said, He is ours. Then he denied us. I say, Next! He sleeps around. I sleep around and around.
62. Tiki porn is the notion that fashion is contemporary, that appropriation is original appropriation.
63. Tiki porn is Picasso claiming to be a discoverer not influenced by African and Pacific Islander and Native American art. Tiki is Picasso making art influenced by art of Africa and Oceania and Native America. Tiki kitsch is the smell of fucking but not fucking itself, unfortunately.
64. Tiki is anthropology as transcription; tiki kitsch is the rest of anthropology; tiki porn is a conference of anthropologists, the smell of something without the something.

65. Tiki kitsch is a beach destination owned by a billionaire who feels like Christ casting out the money-changers from the temple of his environmentalist private islands bought with oil money when he personally smashes and burns down the fishing huts of local fishermen who kill sea turtles once in a while to feed their families as they've been doing for tens of thousands of years.
66. Tiki porn is the contrarian nature of left right left.
67. Tiki porn is Mead not writing about the American political influence over Samoa when she was writing as the American political influence over Samoa.
68. Tiki kitsch is another Hollywood movie by another other sister brother outsider.
69. Tiki sleeping with the enemy.
70. Tiki porn is sleeping with the enemy.
71. Tiki porn is the search for paradise.
72. Tiki kitsch is the notion that everything is for sale, but it is, it is, is.
73. Tiki kitsch is the notion that an international performance artist dressed as a mud-covered Papuan with an artistic history that makes no mention of Papua art, or anything like that where anti-blackness writes black history.
74. Tiki kitsch is the way world politics is influenced by the cheapest, dumbest Hollywood films, which is all the Hollywood films, especially the really good and relevant ones, because vomit is sweet and pink and filled with familiar chunks of actors acting as actors acting.
75. Tiki kitsch is the way anti-blackness cannot see any one just any one.
76. Tiki kitsch is being a sidekick in one's own life.
77. Tiki porn is being a fantasy.
78. Tiki porn is being a lighting check stand-in for a fantasy.
79. Tiki porn is Adam and Eve, and Hollywood, and Adam and Eve, and Hollywood, and Adam and Eve, and Hollywood, and Adam and Eve and Hollywood.
80. Tiki kitsch is the idea the world can be saved by human action.

81. Tiki is not born yet.
82. Tiki is the summer I shall not see.
83. Tiki porn is sexy. Squish. Bad because he is old and has a foreign accent.
84. Tiki kitsch is a chase scene where all the artists follow all the academics follow.
85. Tiki kitsch history is a post-WWII American porn magazine called *Gaze*.
86. Tiki kitsch history is another post-WWII American porn magazine called *Pagan*.
87. Tiki porn is black & white photos of American women deliriously humping pagan idols and then having half-caste children who become artists and academics.
88. Tiki porn is Polynesians killing Daddy Polynesians.
89. Tiki porn is the notion that the body is cursed and it is.
90. Tiki kitsch is the eternal return of the explorer.
91. Tiki kitsch is Aotearoa-New Zealand as a location for *Lord of the Rings*. It makes me feel good.
92. Tiki kitsch is Polynesians in orc make-up, zombies playing zombies.
93. Tiki kitsch is Sauron wearing an inverted tiki on his head, played by a Polynesian, the king of the zombies.
94. Tiki porn is *50 First Dates* with a Hawaiian guy with cataracts played by an actor acting like a zombie.
95. Tiki kitsch is contemporary abstract art, all contemporary abstract art, made with wild abandon, while intoxicated, and pagan, zombie.
96. Tiki porn is this kitsch. And zombie.
97. Tiki is 98 zombies.
98. Tiki is 99 zombies.
99. Tiki is 100.

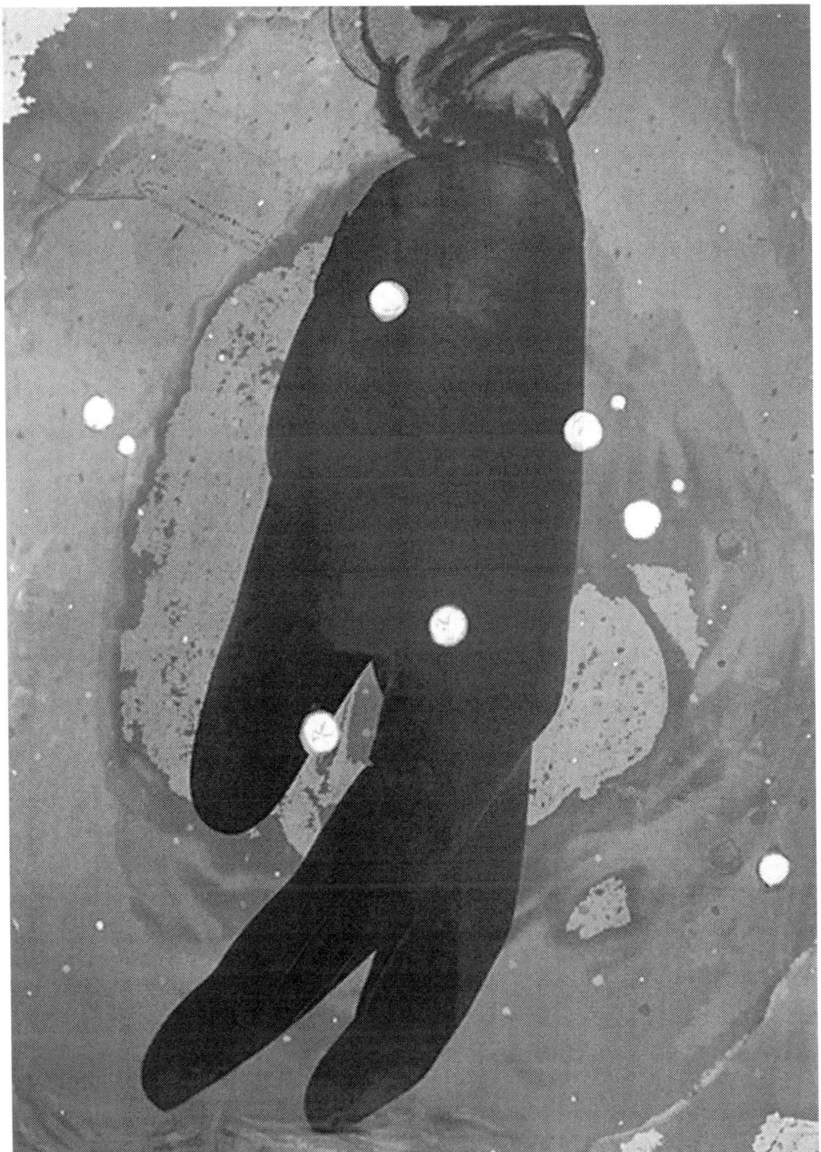

Tiki in Frozen Hell (2013). Image by Dan McMullin.

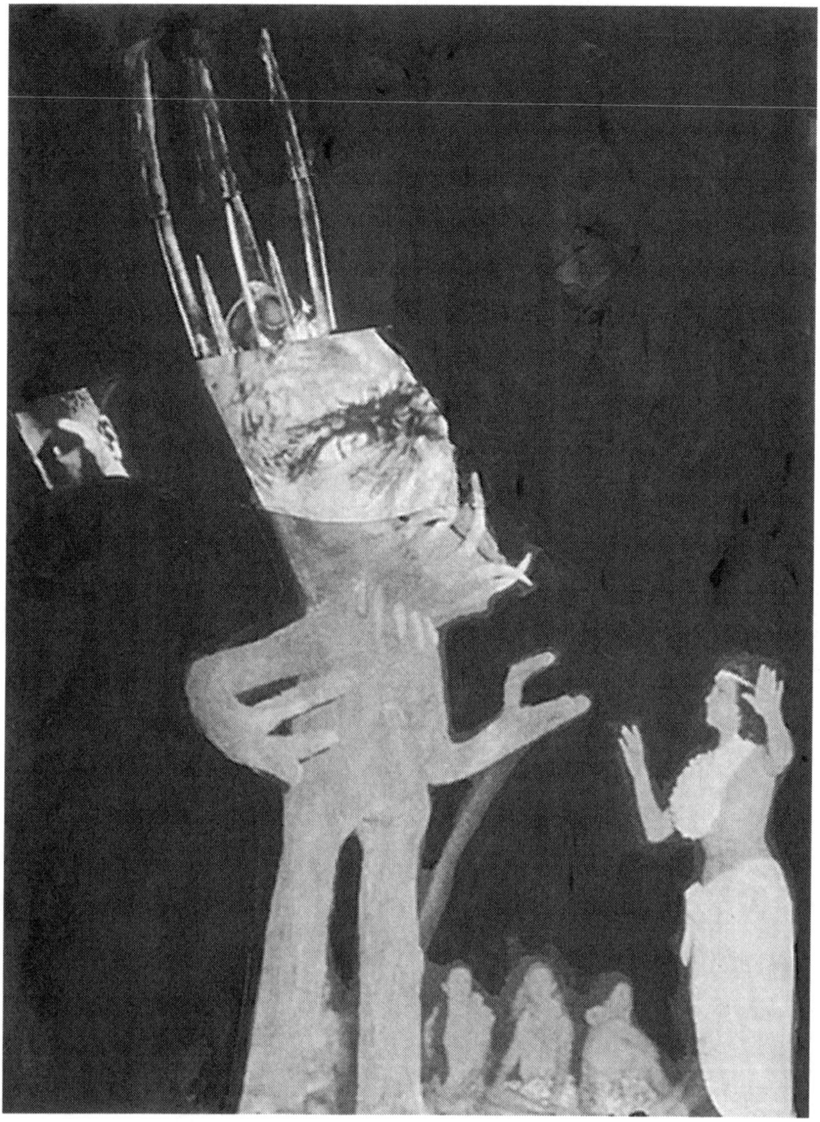

Fake Hula for Alien Tiki (2014). Image by Dan McMullin.

Chapter 5

Cambodian Classical Dance

Unsettlement, Authenticity, Affect, and Exclusion

Tiffany Lytle

A small girl of about five or six walks onto the stage. Her porcelain skin, rosy cheeks, and chubby arms make the audience coo over her adorable stature. She's different from the rest of the girls—lighter, whiter. They put her dead center where she can be seen by the entire audience. She looks like she knows exactly what she's doing up there: each dance movement and smile is deliberate and steadfast. This little girl might have a lot of promise!

As the years go by, the little girl grows up. She is no longer a featured dancer; rather, she has been thrown to the back of the stage, too tall and too thick to fit in. Her differences don't make her "cute" anymore; they make her just another aesthetic problem for the director to deal with. As they squeeze and sew her into her costume, they tell her to suck it in.

"Hold your breath. We need to make your waistline look *tung* (tight)."

"Don't eat red meat," they tell her. "It will make you fatter."

It was blatantly obvious that her body didn't fit the mold that they had envisioned for her.

This little girl was me, Tiffany Johanna Lytle. I am half Caucasian, half Cambodian and 100 percent Cambodian American. My mother is a survivor of the Killing Fields, and she shared those experiences with me through storytelling and declarations of strength and resilience. She says that I am half of her, and it is my duty to keep our Cambodian culture alive. I took this challenge on wholeheartedly and found a sense of identity within the Cambodian community of Long Beach, California,

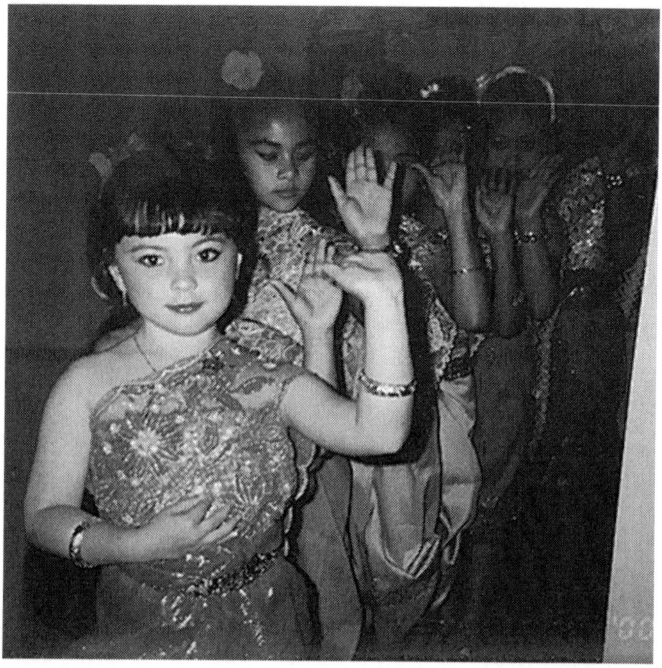

Tiffany Lytle (front) in April 1996, performing in the United Cambodian Community (UCC) group's Cambodian New Year's celebration. From the private collection of the Lytle Family.

despite some claims that I am not "Cambodian enough" to be featured on stage as a Cambodian classical dancer. By participating within Long Beach's Cambodian arts scene, I am unsettling purist notions of Cambodian culture to show that I, too, am Cambodian, and I, too, have the right to represent my heritage through dance.

Long Beach, California, is home to over 20,000 Cambodian Americans. This is the largest grouping of Cambodians in the United States, seconded only by a population of 11,000 in Lowell, Massachusetts. The immigration of Cambodians to the US came in two waves. The first took place in the mid-1970s and consisted of more affluent Cambodians who were able to escape the imminent takeover by the Khmer Rouge. The second influx of Cambodians to the US came in the 1980s and, unlike the first wave of Cambodian immigrants, these citizens were primarily composed of farmers and residents of smaller villages who did not receive formal educations.[1]

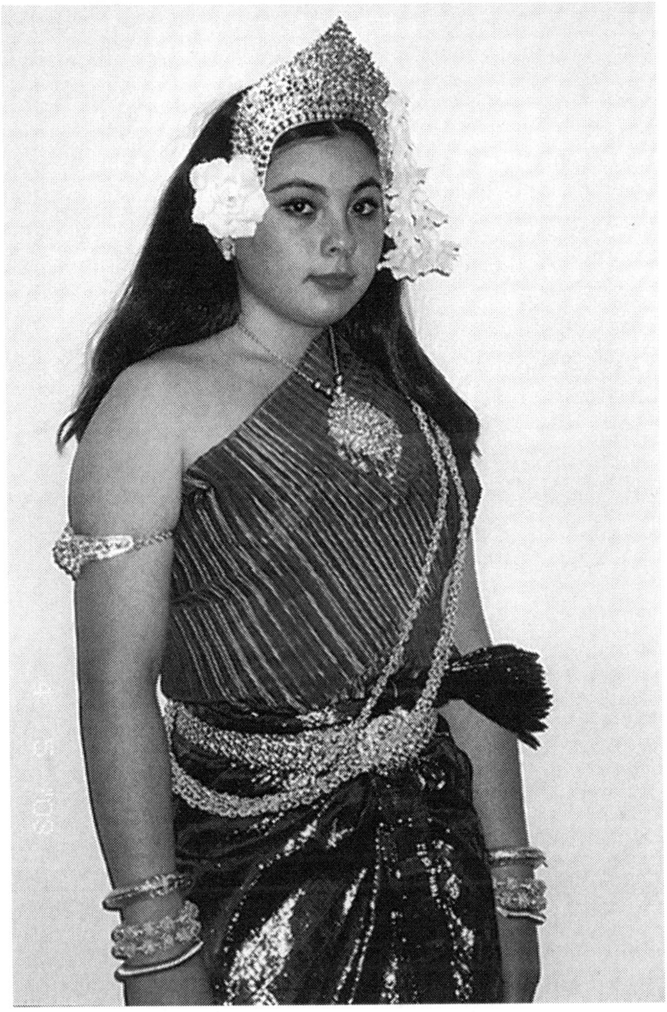

Tiffany Lytle, approximately age twelve. She is dressed for the traditional blessing dance, Chourn Por. From the private collection of the Lytle Family.

Cambodian immigration to America was based upon escaping Cambodia before or after a traumatic period of darkness in Cambodia's political history more commonly referred to as the Khmer Rouge Era, or the Killing Fields Era. April 17, 1975, marks the day Pol Pot's Communist regime, led by soldiers called the Khmer Rouge, took over the capital of Cambodia.[2] Under the name Democratic Kampuchea (DK), the new government power began to implement an experimental system of collectivizing assets and labor to move Cambodia away from industrialized cities to a more agrarian system, in the hopes of bringing Cambodia into Pol Pot's vision of a "Golden Age." Thousands of people were ripped from the cities and forced to work in labor camps that were fueled with little food and governed with great violence. David Chandler notes in his book *A History of Cambodia* that nearly two million people died as a result of the actions of the DK regime.[3] Its policies included the eradication of individuals who could possibly be a threat to Pol Pot's power. Targets included political officials, artists, doctors, and other educated individuals. These people were hunted down and killed so that they could not promote ideas that could cause potential conflict or uprisings.

The DK would further unsettle Cambodia by completely banning all forms of Cambodian traditional culture and art during Pol Pot's three-and-a-half-year reign. The only type of music or art that was permitted to be displayed took the form of pro-Khmer Rouge propaganda. Any violation of this ban would result in death, forever silencing the artists and their art. The death of artists would ultimately mean the deaths of entire art forms, since the skills and knowledge required to carry them out were passed down through oral tradition. Without people who knew about the techniques for traditional Cambodian art production, the Cambodian people's coveted cultural practices would be lost forever.

Cambodians have the strong belief that their traditional arts, like Cambodian classical dance, folk dance, and pinpeat music production, are unique artistic practices that separate Cambodian culture from that of their neighboring countries. Unsettling Cambodian cultural practices and traditions would shake the values and identities of the people. From interviews with some Long Beach–based Cambodian American artists, I've learned about how their sense of national pride and identity is deeply entrenched in these cultural productions. Natalie Lor is a Cambodian classical dancer whose training comes directly from the Cambodian Royal Palace. She says, "Believe me, Apsara [a famous Cambodian classical dance piece that has been appropriated in both Thai and Vietnamese styles of dance] is from Cambodia . . . from Queen Kosamack Neary Roth! She is the one that create[d] that! [Holding on to our cultural dances] is why Cambodian[s are] still alive!"[4] This statement took the form of an impassioned, blood-pumping rhetoric that nearly made Lor lose her breath. Her passionate response clearly exemplified the importance of Cambodia's traditional arts to their people. Lor states, "You know, I don't want to . . . to lose my country and my Cambodian culture."

The aftermath of Pol Pot's radical unsettlement of Cambodian culture resulted in a cultural preservation movement by the Cambodian people and their diaspora. Similar to the Indian subjects in Purnima Mankekar's *Unsettling India,* the unsettlement of Cambodians and their culture has called into question the idea of what it means to be authentically Cambodian.[5] Mankekar posits that the sense of unsettlement experienced by her informants has affected the way "Indianness" is produced through transnational public cultures.[6] Just as "Indian-ness" is produced transnationally then projected upon India, "Cambodian-ness" too has been produced through diaspora's projection of Cambodian authenticity.

So, what is Cambodian cultural authenticity? According to Kirin Mirchandani in *Phone Clones,* "the word authenticity is ordinarily used to signify something that is real or original."[7] Cambodians would seek to produce historically accurate rituals from their culture, like Cambodian classical dance, as a reaction to the inauthentic cultural practices that the DK forced upon the Cambodian people during their reign. Because of immigration away from Cambodia and the death of many of Cambodia's master artists, the authenticity of Cambodian dance is complicated. Who do we ask about the origins of Cambodian dance? As Mirchandani writes, "claims of authenticity involve the establishment and recognition of the social location of actors."[8] Dancers who were able to escape Cambodia before the DK regime took over, or those who kept their skills secret and survived the Killing Fields, would be deemed the "authenticity makers." Those who left Cambodia prior to the DK takeover often came from affluent families, and many of those fled to France. Their political positions in Cambodian communities were already powerful because they were usually members of the royal family, further solidifying their places as the "authenticity makers" of Cambodian dance. Though riddled with complications of rank and class, the authenticity politics of Cambodian dance would be crucial to repairing the fabric of the Cambodian cultural community.

In order to prevent the loss of Cambodian national identity, the action of remembering and participating in traditional cultural practices is important for Cambodian Americans. Cambodian American artists like Lor work to preserve Cambodian classical dance here in the United States by teaching younger generations the techniques and choreography that are considered to be vital both for understanding Cambodian dance and for creating a sense of Cambodian national pride.

Learning Cambodian dance and other Cambodian traditional cultural forms helps to teach Cambodian Americans to identify signifiers of Cambodian cultural identity and produces affective responses to images of Cambodian culture. Just as South Asians in Mankekar's *Unsettling India* cultivate affective responses to objects in Indian supermarkets, Cambodians gain affective responses to popular images of Cambodian classical dancers.[9] These responses help create ideal frames of "Cambodian-ness," national belonging, and authentic Cambodian dance culture.

The ideal appearance of a Cambodian classical dancer is featured in the image of the Apsara character. She is a slim, light-skinned woman whose long black hair cascades down from under a tall golden headdress. The gold jewelry and sequined garb that she wears has distinct Cambodian patterns. The floral designs and symmetrical stitching on the Cambodian silk have special significance in the world of Cambodian dance. This image is promoted transnationally and becomes a signifier of "Cambodian-ness." This appearance is what people seek to promulgate when trying to participate authentically in Cambodian performance culture.

These affective qualities bring about purist notions of what is authentic Khmer culture. The previously stated description of the ideal body for a Cambodian dancer is shaped by Cambodian "authenticity makers," many of whom also happen to be related to the royal family.[10] This Phnom Penh style of music and dance is considered by royal loyalists to be the true expression of Cambodian culture. Lor is related to the royal family and received her dance training within the walls of the Cambodian Royal Palace. She considered this technique of Cambodian dance to be an expression of both Cambodian and Cambodian American art.

Many first-generation Cambodian dancers subscribe heavily to the idea that Cambodian dance technique should be carefully preserved, rather than being reinterpreted. They feel that if Cambodian art is not kept in its "pure" form, it will be lost forever. Much of the contemporary work that has been produced by this generation's artists still features the same movement languages, while telling new stories. The dancers seek to gain stability within the art to help reconcile some of the damage caused by Pol Pot's rule.

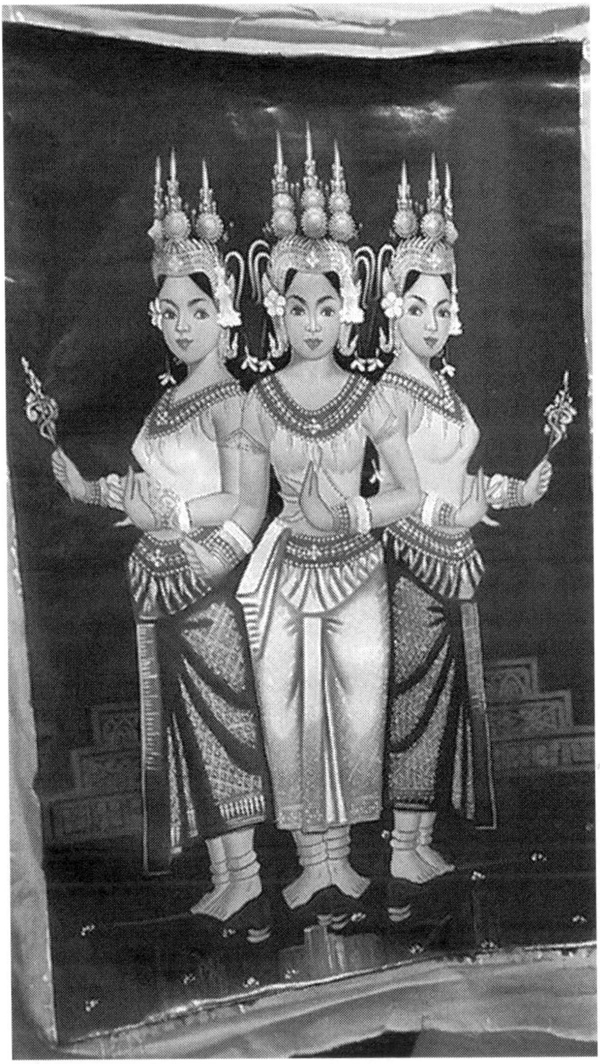

Image of the traditional Apsara character. Stock photo.

Although I see the value in promoting this idea of authentic cultural practice, I still wonder why this idea of Cambodian dance is synonymous with Cambodian American dance culture.

For second-generation Cambodian Americans like myself, ideas of identity and cultural belonging within art are not as simple as following a recipe for Cambodian classical dance production. Growing up in the United States means exposure to many types of cultures that we learn from and connect with daily. Our identities are then established with an awareness of what it means to be both Cambodian and American. Through acculturation practices, many of the so-called 1.5 and second generations of Cambodian Americans have begun to practice American-style art forms, like hip-hop, jazz dance, and modern dance. Because we are more commonly surrounded by these non-Cambodian art forms than we are by traditional Cambodian art forms, these artistic mediums become woven into the makeup of our identity.

Artists like myself, who practice both Cambodian classical dance and Western styles of dance and write Western styles of music, often feel as though our identities are bifurcated. On one hand, I am American and participate in American cultural art; but on the other hand I practice Cambodian classical art, too. I do not fit in with the "authentic" form of either a modern dancer or the form of a Cambodian classical dancer, so I must create a space for myself to negotiate these complicated identity politics.

My creative work has led me to develop unique Cambodian contemporary artwork that not only incorporates Cambodian classical dance technique, but fuses my training in Western dance styles within the traditional Cambodian dance movement vocabulary. I have chosen to focus specifically on unsettling notions of authenticity surrounding Cambodian classical dance, because it is the core dance form of my training and produces deep affective meaning for me. In order to express myself authentically and wholly, I need to address both aspects of my cultural identity by referring to myself as both a Cambodian classical dancer and a modern dancer. I do not fit the bodily image of either form, as I am not thin, nor am I tall, but I do assert that I am both of these things.[11] This denial of core physical traits found in these dance styles, paired with my assertion of identity formation, disturbs the normative associations of what constitutes a dancer in these styles. By claiming both these identities in one body, I am carving a space for myself within the production of contemporary Cambodian performance art.

In my attempt to carve a space for myself and others like me within Cambodian art, I have developed Cambodian Fusion dance choreography and musical compositions. In an amalgamation of both Khmer and English lyrics, my songs talk about the Asian-American experience, while my movement technique tears down the boundaries that separate Cambodian classical dance from other movement styles. This synthesis of all my learned artistic skills from all the communities that I am a part of helps me merge my once bifurcated identity into one.

Although I agree with the importance of the Cambodian classical dance preservation movement, because I don't fit within the purist ideals of "Cambodian-ness," I have pursued the development of artistic work that places me within the realm of Cambodian American contemporary art. This fusion form of art becomes an authentic expression of my identity and is reflective of the communities that I come from. Development of this new genre explores dance tradition as a form of expression for Cambodian Americans while unsettling ideas of authentic Cambodian art.

Notes

1. Susan Anne Needham and Karen I. Quintiliani, *Cambodians in Long Beach* (Arcadia Publishing, 2008).
2. David Chandler, *A History of Cambodia* (Westview Press, 1983).
3. Chandler, *A History of Cambodia.*
4. Natalie Lor, discussion with the author, February 2016.
5. In *Unsettling India,* Mankekar conceptualizes India's unsettlement within the historical and political conditions of India. The idea of unsettlement in India comes from globalization, while the Cambodian nation's unsettlement comes from war and genocide. Purnima Mankekar, *Unsettling India: Affect, Temporality, Transnationality* (Duke University Press, 2015).
6. Mankekar, *Unsettling India,* 5.
7. Kiran Mirchandani, *Phone Clones: Authenticity Work in the Transnational Service Economy* (ILR Press, 2012), 135.
8. Mirchandani, 135.
9. Mankekar, *Unsettling India,* 79.
10. As Cambodian classical dance was a privilege that only well-off families or members of the royal family were able to participate in, it originally represented only the culture of high-ranking Khmers, rather than that of the entire country.
11. Modern dancers are usually considered to be tall and thin. The more commonplace physical quality of a modern dancer is slenderness.

Chapter 6

Lao Fighters/*Refugee Nation*

Leilani Chan and Ova Saopeng (TeAda Productions)

A mother lives alone in the darkness. A father struggles to forget a lost war. A son battles in the streets of urban America. A daughter searches for answers in her community. *Refugee Nation* is about a young generation struggling to understand their history and the silence of an elder generation still healing from the traumas of war. Based on the stories of Laotian refugees in the U.S., *Refugee Nation* began with workshops and interviews in 2005. The work continued to develop through residencies across the country, which included performing scenes at outdoor festivals and community events, while we continued to research and collect oral histories from Laotians in the U.S. In 2012, the full-length play eventually had its completed premiere in Los Angeles and included our third cast member, Litdet Viravong.

More than just a telling of Laotian American history, this three-person performance eloquently touches upon issues relating to the refugee experience, assimilation, generation gap, and mental health using drama, film, music, and audience interaction, and personalizes these issues through a genuine Laotian American perspective. The result is a performance that brings to light the hidden stories of Laotian Americans around the U.S., while uniting people from all types of backgrounds, ethnicities, and histories by relaying the ideas of change, loss, struggle, healing, and the unrelenting strength of the human spirit. The *Refugee Nation* continues to grow. With the certainty of new refugee arrivals from the Middle East, what can we learn from the wounds of a war 30 years ago that are still yet to be healed?

Artist Statement: Leilani Chan (creator, writer, and performer, *Refugee Nation*)

As theater artists, we have a terrible habit of counting butts in seats as a reflection of our success. This is only reinforced by funders asking for audience numbers and our presenters' reliance on ticket sales. For theater artists, the building that is a theater is our temple. The place we are honored to be in to get a chance to work on our craft. Where we can control lights, sound, and all the elements needed for dramatic presentations. For our communities, however, a theater most certainly is not a place that feels like home. For most, a "theater" is not a place they go to regularly and certainly not a place they expect to see their experiences and faces reflected from the stage. In creating and presenting *Refugee Nation,* our arts allies have been community organizations and progressive arts venues. We had yet to encounter an art venue that regularly serves the Southeast Asian community. To produce *Refugee Nation* we consistently find ourselves having to educate the venue about the Southeast Asian community in their midst, while also educating the community about theater. The idea that "theater" can reflect their experience, that seeing a live performance could transform their self-perception, seems far-fetched until we can actually get them to see a performance. We have brought theater to the community, and we have brought the community to the theater. As artists, we exist in between and are always negotiating this tension; this has become a skill in itself. As we do this work, the brick-and-mortar buildings have become a primary obstacle in our community building.

One of our first residency experiences in developing this piece was in the Bay Area. Our presenter was La Peña Cultural Center, based in Berkeley, CA, and known primarily as a Latino venue. The neighboring Laotian community is primarily in Oakland and Richmond, less than half an hour away. Ova (performer and co-writer) and I arrived as early as possible to start our residency activities, which included workshops with schools and community groups, short performances at events, and meetings with community leaders. All this was done while we were still writing and rehearsing a new version of the play.

A week prior to our opening, we were invited to perform an excerpt of the show at the Lao New Year Festival in San Pablo City Hall, which was also only half an hour away from the Berkeley venue. Lao New Year Festivals happen annually all over the continent in any area that has a sizable Laotian community. It is the one event where the community comes together consistently. So we had the chance to test out a new scene in which we both play *Ajan* (expert) emcees who attempt to be entertaining while trying to educate the audience about Laotian history and culture. However, both characters inadvertently spark controversy by expressing their individual takes on history.

The festival was host to 300 Lao community members. We were quite apprehensive about the performance, which was slated to take place at an outdoor stage where environmental elements could not be controlled, and which featured unreliable sound equipment. Our presentation was sandwiched between traditional Lao music and dance performance and martial arts exhibitions. We were not sure how our scene would be received in this environment. For one thing, we would need to hold mics, something we do not have to do in the controlled environment of a theatrical venue.

As we took the stage, we were nervous, wondering whether, in this noisy atmosphere, people would be able to focus on us well enough to hear what we were saying. The din of chatter had been consistent throughout the previous performance, accompanied by the voices of the event's real emcees. We began our scene, and a strange thing happened. The chatter quieted. As we delivered our lines, we found ourselves pausing in places we'd never had to stop before to wait for the laughter to die down before moving on. This audience understood references and gestures our theater audiences had not. People were nodding and cheering as we continued. More than once, I received applause after delivering a line. This had never happened in a theater venue. For the first time, we had an audience that not only knew what we were talking about, but also knew the back story, hidden meanings, and inside jokes. It was thrilling.

After the performance, people came up to us, exclaiming that they never knew their story could be told on stage. One elder came up to me and said that our performance was so important; the youth need to know this story, he told us, and the community needs to hear it. I was so excited by his exuberance that I reminded him that this was only a ten-minute excerpt, and that we would be presenting the full show in just two weeks at La Peña Cultural Center. I asked him to please bring his family to see the rest of the performance.

His response was, "Ten minutes is enough." Argh, a dagger to my heart! We so wanted to share the full show with this audience. But to do that, they would have to come to the performance venue. Ultimately, we did have a fairly well-attended showing at La Peña Cultural Center. But this audience was by far the largest and most enthusiastic thus far.

Several years later, having learned from this experience, we were invited to participate in the San Diego Lao New Year Festival, attended by over 3,000 people. Here we again faced the challenges of venue, working with community, and intergenerational issues, as well as the challenge of performing at a real *Ajan* event. As preparation for the performance we were invited to an *Ajan*'s, a Laotian elder's, house. Unknown to us, the gathering was a dinner with many of the leaders and first-wave elders in the community. During the meal, we were spontaneously asked to perform. Some artists complain about the "dog-and-pony show" they must do for special donors; this was our "make it or break it" moment in front of the elders and leaders, in the foyer of a modest suburban home. Somehow, we did it.

We were able to secure a venue near the festival grounds and, in collaboration with Legacies of War and the film *Nerakhoon: The Betrayal,* we participated in an event the evening before the festival. The venue was a ballroom, not a theater. Upon arrival, we realized that while the center described itself as state-of-the-art, it had a fabulous lighting grid accessible only by a cherry picker—and there were no lights on the grid. Luckily, we had a friend helping us out, and he had a truck. He picked up the lights and, right up until 30 minutes before the performance, he and Ova were under the stage searching for ways to plug them in without blowing the electricity. We were our own crew!

Just as we started saying to ourselves "Never again, never again," the people began to arrive. As we got into our costumes, additional chairs were being pulled out. Soon the room was full to capacity, standing room only, with 500 people in the audience. We had selected only 30 minutes from the existing play for this presentation. This included a scene between a young woman trying to start an oral history project and an elder man still suspicious of any organizing and still suffering from PTSD. We had been struggling with this scene, but finally we chose an outlined improv structure to play with.

Using all that we had learned about the struggles of the community, and from our own struggles with the venue, our characters found words they hadn't had in rehearsals. Ova began speaking in Lao as elders in the front row, many of whom had watched us in that living room full of *Ajan*, were nodding and applauding in agreement with Ova's character. As this happened, the young woman, the character I was playing, found responses like, "I don't know what you just said," since both she and I didn't speak Lao. And in the frustration of being stuck in very tight lighting, not being able to move from our spots on the stage, we found the metaphor of the relationship between youth and elders. We found the desire to move the community forward, versus being held back by a past that cannot be forgotten yet cannot be named. Soon both characters and actors found themselves in tears.

In 2011, we were invited to perform at Sacramento's first-ever Lao New Year Festival. The festival organizer, Lily, who is also a community activist, asked us to perform a scene that includes the voices of two men in prison. One is a Royal Lao Soldier imprisoned in a communist re-education camp during the mid-1970s in Laos; the other is a gang member in a contemporary federal prison facing deportation. Each tries to understand how they ended up in their respective cells and the injustice of their imprisonment. The scene ends with a physical fight between the two. We had chosen not to perform this scene at outdoor family events because of both the content and the challenges of the choreography. The fight scene is difficult on a small stage, where the wires for mics and instruments cover the floor and present a hazard. And the swearing of the characters could be unwelcome by parents. But Lily insisted she would make it okay, and the stage was unusually big. She explained that there was a pervasive gang problem in her community, and she knew many gang members and their families would be in attendance. We chose to perform that scene and the *Ajan* scene.

Seven thousand people attended the festival, and the sound was a bit sketchy. But the report back was that many in the audience had known exactly the story we were telling. Lily's own mother, who was also in attendance, shed tears at hearing of the experiences of the communist re-education camp.

Keeping communities coming to shows is hard, because venues must provide follow-up programming even after the artist leaves town. One of the most successful examples of this was at Out North in Anchorage, Alaska, where we held a workshop in 2007 as part of our residency activities leading up to the performance. This included working with a group of 20 Hmong students at Begich Middle School. This school was known for being one of the most diverse in Anchorage, with over 26 languages spoken by the student population. These students had never been asked to come together before.

One of them happened to be the son of one of our community organizers. He brought the *Refugee Nation* flyer home, and his mom asked him if he would participate. He initially said "no" because he was not a refugee, but his mother sat him down and told him about how his grandfather had escaped Laos to come to the U.S., and about what his grandparents and parents had had to do to bring him to this country. With pride, the young man attended our theater workshop.

We conducted a two-day residency at Begich Middle School. On day 1, we offered a three-hour workshop. On day 2, Ova and I would share an excerpt of *Refugee Nation,* and the students were expected to share what they had learned during two assemblies, attended by the entire school.

On the first day of the workshop, they goofed off a bit, often laughed nervously, and didn't understand our exercises, but they did them anyway. Many were asked to share stories of their families' escapes from Laos, but some didn't remember and had to go home that night to ask their parents or grandparents. The second day, the students quickly applied some of the theater games we taught them. Between assemblies, they even asked for a game we had taught them the day before to help them gain focus and calm nerves.

When the assemblies were over, the principal asked the students if they wanted to continue doing theater. They said "Yes." So, Out North partnered with the middle school to keep an afterschool program running for the Hmong students. In addition, Out North began *khene,* traditional Lao music, classes for the community at their center. A few years later, they invited one of our collaborators, May Lee-Yang, a Hmong playwright from Minneapolis, to perform her solo performance piece.

One of our most successful residencies took place in Minneapolis, Minnesota. We were presented by Intermedia Arts, Pangea WORLD Theater, and the Lao Assistance Center. Again, the majority of the community lived in Saint Paul, while Intermedia Arts Theater was in Minneapolis. Luckily the Lao Assistance Center (LAC) was an active and essential partner, due in large part to LAC's development director, Bryan Thao Worra, who is also an artist and award-winning writer himself. In addition, our key commissioning partner, Legacies of War, was able to install their exhibit in the gallery outside the theater during the run of the show. Through the combined efforts of these four organizations, we received press coverage and full houses comprising the most diverse audiences we have ever had. Post-show discussions were vibrant, and refugees from Somalia, Nepal, and more were in attendance. Many of the attendees discussed how they shared similar experiences.

When we began to develop this play, the U.S. was engaging in the Iraq War. Meanwhile, it seemed to us that the Southeast Asian communities in the U.S. were, and still are, just beginning to discover ways to heal from the effects of the Vietnam War era, fought 30 years prior. After over a decade of touring this work, *Refugee Nation* continues to be relevant, as the U.S. continues to engage in wars that result in more refugees seeking asylum. The development of *Refugee Nation* was pivotal to our creative practice as artists of color. It has created a template for us to continue to work with newcomers from other countries and regions, many of whom face similar challenges upon arrival in the U.S. We call this the TeAda methodology, which we continue to utilize to collaborate with other refugee and immigrant communities. New plays that have come out of this process and have toured nationally include *Global Taxi Driver* and *Masters of the Currents.*

In addition, we know that many of the community participants, collaborators, and audience members that *Refugee Nation* has touched have gone on to become playwrights, performers, and artists in their own right. Meanwhile, mainstream (historically white regional theaters) are only just beginning to include Southeast Asian stories from an Asian American perspective on their stages. Through our work as artists and as TeAda Productions, we know that our practice can bring attention to communities struggling to survive and tell their own stories. By doing so, we know that this kind of performance practice can create healing and intergenerational understanding.

"Lao Fighters," an excerpt from *Refugee Nation*

Scene 2: Fighters

VIDEO plays of Khene player, into LA Riots, into bombs and military in Southeast Asian jungle.

Both characters enter in black. KHAM, a Royal Lao Army soldier, dressed in rags, is being held captive in a communist labor camp. He squats downstage left. SANG, an ex–gang member, is being held in a modern-day jail cell; he stands upstage right. Lights up.

KHAM
How long have I been in here?

SANG
I spent two years in county.

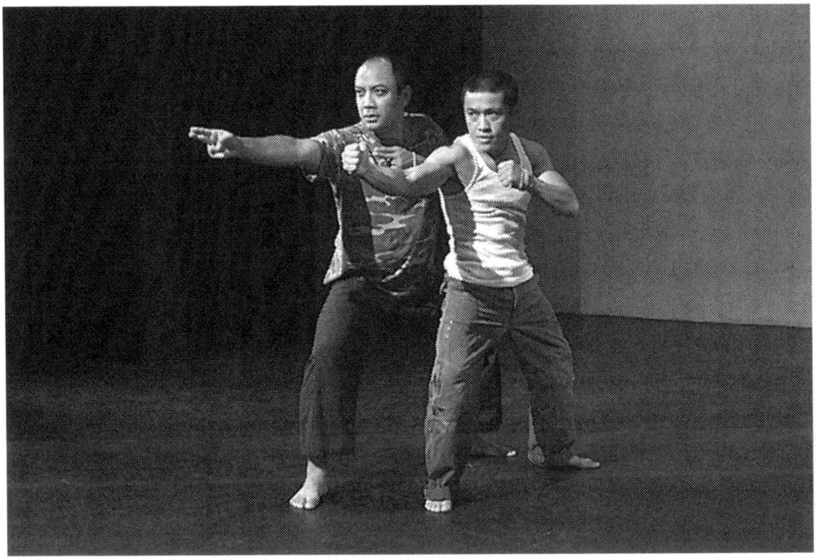

Scene from "Lao Fighters," with Ova Saopeng (rear) as Senior and Lidet Viravong (front) as Junior. Photo by Sean Samuda.

KHAM
Why do you keep moving me?

SANG
Three years in state.

KHAM
Where is my family?

SANG
Now I'm here

KHAM
When am I going to be let out?

SANG
I done the time for the crime.
I supposed to get released, but immigration just straight up picked me up and brings my ass here. Motherfuckin' Arizona? Deportation camp? You know, INS Detention Center. Shit.

KHAM
Damn communists. The war is over. Let me go. I want to see my family. I want to go home.

SANG
They want to ship my ass to Laos. I don't even speak Laos. I didn't know any of this shit until I got here. I told my mom not to come visit any more. She just cries and shit. But I had to ask her about what had happened 'cause I need it for my INS case. Why'd we leave Laos, Ma? Whoa, what? We escaped Laos on some bamboo and tires tied together and shit, and we crossed the Mekong River like that? At night? Holy shit, that's fuckin' crazy, man,

Both characters begin to move across the stage as if reliving their experiences. During the following lines they have choreographed movements interlaced within their dialogue.

KHAM
Ai Nong kao duah/The communist, they lie. They lie to the people of Laos. Lao is neutral, but they bring war into our country. That's why I fight against them. When they take over, they say we must go to *seminar seminar. Ma-na . . . Ma/Come here . . .Come.* Come learn about the new government. The new future. They lie again! Seminar is not school. Seminar is labor camp. Prison camp for Royal Lao Army soldiers, like me. I fight with Americans. Future? There is no future.

SANG moves as if reliving his family's escape from Laos.

Kham beckons as if to say "You should come."
He moves upstage center, then wraps his wrists together as if being tied up as a prisoner to a post.

SANG

People was getting shot or drowned or killed. By the time we got to the Thailand shore, half of the group was missing. We was in the Thai refugee camp for a long time. Took us a while to get the documents, to get U.S. sponsorship. The only way we got out was that we had to say we would, uh, resort to being Christians. Oh, hell yeah. We'll be Christians. So a white family sponsored us and we ended up in Dumas, Texas.

Sang, continuing journey of escape, rolls, crawls and hides across to stage left.

KHAM

They take people away. Everybody is scared. No one trust each other. Neighbors tell on neighbor. Family tell on family. They take me away. They take me away from my family. My wife. My children. *Luk er, mia er jao yu sai?/My child. My wife. Where are you?* When I see birds flying in the sky, I am jealous they have wings.

Sang lifts hands as if to say "Praise the Lord," then seems possessed, while Kham unlocks his arms into Jesus on cross.

Kham moves stage right as if being dragged away, then searches for his family.

SANG

A'ight. It's like this in the pen, right? You got four different groups: the blacks, Mexicans, whites and Other—they don't call us Asians; they call us Other. It's like the population of LA: 60 percent Mexican. When I was at county, we was at war with the Mexicans. So you can imagine: inside, the war is on every day, everywhere. So I thought of my drunk-ass pops forcing me to learn Muay Thai. You know, the hard way. So I'd try to remember.

Sang starts doing calisthenics, lifting weights, doing one-arm pushups as if in the prison yard.

Kham does Lao dance moves, then poses as if he is a Mexican gangster.

Kham moves as if he were going to punch Sang.
Sang moves, defending himself.

KHAM
Buk na mah, goo see ka mung!/You dog face. I'm going to kill you! Every day they put us to work. Lifting. Digging. They keep us working because they don't want us to think. Many of the older men, they are dying. Others they take away . . .maybe to another camp. The guards, they are only kids. They treat us like dogs. They beat us. Spit at us.

Sang practices Muay Thai and shadowboxes. Kham lifts rocks and debris.

Sang's shadowboxing intensifies, kicking and punching. Kham spits, and Sang reacts to spit as if it hits his face.

SANG
Folks would spit on us and all kinds of shit. It's not like the deputies actually care. Shit, they in there with us 8 hours, 10 hours a day. It's like entertainment to them. I got into so many fights they kept moving me from prison to prison. Now I get these seizures.

Kham stands as if he is a prison guard.

KHAM
In the Royal Lao Army I fight with America. I use radio and call location to drop bombs on the Ho Chi Minh Trail. Then the Royal Lao Army come in. But the bombs don't work. The enemy is smart. America pull out. That's why we lose the war. America is coward.

Sang shakes as if having a seizure.

Kham salutes.

Kham moves in and reacts to the devastation.

SANG
Yeah, yeah. LA riots was fun, man. You know that video game Street Fighter? We, uh, borrowed one of them. Was me and six Filipino cats with a big old machine above our heads running down the street. Shit, took so much electricity to run that dang thing we had to take it back. Stupid, man. We did some retarded shit. I mean, uh, I didn't do nothin', right? *(looks at audience)* But they did. That was fun, though. Not like the time I got shot.

Kham and Sang cross each other center stage.
Kham in the jungles of Laos seeking safety.
Sang grabbing machine and throwing it.

KHAM
I go into hiding with the Hmong up in the mountains. They good to me. They tell me stories about their leader. General Vang Pao. I never got to meet him, but I knew he was a good leader because he was well supplied by the Americans. The CIA.

Sang feigns being shot, slow-mo Matrix*-style.*

SANG
We were in the parking lot of the Yoshinoya. Me, my two homies and a girl. Another Asian gang pulls up. You know, the Filipino gang that got taken over by the Koreans. "What you want? Get out of the car. Let's handle it." Two cars pull up: ten of them, three of us. They didn't want to get down so they pulled out a gat. . . . I like to think of myself like a martial arts Bruce Lee action hero. So I open up the door and I dive in and hold my girl's head down. Fools start busting caps. I wait for them to pull out. Shit, my homies are lying on the floor, aw fuck I got hit.

Kham and Sang both envision their enemies approaching. Sang moves as if in driver's seat of car. Sang gets out of the car and crosses to passenger seat.

Kham mimes a rifle. Sang does Bruce Lee move and dives to cover girl.

Kham mimes shooting rifle. Sang reacts to being shot.

KHAM
They kill my general. They killed him in this camp. Who do I follow now? The army was my life. The army taught me everything. I came from a poor village. When I was 8 years old, both my parents died.

Sang lies on the floor as if hit and dies. Kham crosses to Sang and stands over him.

By the time I was 12 years old, I joined the Royal Lao Army.

Kham salutes and military-marches stage left.

SANG
I joined a gang when I was 12 years old. My first day at school in LA I got hit up. Filipino guys come to me and they like, "Where you from?" And I thought, dang, y'all friendly around here, and I'm like "I'm from Texas." They took one look at me, and straight jumped my ass. Well, you know, fast forward a few months later, I end up joining the same gang. They my family. They got my back.

Kham does martial arts training in slow motion and repeats sequence.

Sang gets off ground to tell story as if he is 14 years old again.

Sang turns his back to audience.

KHAM
I was on a mission as the platoon leader.

Kham moves downstage right of Sang and positions himself with rifle, ready to attack.

SANG
I was in a warehouse with three hundred guys stacked three bunks high.

Sang faces the audience and poses next to Kham in fighting stance.

KHAM
We were fighting the communist forces. The Pathet Lao and North Vietnamese.

They pivot like a pinwheel.

SANG
I could tell it was going to go down. The Mexicans were getting ready to throw down.

They end up side by side, upstage center, delivering the rest of the lines as dialogue.

KHAM
The plan is to attack them on both sides.

SANG
The wall is our friend.

KHAM
Flank them on both sides.

SANG
Make a barricade. That way, they can only come at us one by one.

BOTH run to far sides of the stage and cross back down stage.

KHAM
We will trap them against the mountains of Khammouane.

They end up side by side at center stage, in battle formation.

SANG
Give us a couple minutes to defend ourselves before the guards get here.

KHAM
The eastern border of Laos and Vietnam.

They split center and get ready to attack.

KHAM
Bpai, bpai, bpai!/Go, go, go!
Kham charges forward.

SANG
Line up, line up, line up!
Sang sprints forward.

SANG
Here they come, here they come!

They end up on opposite sides, ready for battle in their respective worlds.

KHAM
Jup kao!/Charge!

SANG
Motherfucker!

Both men shadowbox in their corners and fight invisible enemies separately. They cross stage doing somersaults, high kicks, and aerial punches. After each fights off several opponents, their eyes land on each other. They attack each other in a full contact fight sequence that ends up in a stalemate. They circle the stage and return to their positions at top of scene. Lights out.

CHAPTER 7

21 Reasons Why This Movie Sucks

PRINCE GOMOLVILAS

"WHAT IS THE GREATEST PIECE of Asian American literature of all time?"

That's a question I've often asked when standing in front of students in ethnic studies classes, various communities within the Asian diaspora, and savvy theater audiences. The usual suspects are invariably mentioned: *The Woman Warrior* by Maxine Hong Kingston, *Native Speaker* by Chang-Rae Lee, *The Joy Luck Club* by Amy Tan. Those bold enough to speak up and name one of these books (or other books of similar import) are not only told, by me, that they're flat-out wrong, but they are also subjected to my butchered (and heavily accented) retelling of the swan/swan-feather parable. (With apologies to Ms. Tan, if a comic bit can elicit a cheap laugh from just *one* person in an audience, then the remaining looks of discomfort—or outright horror—are worth it. [Revisit my career in ten years, and ask me if I still feel the same way.])

Let's definitively settle the question, here in print, once and for all. The greatest piece of Asian American literature of all time is *Bringing Down the House* by Ben Mezrich. Before you doth protest too much, let me explain.

Bringing Down the House documents the true story of six MIT math students who devise an elaborate system of card-counting in blackjack, a nerdy scheme that eventually wins them millions of dollars in the casinos of Las Vegas. Have you made the connection yet? Do you now understand why this book is the greatest piece of Asian American literature of all time? It's simple. *Asians love gambling.* Let me write that again, this time in capital letters. *ASIANS LOVE GAMBLING.* You know it's true. If you don't believe me, just visit an Indian casino and look at the clientele—it's like a Filipino fish market in there.

Take my dad, for example. Here's a man who suffered two major heart attacks and a stroke, is partially paralyzed, has trouble walking, and cannot speak—but despite all that he still manages to board a bus almost every day to go to the Santa Anita Race Track in Arcadia, California. And the first year of my college education was not financed through accumulated savings that my parents had accrued over time. My mother actually hit the jackpot on a quarter slot machine at the (now-demolished) Frontier Hotel and Casino in Vegas. You see, all people of Asian descent are afflicted with a kind of gambling sickness, a core malady that is trapped deep inside their smooth and tender bodies.

Before you accuse my thesis and supporting argument of being thin or perhaps even painful to witness, allow me to continue building my case. The gambling thread isn't the only element that secures *Bringing Down the House* a place in Asian American literary history. The protagonist of the book is Asian American, and, in fact, many of the characters in the book are Asian American. (But I'm certain you already drew that conclusion the moment I said "MIT math students"—*of course they were Asian!*)

If all that doesn't persuade you to side with me and trumpet my original premise until the day you die, let me point out that I also teach at a major university. (And if that statement is too subtle, let me make what I'm saying clear: I am right, and anybody who disagrees with me is wrong.)

So when it was announced several years ago that *Bringing Down the House* was going to be adapted into a feature film by a major production company and distributed by a major studio, I was elated. It was clear that this movie would become the greatest piece of Asian American *cinema* of all time. (As an act of celebration, I went out and bought a new rice cooker. [It's easy to break free from the feeling of rootlessness when your local grocery store has an Asian aisle.]) Finally, Asian Americans—particularly Asian American men—were going to be front and center in a mainstream motion picture. And this held significance, for me and my colleagues in the entertainment industry, because despite a few small breakthroughs over the years many Asian American actors were still relegated to playing the Chinese waiter or the Japanese tourist or the Asian gangster or the computer nerd or the dirty refugee or the token ethnic person in the background. But in the film version of *Bringing Down the House,* the characters could be portrayed just like they were portrayed in the book—they were real, three-dimensional Asian Americans. And, sure, they all stereotypically excelled at math, but they were also the heroes of the story and they were given depth.

For example, the main character in the book is Kevin Lewis. (It was later revealed to the public that his real name is actually Jeffrey Ma.) He is described as a bright, good-looking, charismatic MIT whiz kid, a Chinese American who was in a fraternity, played water polo, and defied stereotypes. So now, with this new movie, in one fell cinematic swoop, Hollywood could finally atone for its casting sins of the past.

But then, a dastardly thing happened on the way to the film set. *Bringing Down the House* was eventually transformed into a movie that was now titled *21*. For those of you who didn't see *21* or don't remember it, I present to you:

"21 Reasons Why This Movie Sucks"

1. Jim Sturgess—the star of the Beatles musical, *Across the Universe*—was cast in the lead role. Incidentally, Jim Sturgess happens to be Caucasian.
2. Not only is Jim Sturgess Caucasian, he is *so* white that professional photographers could use him to light dim interiors.
3. Just to be clear: *Caucasian* Jim Sturgess was cast as the character based on *Asian* Jeffrey Ma. But that's not what bothers me most about this. I was hoping the filmmakers were going to give him buckteeth, tape his eyes back, and have him do a funny accent—this would've been offensive, sure, but at least the audience would've noticed that there was something fishy going on. But the filmmakers didn't do that.
4. What they did was worse. In the movie, the character has been completely changed into a white guy with absolutely no trace of his original Asian American identity, as were other key Asian Americans from the book.
5. The byproduct of this reckless decision? Most of America will never know the act of complete cinematic whitewashing that has taken place.
6. Before I continue, I want to make sure you don't get the wrong idea about me. I *like* white people, I *know* white people,

I've *slept* with white people. But this is not the kind of movie that an actor like Jim Sturgess should be in. It would have been more appropriate if he had been cast as Ray Charles in *Ray* or as Idi Amin in *The Last King of Scotland* or as Frank Lucas, the Denzel Washington character in *American Gangster*. Or, even, the Denzel Washington character in *The Great Debaters* or *Remember the Titans* or *The Hurricane* or *Malcolm X* or any other Denzel Washington movie based on real people—because, apparently, judging by the movie *21*, it's perfectly okay to cast Caucasians as people of color. And since black folks are the ultimate people of color—why not Jim Sturgess?

7. Since the filmmakers simply erased the characters' racial and ethnic identities altogether, this suggests that they believe that issues of race and ethnicity do not matter.
8. Because I have chosen to speak about *21* in the way that I have, I have been accused of race-baiting and things of the like. But in a world where I still hear people hurl racial slurs at me from their car, I am convinced that we are not "post-racial" and that race *does* matter.
9. All this wouldn't be such a big deal if race *weren't* a significant factor in the book, but it *is*. *Bringing Down the House* offers a very real glimpse into the Asian American psyche.
10. Additionally, the book details how other people's perceptions of these MIT students' racial identities factored into their blackjack scheme.
11. Some people may say that I should be happy because the producers, out of an apparent act of charity, *did* cast two Asian Americans in smaller roles. But I seriously ask you: Why the hell should I be happy? That's like somebody jerking you off halfway and then leaving.
12. By the way, what's so wrong with somebody jerking you off halfway and then leaving? Well, I'm pretty sure that it has been scientifically proven that you can *die* from blue balls. (I'm not sure if my editors fact-checked this, but since this is such common knowledge I assume not.)
13. One of the producers of *21* was quoted as saying, "Believe me, I would have *loved* to cast Asians in the lead roles, but the truth is, we didn't have access to any bankable Asian

American actors that we wanted." If it's possible to smell bullshit in print, then you should smell it right about now.

14. If the producer's issue was that he couldn't find any Asian American actors who were bankable and there was extreme importance around the idea of bankabilty, then why was Jim Sturgess cast? He was brought onto the project as a relative unknown, long before the release of his high-profile movie, *Across the Universe,* which means he was not bankable at the time of casting. And even after the release of *Across the Universe,* all the way up to the time of publication of this essay, he's *still* not bankable. (And, by the way, *Across the Universe* is considered a box-office flop.)
15. And if the producer's issue was that Asian American acting talent was scarce in Hollywood, then he certainly had never spent a day at a casting call for an Asian American role. There are so many exceptional Asian American actors that, if I hated Asian American actors, I would throw up on a regular basis just walking through the streets of L.A. If you can't find them, then you're not really looking.
16. And if the producer's issue was that Asian American audiences have no impact at the box office anyway, so why cater to them—does he not know the facts? Even cursory research on the Internet would reveal that, on industry sites like Deadline.com over the past year (as of this writing), on any given week at the box office Asians account for about 11 percent to 14 percent of ticket sales—even though Asians make up only about 5 percent of the population in the United States. Those figures are remarkable. That means for a film that ultimately grosses $100 million, Asians are responsible for putting $11 to $14 million into the pockets of people who actively reject the practice of proper representation.
17. It would've been relatively easy for me to get over this controversy if not for the fact that it happened again with another high-profile movie just two years after the release of *21*. Nickelodeon's wildly popular animated series, *Avatar: The Last Airbender,* which features characters of Asian and Inuit descent in a definitively kung fu–filled Asian fantasy world, was made into a live-action feature film starring Noah Ringer, Jackson Rathbone, and Nicola Peltz. In case you haven't already

guessed, the movie's three lead actors are *so* white that they make Justin Bieber look Cambodian.

18. The filmmakers threw people of color a bone by reluctantly caving into pressure and casting *one* ethnic actor in a lead role—Dev Patel from *Slumdog Millionaire.* But guess what? He plays the lead *bad guy.* If anything can be defined as a "douchebag move," that's it.
19. What's so mind-boggling about all this is that the film was helmed by South Asian director M. Night Shyamalan, who really should've known better. But he didn't. And there's really nothing I can do about it now . . . *except* spoil the surprise endings of his movies! So: In *The Sixth Sense,* Bruce Willis turns out to be a ghost—yeah, that's right, *he's* one of the dead people that creepy boy sees! In *Unbreakable,* Samuel L. Jackson turns out to be a super-villain—yeah, that's right, he's *not* a mentor to Bruce Willis after all! In *The Village,* the village is actually in the present day—yeah, that's right, the film *seems* like it's set in the distant past, but it's a trick! And in *Signs,* the death of Mel Gibson's wife isn't a Godless coincidence—yeah, that's right, her car accident leads to Joaquin Phoenix swinging a baseball bat at aliens and killing them with water! (Don't ask.)
20. Both gambling and kung fu are cornerstones of Asian culture. We can play Texas Hold 'Em and snatch the pebble from your hand with one arm tied behind our freakin' backs.

And, finally,

21. Isn't it about time Hollywood did the right thing?

CHAPTER 8

From the Island of Berkeley

Hawaiian Belonging in California

KEVIN FELLEZS

THERE IS A YOUTUBE VIDEO of kī hō'alu (Hawaiian slack key guitar) musician Patrick Kahakauwila Kamaholelani Landeza singing "How Would You Feel?"—a song in which he proclaims his Californian Hawaiian identity.[1] Accompanied by a mixed-race band of musicians, Landeza answers his own rhetorical question in "How Would You Feel?" by claiming his Hawaiian ancestry while being true to his upbringing in his birthplace, Berkeley, California:

> How would you feel if I came up to you and said you weren't real?
> How would it be if I grew up with my friends and family in Hawai'i?
> Then I wouldn't be me. Just because I'm not from Hawai'i doesn't mean Hawai'i's not in me.
> My grandmother told me so, that home will always be in me.[2]

While his grandmother assures him that Hawai'i is an innate part of his identity, Landeza also recognizes Berkeley as central to it, as well—a place that formed him in distinct ways from an imaginary Patrick Landeza who might have been born and raised in Hawai'i. Landeza creatively merges Hawai'i and California into a single "home," asserting a sense of identity that stands in contrast to prevailing notions of Hawaiian belonging.

While there are other California-based kī hō'alu artists (both native Hawaiian and non-Hawaiian), I want to focus on Patrick Landeza because his performance of diasporic Hawaiian-ness moves away from the race- and land-based ideologies of belonging that are arguably necessary politically for Kānaka Maoli (literally, real or true people) in Hawai'i but can be problematic for Kānaka Maoli born and raised off-island.[3] How might Californian Kānaka Maoli support the actions of Kānaka Maoli in Hawai'i for self-determination and reassertion of native Hawaiian values and institutions without suppressing or obscuring also-valued connections to California? It is within this predicament that I want to think through the ways in which Landeza's engagement with kī hō'alu allows him to claim Hawaiian and Californian belonging simultaneously in order to articulate what I am calling an intertwined Californian Kanaka Maoli positioning that moves beyond mere "Caliwaiian" or "Hawafornian" hybridity.[4]

It was Landeza's deep commitment to slack key, after all, that helped establish him as a much-in-demand Hawaiian music performer who performs regularly on the West Coast "poi" circuit of Hawaiian restaurants, Hawaiian-themed clubs and performance halls, Hawaiian-themed parties and weddings, and "roots music" venues such as Berkeley's Freight and Salvage theater. He was an opening act for the West Coast tours by the late Hawaiian music star Israel Kamakawiwo'ole (better known simply as Iz), and other popular Hawaiian acts such as Cecilio and Kapono, Keali'i Reichel, and Hapa. I asked him why he performs such a traditional style of music when even in Hawai'i itself, the popularity of kī hō'alu is overshadowed by other idioms, including na mele paleoleo (Hawaiian rap) and Jawaiian (Hawaiian reggae) music. Currently, he enjoys a performance career that has expanded beyond the West Coast of the United States to include Hawai'i, Japan, and the rest of the continental United States.[5]

His answer was illuminating: "When I was younger, my parents would always play Hawaiian music. Constantly. When I was at home, I'd always hear it; and at all the parties and stuff. They were always playing Hawaiian music, Hawaiian songs; you know, like all the old stuff: Gabby [Pahinui], the Sons of Hawaii [a popular and highly influential group formed in 1960, originally co-led by Gabby Pahinui and Eddie Kamae, an 'ukulele virtuoso]. And I guess growing up I was influenced by all that. But I didn't know it, you know, until high school. So I mainly learned because I was ha'ina [influenced] by family."[6]

Still, despite a home culture saturated with Hawaiian culture, Landeza often faced questions about his Hawaiian cultural legitimacy. "It's a hard thing at first, not being from Hawai'i. I had to put up with that a lot. 'Why do you play Hawaiian music?' 'How come you play Hawaiian music?' [My response is] 'Number one, I'm Hawaiian and that's my heritage. I may not look it but I represent [it].' That [upsets] me sometimes; some people are so ignorant."[7] While Landeza acknowledges that many Hawaiian listeners have been supportive, questions about his legitimacy were a continuous source of tension, particularly in the early days of his career.

Have Guitar, Will Travel

Kī hō'alu, or Hawaiian slack key guitar, is an open-tuning fingerstyle acoustic guitar tradition that is unique to Hawai'i and heard as an indigenous Hawaiian musical tradition despite the guitar's introduction by non-Hawaiians. (I will also be using the term *slack key*, the shortened English language term that most practitioners use in referring to the music.) Kī hō'alu is considered a native Hawaiian practice for a number of reasons: its transmission within an oral tradition in Hawai'i; its origins and historical development in rural Hawai'i, far from the pressures of an urban or non-Hawaiian tourist music market; a reliance on hula dance rhythms for much of its traditional repertoire; lyrics in the Hawaiian language with themes drawn from native Hawaiian myths, romances, and folk tales, including the fondness for doubled meanings; and a nahenahe (sweet, gentle) aesthetic that favors a relaxed rhythmic pulse and pleasant melodies. There are virtuoso pieces, such as Sonny Chillingworth's "Whee Ha Swing," that require the guitarist to remain relaxed even as the picking and fretting patterns acquire increasing speed and the melodic embellishments increase in complexity and momentum, building into the Hawaiian corollary of a bluegrass breakdown.

In any case, these elements' overwhelming tendency toward the languid underscores the representation of Hawaiians as a sweet, gentle people whose culture is ripe for appreciation. Fittingly, the liner notes to *Hawaiian Slack Key Guitar Masters: Instrumental Collection* (Dancing Cat, 1995), an important early recording in slack key's emergence in the 1990s as a bona fide genre in the world music market, described slack key guitar as the sonic rendering of "vivid, warm tropical images that transcend the Islands to express universal feelings." Nonetheless, traditional kī hōʻalu features an alternating bass line that can be traced to the influence of the Mexican vaqueros, imported to train Hawaiian paniolo (cowboys; the term is derived from the Hawaiian translation of "Español") in cattle husbandry, who brought their guitars and music in the 1830s.[8]

Keeping this transcultural history in mind, I want to think through the ways in which Landeza's self-positioning as a diasporic, or more specifically Californian, Kanaka Maoli recalibrates the connections between blood, land, and song. As he has often maintained, he is from the "island of Berkeley," offering a shared pan-Pacific culture that embraces both Hawaiʻi and California. Fortuitously, his emergence as a professional kī hōʻalu guitarist arrived at the very moment the Dancing Cat record label was aggressively recording as many Hawaiian slack key guitarists as possible, actively promoting their work by sponsoring national and international tours, and distributing their recordings beyond Hawaiʻi and the U.S. national market. Dancing Cat was a major factor in not only preserving kī hōʻalu because it had rarely been featured in solo recordings before, even in Hawaiʻi, but it also created a slack key genre and market that had not existed prior to label founder George Winston's interest and promotion.

As an aspiring young guitarist, Landeza participated in various ways in the recordings at the label's studio in Santa Cruz, California, while also learning from older Hawaiian slack key artists such as Raymond Kane and Sonny Chillingworth. He would also journey to Hawaiʻi, staying at the home of his great-aunt, Judith O'Sullivan Sham, while studying with many of the leading kī hōʻalu musicians, including Kane, Chillingworth, and George Kuo. It was on an early family trip to Hawaiʻi that Landeza was first exposed to the guitar tradition by two uncles, Clarence and Francis AhYee, who performed kī hōʻalu at family lūʻau.

Unlike the more formalized hula tradition, with its sponsorship by Hawaiian aliʻi (elites) and its strict code of matriculation and education by kumu hula (hula masters), slack key was a rural vernacular guitar tradition that was passed down by example in the nānā hoʻo pili (look, listen) pedagogical approach of traditional Hawaiian music culture. There is little, if any, direct teaching; rather, students would quietly sit, listen, and try to imitate as best they could manage the tunings and playing of elder musicians. As Landeza and other guitarists confessed, these elder musicians often teased, yelled at, or simply ejected beginning guitarists from the musicians' circle, sometimes for minor infractions or for reasons seemingly unrelated to music performance.

As this suggests, kī hō'alu is not innately Hawaiian but is learned by careful observation and imitative repetition—a performative activity, to borrow from Judith Butler. The anecdotes by various guitarists about their learning experiences also indicate that the stereotype of native Hawaiian culture as celebrating indolence, lacking in standards, and without clear aesthetic goals, is incorrect. Hawai'i's isolation, too, has been overemphasized, particularly in the period between Captain Cook's landing in 1778 to the end of World War II in 1945. For example, despite being consistently figured as a native Hawaiian musical tradition, kī hō'alu requires the guitar, an instrument imported from Mexico, Portugal, and Spain. While adapting the guitar to Hawaiian aesthetics, Kanaka Maoli guitarists absorbed musical influences from a variety of other places, including Spain, Mexico, and the continental United States, perhaps through the people bringing guitars to the Islands: New England sailors and missionaries, Mexican vaqueros, Portuguese sailors, Filipino and Puerto Rican plantation laborers. In moving to the present day, I posit that California is one of the sites where kī hō'alu is undergoing a series of regional re-inventions that reflects diasporic Hawaiians' struggles for recognition as "real Hawaiians" distinct from, yet still related to, on-island Kānaka Maoli and the shared history that has resulted in the separation of Hawaiians from Hawai'i.

In making the claim that kī hō'alu has been transformed in its travels outside of Hawai'i, I point to kī hō'alu's similarities to another "traveling music," the blues: the adaptation and creative "re-use" of instruments from outside a community in order to give expression to the community's aesthetic values evidenced by, for instance, the "slackening" of the guitar's strings so when strummed unfretted, they sound a major key tonality, a dominant feature of traditional Hawaiian music; an unwritten, oral tradition that is transformed when the music enters the marketplace through recordings and performances in public spaces by taking the music outside of the community that gave birth to it; the increasing professionalization of the musicians as recordings and professional concertizing replace, in kī hō'alu's case, backyard jams, family lū'au, and other informal spaces for the performance of the music; the introduction of musicians from outside of the original community, who often further transform the music; a playing style that, while idiosyncratic or even "wrong" in terms of standard Western performance standards and aesthetics, defines the nature of the music; and, historically, a second-class status among academics and laypeople alike in terms of scholarly interest and perceived cultural importance.

Additionally, Hawaiian slack key guitarists share identical open tunings with blues and other folk traditions. Most significantly, because kī hō'alu is intimately linked to Hawaiian culture, it has fueled debates regarding artistic legitimacy and authenticity within kī hō'alu that bear a remarkable resemblance to similar debates in African American music.

Kī hō'alu, as it journeys beyond the Hawaiian archipelago to California and beyond, undergoes a transformation similar to the blues as it traveled north from the South. The blues, originating in the Mississippi Delta region, traveled north and west as blues artists joined the Great Migration and began developing regional styles of the blues, creating, for example, a Texas or Chicago blues style distinct from each other as well as from the blues of Mississippi. There is a long history of a proliferation of kī hō'alu styles unique to each of the Hawaiian Islands due to the relative lack of intra- and inter-island travel by rural paniolo for much of kī hō'alu's history. In fact, the "Big Island" of Hawai'i became home to a number of regional styles due to its large geographic territory. Just as obvious, however, is that guitarists and the music they created circulated among the Islands; still, local tastes prevailed enough for distinct repertoire, tunings, and styles to emerge.

Therefore, the idea that there are different styles or kinds of slack key guitar is not entirely novel. Yet many contemporary kī hō'alu artists in Hawai'i, who justify their blending of kī hō'alu with rock or hip-hop by pointing, for instance, to the example of Gabby Pahinui, the father of modern slack key guitar, who introduced jazz elements into the music, or to the distinctions between Pahinui from earlier guitarists such as Alice Namakelua, balk at the idea of a Californian kī hō'alu.[9]

Admittedly, even Landeza is skeptical about the idea of a California slack key style. He denies that he is performing anything other than authentic Hawaiian slack key guitar, telling me straightforwardly, "I don't think there's anything like a California slack key style. I think that it's just strictly kī hō'alu."[10] Why might Landeza be hesitant to accept that there might be such a thing as California kī hō'alu, while arguing for the legitimacy and authority of a Californian Kanaka Maoli perspective?

Californian Kanaka Maoli

Similar to many diasporic Hawaiians, Landeza boasts a mixed heritage, including Filipino, Chinese, and Irish lineages. In truth, both his off-island birthplace and his Asian-European racial mixture tend to obscure his connections to his Kanaka Maoli legacy despite his wide acclaim as a leading practitioner of Hawai'i's unique guitar tradition. Landeza and his music offer an alternative to the limitations of current understandings of Hawaiian identity and Hawaiian-ness. Scholars such as Rona Halualani summarize the ways in which a variety of popular Hawaiian representations have impacted the formation of Hawaiian identity, particularly for Hawaiians born and raised off-island. Halualani lucidly delineates the various ways in which Hawaiian identity is defined—native-born, meaning, either native Hawaiian or Local (someone born and raised in Hawai'i, but without native Hawaiian "blood") born and raised in Hawai'i; or U.S. state and federal qualifications based on blood quantum—all of which provide little space for those in the Hawaiian diaspora who are a generation or more removed from living in Hawai'i.[11]

In *Hawaiian Blood: Colonialism and the Politics of Sovereignty and Indigeneity*, J. Kēhaulani Kauanui tracks the history of the legal definitions dictated by U.S. state and federal government agencies such as the Office of Hawaiian Affairs (OHA) that require a blood quantum of 50 percent in order to qualify as "real" Hawaiians. As she convincingly argues, this regulatory standard effectively adheres to a narrative of Hawaiian disappearance by "disappearing" subsequent generations of Hawaiians as Kānaka Maoli by ignoring native Hawaiian notions of 'ohana [extended family], which are predicated on genealogical lineage rather than blood quantum.[12] Indeed, even native Hawaiians who live in Hawai'i but whose blood quantum fails the fifty percent requirement of the U.S. government's definition for legitimate Hawaiian identification can find themselves external to legal claims of Hawaiian identity.[13]

In addition, these regulations have hindered linkages between diasporic Hawaiians and on-island Kānaka Maoli by creating a competitive environment for resource allocations and political rights. This is accomplished by instigating the careful policing of Hawaiian belonging along blood quanta definitions rather than through the prevalent genealogical understanding of 'ohana, shifting understandings of lineage to be ascertained by U.S. judicial review rather than native Hawaiian practice. This situation resonates in the ways Landeza was challenged about his legitimacy in his early career. The concern about his legitimacy among native Hawaiian listeners from Hawai'i as both a practitioner of Hawaiian music as well as his self-identification as native Hawaiian exemplifies the discourse Kauanui describes as a "fixation on the 'full-blooded' or 'pure' Hawaiian [that] erases the survival of Kanaka Maoli people overall by relying on unmixed Kānaka Maoli to bear the burden of representing the 'true Hawaiians'" (16), leaving no room to accommodate many surviving Kānaka Maoli, the majority of whom enjoy mixed-race heritages and blood quanta far below the 50 percent mark. On one hand, the racial mixedness of the majority of Hawaiians has been celebrated as a sign of Hawaiian inclusivity since the early twentieth century.[14] On the other hand, "impure" Hawaiians are not real Hawaiians, a particularly salient point with respect to struggles for Kanaka Maoli political autonomy or for building solidarity between on- and off-island native Hawaiians.

Another route into Hawaiian culture exists: similar to other diasporic Hawaiians raised in California, Landeza accessed Hawaiian culture primarily through family associations and popular culture. The complicated relationship between an individual and Hawaiian culture is informed by the commodification of Hawaiian culture, which allows diasporic Hawaiians to develop a sense of their own Hawaiian-ness through events such as Aloha festivals, cultural forms such as hapa haole songs, and Hawaiiana kitsch even as they become conscious of the more troubling aspects such misrepresentations instantiate. That non-Hawaiians form their impressions of Hawaiian culture, including a sense of being "Hawaiian in the heart," from the same processes and objects complicates the distinctions diasporic Hawaiians might hope to make between their search for cultural roots and the easy donning of Hawaiian-ness by individuals who cannot claim a genealogical or geographical affiliation to Hawaiian culture.

As Paul Gilroy notes in his study of Afrodiasporic music, "The unashamedly hybrid character of these black cultures continually confounds any simplistic (essentialist or anti-essentialist) understanding of the relationship between racial identity and racial non-identity, between folk cultural authenticity and pop cultural betrayal" (*Black Atlantic,* 99). In order to understand how the connection between kī hō'alu and 'āina can be thought of in the fluid and flexible ways Gilroy argues is fundamental to nuanced and sensitive hearings of hybrid musical cultures. I recall a conversation I had with Hawaiian music legend Dennis Kamakahi, who, as a young, up-and-coming guitarist, replaced Gabby Pahinui in the Sons of Hawaii in the 1970s. He recounted a time when he met blues musician Muddy Waters, who noticed that they both tuned their guitars to identical tunings but remarked that their music sounded so dissimilar. Kamakahi, in relating his answer, brought up a point that was reiterated by many of the kī hōʻalu musicians I spoke to in Hawaiʻi, namely, that a personal connection to Hawaiʻi is one of the criteria they use to weigh claims of authenticity.[15]

But Kamakahi also noted the mutability of that attachment. Speaking to the difference between Muddy Waters and himself, Kamakahi emphasized,

> The music takes on the form through the person who plays it, wherever he comes from, you see. So, I said [to Muddy Waters], "If you stayed in Hawaiʻi a couple of years, you'd play the same way. If I went to the [Mississippi] Delta and lived with you, I'd play like you!" And he said, "Yeah, I never thought about it like that." But it's the same key, same style, same instrument [yet sounds different].[16]

Divorcing kī hōʻalu from blood, Kamakahi recalibrates the relationship between blood and land. His recognition that the "same key, same style, same instrument" might yet produce "different sounds" in different locations points to ways of constructing Hawaiian-ness that highlight the active construction of identity, which is undoubtedly affected by the materiality of geography and genealogy but can be rescued from the over-determination of notions that seek to forever bind the ties between blood, land, and music to recognize, instead, the fluidity of blood in a space surrounded by water, the shiftings of land in an island archipelago dotted with active volcanoes, and a music that is born out of the musical mergings between Hawaiians and the rest of the world.

The liner notes to Landeza's latest recording, *Kamaʻalua*—a concept album of sorts—state,

> "Who Patrick is" is the exact theme of *Kamaʻalua*, which means "to become familiar with." The title was gifted from the Reverend Dennis Kamakahi, and this disc is the result of Patrick having become familiar with, taking pride in, and representing who he is—a mainland-born Hawaiian.

The notes to the song that began this essay, "How Would You Feel?" read in part,

> One's ancestry and cultural identity are one's own, and yet there are those who believe that they know us better than we know

> ourselves. As a mainland-born Hawaiian, Patrick has been tried and questioned to prove his 'Hawaiian-ness.' With this song, he hopes to convey the message of pride and fortitude to other mainland-born Hawaiians.

As J. Kauanui, Halualani, and Landeza have pointed out, there is a difference between calling oneself a "Californian" and claiming to be "Hawaiian." If claims to being Hawaiian can be displaced from direct connections to the 'āina (the land) by remaining linked through genealogical ties, claims about being a Californian remain rooted to some period of residency in the Golden State. In this way, the particulars of identification inherent in place remain bound to "the (California) land" in ways that are liberated from questions of "blood" because "Californian" is not a racial category. In order to be seen as a Californian, as long as you reside within the Golden State, there is little reason to think yourself "less" of a Californian than any other resident.[17] In claims for Hawaiian belonging, however, blood remains a powerful metaphor for an innate biological or cultural connection in ways that claiming to be a Californian rarely entail.

And local urban culture matters. Berkeley is *different* from Honolulu, Hong Kong is not London, and Mumbai is quite a trip from Timbuktu. But some of those differences can translate, however limited, partial, or distorted. For instance, in Hawai'i, the relationship between the 'āina and Kānaka Maoli, individually as well as collectively, is considered sacred and engenders kuleana, or responsibility, toward the land that does not necessarily carry a meaning for environmental stewardship incompatible with its meaning in Berkeley, tree-hugging stereotypes of its residents notwithstanding. Simply put, despite Landeza's reluctance to call his music "California kī hō'alu," his other assertions—his pride as a "mainland Hawaiian" and a rhetorical insistence that music reveals an artist's inner subjectivity, including its formation while embedded in specific circumstances—tend to undermine the idea that the performance of kī hō'alu fails to reflect, in his case, an upbringing in Berkeley, California. It is understandable, however, given the racial politics of the marketplace within Hawaiian music, that there are compelling reasons to stake a claim to a notion of authenticity that paradoxically challenges the very openness to Hawaiian identity he is also asserting.

In 2011, as an indication of his status in the Hawaiian music world, Landeza became the first nonresident Hawaiian musician to be nominated for a Nā Hōkū Hanohano Award, the Grammy equivalent for Hawaiian music awarded annually by the Hawai'i Academy of Recording Arts. It is fitting, then, that as Landeza becomes more comfortable identifying as a Californian Kanaka Maoli, he finds acceptance among his peers in Hawai'i, as well as fans within a "home" that encompasses both California and Hawai'i. Hawaiian hip-hop group Sudden Rush once asked who was a "real Hawaiian" in a na mele paleoleo (Hawaiian rap) song, an idiom clearly indebted to African American and Caribbean expressive culture, implicitly registering cultural hybridity and transcultural connection as a component of "real Hawaiian-ness."[18] Landeza's musical articulation of a pan-Pacific "home," a space from which Californian Kānaka Maoli announce their presence, transforms kī hō'alu into an expansive sounding-out of Hawaiian belonging that gainsays the landlocked and the blood-bound—a space in which Californian Kānaka Maoli can, in fact, be "real Hawaiians."

Notes

1. Patrick Kahakauwila Kamaholelani Landeza, "How Would You Feel?", YouTube, (RT: 10:01) Published February 28, 2012. Available at: http://www.youtube.com/watch?v=R40kRHOJS4I&feature=related. The song is also available on Landeza's 2011 release, *Kama'alua* ("to be familiar with").
2. I am linking disconnected lines from the song here, but I do not believe I have distorted his intended sense or meaning.
3. I will use the terms *native Hawaiian* and *Kanaka Maoli* (pl. *Kānaka Maoli*) interchangeably. Other names used by Hawaiians today include Kānaka 'Ōiwi (bone people, or people of the bone) and 'Ōiwi Maole (true bone). As J. K. Kauanui points out, these designations express a genealogical rather than a blood quanta basis for articulating Hawaiian identity. The term *Native Hawaiian* (both terms capitalized) is used in legal documents, and, like Kanaka 'Ōiwi and 'Ōiwi Maole, will not be used here. For more on this, see J. Kēhaulani Kauanui, *Hawaiian Blood: Colonialism and the Politics of Sovereignty and Indigeneity* (Durham: Duke University Press, 2008), particularly "A Note to Readers," which traces the history and uses of the various terms used to describe native Hawaiians. I also want to note that I will be using the terms *on-island* and *off-island* in the same way Kauanui delineates as indications of whether an individual or practice is "in Hawai'i (on-island)" or "outside Hawai'i (off-island)" rather than, as she describes in detail, the conventional uses of the terms in Hawai'i.

4. This essay is part of a larger project that tracks kī hōʻalu in Hawaiʻi, California, and Japan in order to think about the distinct and disparate ways in which guitarists perform Hawaiian-ness. Their performances hold distinct meanings for Hawaiian identity, particularly at the individual musician's level, but are also salient in terms of collective meanings for Hawaiian-ness, its representations, and its values.
5. Cf. *Billboard*, "Broader Audience Catching Wave of Hawaiian Music," November 14, 1992.
6. Patrick Landeza in discussion with the author, October 10, 2004.
7. Patrick Landeza in discussion with the author, January 12, 2006.
8. There is a longer history of the guitar in Hawaiʻi, including lap/pedal steel guitar. Much of this early history comes through tangential evidence, for example, a playbill that cites a solo classical guitar performance or an advertisement for steel guitar strings in the 1860s. See Elizabeth Tatar, "Slack Key Guitar," in *Hawaiian Music and Musicians: An Illustrated History*, ed. George Kanahele (Honolulu: University of Hawaiʻi Press, 1979).
9. I came across this many times in my interviews with guitarists in Hawaiʻi.
10. Patrick Landeza in discussion with the author, August 9, 2010.
11. See, in particular, Halualani's introduction to *In the Name of Hawaiians*. For a perceptive and illuminating study that insists on explicitly marking whiteness in Hawaiʻi, see Judy Rohrer, *Haoles in Hawaiʻi* (University of Hawaiʻi Press, 2010), particularly chapter two, "'No Ack!': What is Haole, Anyway?"
12. It also ignores the common practice of *hānai*, or adoption, which is understood differently in Hawaiʻi than in contemporary Western societies. For more on *hānai*, see Jill E. Korbin, "Hana 'Ino: Child Maltreatment in a Hawaiian-American Community," *Pacific Studies* 3, no. 3 (July 1990): 7–22.
13. The 50 percent rule was attenuated somewhat by the state of Hawaiʻi in 1992 to accommodate native Hawaiians' ability to designate direct descendants as successors to their leases. Blood quanta still counts, however, as the direct descendants must still prove one-fourth Hawaiian blood. See Kauanui, *Hawaiian Blood* (5) for more details.
14. As early as the 1920s, sociologists such as Robert E. Park viewed Hawaiʻi as a model of race relations in which individuals not only married across racial and ethnic lines but, along with their mixed-race children, thrived in a multicultural paradise. While this view would change somewhat over the decades, the current discourse over mixed-race individuals and communities in Hawaiʻi replays these ideas of multiracial harmony papering over a long history of white American and, since the 1960s, Japanese American domination of the political

and socioeconomic landscape, with a corresponding decline in Kanaka Maoli living standards, including educational and economic achievement levels. For a concise accounting of this history, see Hauanani-Kay Trask, "Coalition-Building Between Natives and Non-Natives," *Stanford Law Review* 43, no. 6 (July 1991): 1197–1213. See also Kauanui, *Hawaiian Blood.*

15. It is worth noting that Landeza has recorded with a number of master musicians such as Raymond Kane, Dennis Kamakahi, Cyril Pahinui, George Kuo, and George Kahumoku.
16. Patrick Landeza in discussion with the author, April 25, 2009.
17. I do not intend to forget or lessen the racism and ostracism various groups faced in California, including Mexicans, Chinese, Filipino, Japanese, Sikh, Native Americans, and Native Hawaiians. While this is little known today, so many Hawaiians emigrated to California during the early 1800s because of the lack of opportunities in Hawai'i that in 1850, King Kamehameha III signed an act prohibiting Hawaiians from emigrating to California, where, it was feared, as the language of the Act put it, "They May Die in Misery," and to prevent the increasing loss of Hawaiians to the U.S. West Coast. A number of settlements and sites in the western United States that bear the name Owyhee, an earlier English spelling of Hawai'i, are evidence of the native Hawaiian immigration in the eighteenth and nineteenth centuries.
18. The song "Real Hawaiian" appears on the Sudden Rush recording, *Kū'ē!!* (Way Out West, 1997). The group sampled Gabby Pahinui performing his signature song, "Hi'ilawe," for the band's 2002 release, *Ea* (Quiet Storm), mixing hip-hop and slack key.

CHAPTER 9

Somewhere Tropical

GINA OSTERLOH

"SOMEWHERE TROPICAL" IS THE FIRST STUDIO SET I constructed for photo tableaux.

In the photographs, there is a woman whose body faces the camera, but head and face are turned away, looking back at the faux, crudely painted sunset. Other sculptural elements—bamboo, palm fronds,

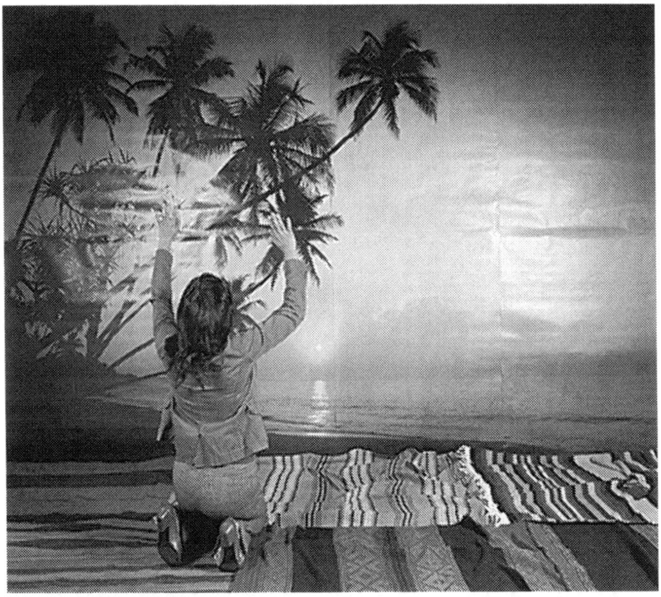

Rapture (2006). Courtesy of the artist, Higher Pictures and Silverlens Galleries.

fake ferns and a crudely painted foam rock—signify a tropical, albeit shoddily constructed, environment.

When I created "Somewhere Tropical," I had just moved to Los Angeles for the Studio Art MFA program at UC Irvine, and was infatuated by the horizon and saturated, ever-changing hues of the sunset. In my early years of graduate school, I reflected upon how this ephemeral yet clichéd landscape of sunset and palm trees was also the landscape I knew through my mother's stories, stories I heard since childhood—of an idyllic tropical landscape, the sea, intertwined with horrific accounts of running from Japanese soldiers and living in hiding as a child during WWII in the Philippines. In many ways, my external landscape—Los Angeles—became a psychic wall, a prop in itself for "Somewhere Tropical." It doubled as the backdrop for internal questions of belonging, issues of identity and visual perception, informed by experiences growing up mixed-race in the Midwest. In Ohio during the 80s, there was a constant hailing or question called out to me: *"So, what are you? Where are you from?"* When classmates or random people in the mall asked these questions, I always tried to insert an awkward pause. I wanted to respond with silence, a blank.

"Somewhere Tropical" is the photo series in which I first developed visual strategies of camouflage and the "blank" or void. Immersed in a studio construction of the tropics, I turned my face away from the camera. Staring at the photograph pinned to my studio wall at UC Irvine, I became enthralled by the head of hair, turning away, refusing identification. It was odd, uncanny, almost vaginal. "Somewhere Tropical" is the origin of resistance visual strategies—shapes of refusal.

While in other photographs in the series I donned military camouflage pants in an attempt to splinter or fracture the picture area where the subject sits in a portrait, in the end, I realized that metaphors of military camouflage are too literal, too full and all too familiar through film, depictions of war, and fashion. To destabilize and defamiliarize the figure ground through camouflage, I wanted to expand the language of camouflage beyond military reference. I needed to pare camouflage down to its most basic operation: mimesis, or the act of resemblance.

In "Corpus Delicti," Rosalind Krauss addresses "informed," or the unformed body as a surrealist visual strategy specific to photography during the 1930s. Emerging from the trauma and horrors of World War I, as well as the rise of fascism pre–World War II, surrealist photographers presented the body as never seen before.[1] For example, in

Man Ray's photograph "Anatomy," the head is unrecognizable or misrecognized as a phallus through two decisive moves: the tilt of the head up, and the camera close-up.[2] To expand the viewer's experience of informed or unformed body within the photograph, Krauss references French writer and theorist Roger Caillois and his studies of insect mimicry. For Caillois, the act of camouflage is at once embodiment and perception; it is the embodiment of mimesis—for example, the praying mantis's perception of space, of its surroundings. Krauss also reminds us that this act of mimicry is not based on the vertical and hierarchal viewpoint of human vision; rather, it is the animal's experience of space, from its position of horizontality. Additionally, this physical embodiment of camouflage is an interdependent, dual relationship between self and surroundings—the insect, whether in defense mode or automated, is unable to hold its own psychic energy. It undergoes "a loss of ego substance," and this "loss of possession" allows the surrounding space to write its visual code onto the insect's body.[3]

Following "Somewhere Tropical" is the photo series "Blank Athleticism," which activates visual strategies of mimesis, the blank or monochrome, the void, and flatness.

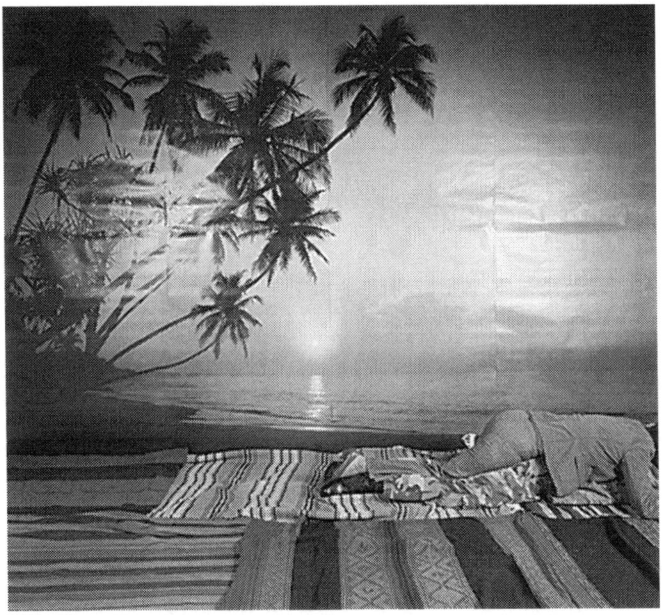

Collapse (2006). Courtesy of the artist, Higher Pictures and Silverlens Galleries.

In terms of mimesis, the act of copying is not a resemblance of nature; in "Blank Athleticism," the figure attempts to mimic a monochrome room. What does it look like if a subject attempts to mimic a blank or nothingness? In *Discrepant Abstraction,* Angeline Morrison writes,

> One of the major ways in which the monochrome acts as a perpetually reappearing embodiment of chaos is in the fact that it seems to resemble, mimic or represent nothing. Mimesis holds the meaningful world together, and monochrome is the nemesis of mimesis. (. . .) When a spectator stands before a pictorial surface, s/he expects some kind of "picture." When confronted by a picture that does not depict, a sort of psychic panic often ensues.[4]

On all fours, folding into a turquoise blue paper floor, the figure (my own body) "faces" the camera directly with head down, hair hiding the figure's face. With the head placed close to the middle of the picture plane, the photograph presents the viewer with a "blank" or visual stop, where identification of a face is expected. As in "Somewhere Tropical," the placement and shape of hair/head creates a void in the picture plane. Contained within a paper room, the head expels strips of paper; confetti flies into the air but also seems to attack the body. Body and space perform an unstable act of mimesis, as they threaten to invade each other.

While constructing the bright blue paper room in which I was planning to wear a similar-colored sweater and create the illusion of a figure vomiting paper, I was reading Gilles Deleuze's *Francis Bacon: The Logic of Sensation.* In Chapter 4, titled "Athleticism," Deleuze describes specific visual strategies in Bacon's paintings:

> The entire series of spasms in Bacon is of this type: scenes of love, of vomiting and excreting, in which the body attempts to escape from itself through one of its organs in order to rejoin the field or material structure.[5]

My interpretation of Deleuze's "material structure" in Bacon's paintings refers to the visual space surrounding the figure, as well as the depiction of a physical structure that houses the body, for example a room. "Blank Athleticism" also marks the emergence of play in its representation of a three-dimensional and two-dimensional body: legs collapse into the floor through illusion and shadow. Yet the illusion is not digital post-production; rather, it is based in the real. In terms of process, I knelt on all fours, while a patient artist friend cut around my legs and wrists with a utility blade. With the cardboard and paper floor raised on wood blocks, my legs sank down onto the actual concrete floor, and in the photograph they appear flattened. In terms of conceptual drive, the drive is nonverbal—a scene of something guttural, an explosion, an energy or force that cannot be easily defined nor contained.

"Anonymous Front" marks a shift in my practice, a heightened awareness of mark-making and repetition of pattern to visually connect the space between an individual and a group, as well as a figure and its surroundings. It also marks my first use of the silhouette. To make each figure, I traced the outline of friends on cardboard. Through cardboard cut-outs and a spray-painted gray dot pattern, the silhouettes flicker between flatness and three-dimensionality. The repeated gray dot pattern—loose in some areas and concentrated in others—collapses foreground, background, and figure ground, as well as boundaries between the individual and a group. The entire photograph embodies and activates strategies of camouflage through mimicry of pattern and flatness. "Anonymous Front" plays with tactics of camouflage, another strategy to resist legibility. Just like Western projections and depictions of the tropics, the figures and surrounding space are anonymous.

"Somewhere Tropical" is the origin of the conceptual and philosophical underpinnings, as well as formal strategies and aesthetic inquiries that drive my entire oeuvre. While creating "Somewhere Tropical," I considered the sociology anthology edited by Maria P.P. Root entitled *Racially Mixed People in America*. Several years before grad school, I was introduced to Root's book, and it was specifically Carla K. Bradshaw's contribution, "Beauty and The Beast: On Racial Ambiguity," in which I first encountered a text that articulates experiences of being biracial through the lens of camouflage. Bradshaw describes camouflage through a dynamic process of passing and not-passing, feelings of integrity and impostor-ship within racial groups, and the impossibility of assimilation:

> Passing is the word to describe an attempt to achieve acceptability by claiming membership in some desired group while denying other racial elements in oneself thought to be undesirable. The concept of passing uses the imagery of camouflage, of concealing true identity or group membership and gaining false

> access. [. . .] To transcend artificial, irrational racial barriers is not an act of deviance; rather, it requires engaging in a process of adaptation.[6]

Carla K. Bradshaw's text, connecting issues of identity to "the imagery of camouflage," remains a fundamental driving force in my work. When I first read "Beauty and The Beast: On Racial Ambiguity," I interpreted Bradshaw's description of "passing" and the "process of adaptation" to heavily emphasize the way one presents self visually, while maintaining a meta-consciousness that race is both an "irrational racial barrier" as well as a lived experience. Like in photography, as well as in "Somewhere Tropical," race is both a profound truth as well as a fictive construct.

Notes

1. To note: I am very aware of the misogyny embedded in many of the surrealist photographs of this era. My goal here is to concretely define photographic strategies that de-normalize and de-familiarize the figure in photography—artistic strategies that de-normalize habitual ways of seeing and expectations vis-à-vis portraiture.
2. Rosalind Krauss, "Corpus Delicti," *October* 33 (Summer 1985): 32–34.
3. Rosalind Krauss, "Corpus Delicti," 49. (Krauss references Roger Caillois's essay "Mimicry and Legendary Psychasthenia" and his study of the praying mantis (1934–1937) in *The Edge of Surrealism: A Roger Caillois Reader*, Claudine Frank, ed. (Durham: Duke University Press, 2003).
4. Angeline Morrison, "Autobiography of an (Ex) Coloured Surface: Monochrome and Liminality," in *Annotating Art's Histories: Discrepant Abstraction*, ed. Kobena Mercer (Cambridge, Massachusetts & London, England: The MIT Press), 135.
5. Gilles Deleuze, *Francis Bacon: The Logic of Sensation*, English translation by Daniel W. Smith (London: Bloomsbury Academic, 1981).
6. Carla K. Bradshaw, "Beauty and the Beast: On Racial Ambiguity," in *Racially Mixed People in America*, ed. Maria P. P. Root (Thousand Oaks, CA: Sage Publishing, 1992), 79–80.

Chapter 10

Dreamers

A Dialogue on Education Rights and the Movement for Undocumented Migrants

Raymundo M. Hernandez-Lopez and Tracy Lachica Buenavista

Rhetoric plays a critical role in our society, through both the written word and speech, with the intent to inform or educate an audience. Verbal rhetoric is one of the main forms of communication that allows us to share and/or formulate thoughts, ideas, visions, feelings, beliefs, disagreements, positions, and perceptions with other people. However, visual imagery in rhetoric has also become significant in that it too can influence, formulate, and modify attention, and sustain thoughts, feelings, beliefs, ideas, and perceptions. The praxis of visual rhetoric takes place in the internet, media, advertisement (print or web), data graphs, pictures, paintings, prints, and/or anything we visually perceive on a daily basis.

In today's world, visual rhetoric is a powerful weapon that can be either constructive or destructive to society. More specifically, *political visual rhetoric* refers to political artwork that aims to document historical events; these images depict the struggles of marginalized communities in a capitalist society and carry messages of empowerment. Aligned with political visual rhetoric, I employ the terms *artivist* or *artivism* to refer to the artist who puts political visual rhetoric into praxis by creating powerful images for a movement as a form of activism. The inclusion of political visual imagery in rhetoric as an art form is critical to all political movements, as it offers people more political, social, and intellectual empowerment. In addition, art can foster consciousness of peoples' aspirations to demand both democratic civil and human rights.

Art that depicts a political movement where dispossessed people expressed resistance to their oppression produces a visual historical record of the event(s) and documents the different struggles people face as they fight for social justice and liberation. Political artwork that depicts these injustices of oppressed communities is a constructive, powerful tool for the artivist and for working-class people, as it becomes an avenue to create consciousness, educate, and formulate solidarity with other groups of people. For example, during the late nineteenth and twentieth centuries, Mexican, Cuban, Chicana/o, African-American, Euro-American, and Asian-American printmakers and social realist artists used art as a weapon. Their art communicated their dissatisfaction with historical events of traumatic social injustices, racism, oppression, struggles, exploitation, violence of the oppressor, and problems that both directly and indirectly affect everyday lives; many of those images reached out to a wider audience who shared experiences of injustice and struggles in their own communities.

In my artivism, political visual rhetoric has been a constructive avenue to empower the dreamers and the dreamers' movement across the nation, as they fight for fair educational opportunities and the opportunity to legalize their status in the United States. The term *dreamers* often refers to undocumented students who are in pursuit of higher education, but I also use the term to name youth who are not included in the DREAM (Development, Relief and Education for Alien Minors) Act rhetoric or part of the dreamers movement. I decided to contribute to the dreamers' movement through my artivism because, as a dreamer and as an artivist, I felt there was a need to incorporate art into the movement as a way to empower undocumented immigrants in the U.S. The following are two designs I created that have garnered national attention in and for the dreamers' movement.

In 2008, while undocumented immigrant students throughout the state of California organized to lobby in support of the Federal DREAM Act, I decided to create my first visual statement to help spread awareness of the movement. Image 10.1, *I Support the DREAM Act/Support the DREAM Act,* is an image I created that can be read in two ways: as a personal statement and as a statement towards the viewer. The cap and gown represent the letter "I" as a personal statement, and also a representation of an undocumented immigrant student wearing the cap and gown without having an identity. This logo has been produced on T-shirts, flyers, banners, mouse pads, and clear window decals in order to reach a broader audience. My vision for the

T-shirt concept was for people to wear the design as a form of endorsement, support, encouragement, and personal ad. It also gave the opportunity to educate others about the DREAM Act and the issue of undocumented students. In addition, sales of the T-shirts helped raise funds for a scholarship that would benefit dreamers in higher education.

As the design became nationally known and worn by students across the nation, media outlets such as newspapers began to use it for their articles; bloggers also began to use it as a logo. As I stated earlier, art can be constructive, and I personally felt this logo was doing the job I intended it to do, which was to promote higher education for undocumented immigrant students. However, the accessibility of the logo led to its use by a group called "The DREAM Army." They wore the design on T-shirts while they organized and lined up a group of youth in platoon formation with an acting drill instructor, to bring attention to the possibility for undocumented youth to enlist in the military under the provisions of the DREAM Act. To me, it seemed that the logo was being used in a destructive way. The *I Support the DREAM Act/Support the DREAM Act* logo was never intended to promote the military option of the DREAM Act, but rather to encourage youth to pursue better educational opportunities.

In February 2010, Lizbeth Mateo, cofounder of DREAM Team Los Angeles (DTLA), Dreams to be Heard (D2BH) at California State University, Northridge, and the Dream is Coming Collective, reached out to me to design a T-shirt for the second *National Undocumented Come Out Week,* which took place from March 15–21, 2010. When I was first approached to design the shirt, which would feature the message "*I Am Undocumented*" (Image 10.2), I felt empowered and inspired by the idea behind the action. As a designer, my first concern was to create a beautiful and attractive shirt, but after analyzing the actions of the group and the message it wanted to produce, I decided to create a simple design and let the content speak for itself. Although I decided to work with simple typography, the visual component of the written word took on more consideration in my design. I wanted to express a strong message towards xenophobic peoples and groups.

As I was brainstorming and creating sketches for my concept design, I came across images of xenophobic people protesting and holding up signs with anti-immigrant messages such as "Illegal is illegal," "Go back to your country," and "All illegals are criminals." There were two that particularly grabbed my attention: one with a message "Learn to speak English" and another that had a different message with the word "undocumented" misspelled. When I saw the two images, I realized how hypocritical xenophobic groups and members could be: while they preach about learning to speak the English language, many can't spell simple English words. Therefore, I decided to incorporate the word "undocumented" in a phonetic format, as if it was

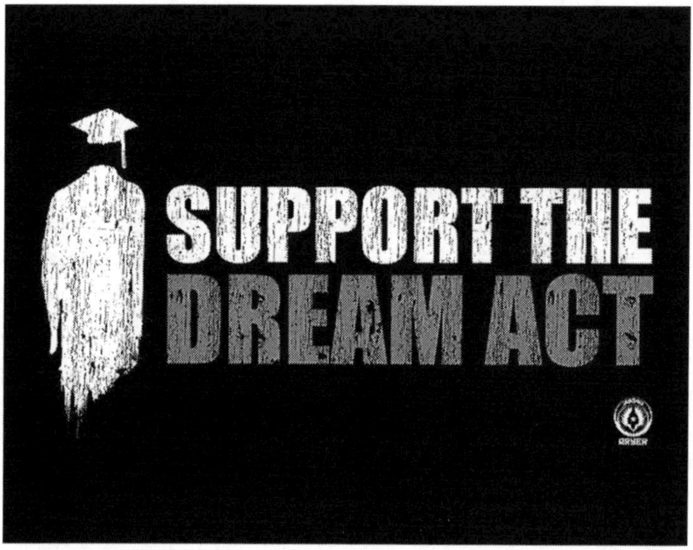

I Support the Dream Act/Support the Dream Act (2008). Image by Ray Hernandez.

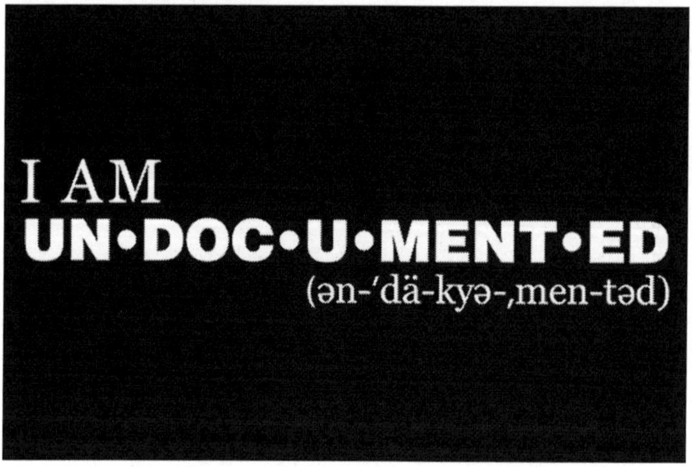

I Am Undocumented (2010). Image by Ray Hernandez.

taken from a dictionary. My intention with this visual piece was to tell anti-immigrant people to learn to write the English language the right way themselves before they preach to others to learn to speak English. The *I Am Undocumented* shirts became an empowering tool for dreamers or undocumented people, urging them to come out of the shadows. For those who chose to out themselves by wearing the shirt, the design itself is a personal statement, a mode of empowerment, and a step forward from leaving out of fear.

Tracy Lachica Buenavista

The term *dreamer* has become a moniker for undocumented immigrant youth in the United States. Originally inspired by the proposed Federal Development, Relief, and Education for Alien Minors (DREAM) Act, undocumented youth named themselves "DREAMers" as a means to humanize the very people who would be impacted by the passage of such legislation. The DREAM Act would provide a pathway to legal residency for many young people who are "out of status," a possibility that ignited youth activism and the proliferation of symbols that embodied the national undocumented movement. While the movement has since become more diverse and complex, initially obscured were the experiences of millions of undocumented immigrants who would not benefit from the passage of the DREAM Act.

Often referenced during undocumented events is John Lennon's (1971) song "Imagine," which contains a reference to dreamers. In the song, Lennon states that dreamers play a necessary role in the construction of a more humane society, one in which every human being experiences infinite possibilities. Thus, the song has become symbolic of the struggles and desire of undocumented immigrants to be recognized as people within American society. In the chorus, Lennon asserts, "You, you may say I'm a dreamer, but I'm not the only one. I hope someday you'll join us. And the world will be as one." The chorus has come to represent how dreamers, or migrants with undocumented status, are not social anomalies; their struggles for belonging mirror the struggles of all those who have been marginalized in one way or another. Further, while the chorus of the song emphasizes the need for solidarity building to create social, political, and economic justice, it is also important to focus on the lyrics that depict processes of humanization.

In the second verse of the song, Lennon argues that a more humane society is absent of war. He writes, "Imagine there's no countries;

It isn't hard to do. Nothing to kill or die for. And no religion too. Imagine all the people living life in peace." In this verse, Lennon essentially critiques war and alludes to the military industrial complex that positions people to "kill or die" under the guise of "peace." While the song does not necessarily call attention to the political economy that shapes global imbalance, his perspective promotes what can be perceived as an anti-war stance.

Not considered in its use by the dreamer movement, and what I'd like to point out, is the irony between Lennon's song serving as an anti-war anthem and the initial agenda of the movement to promote the DREAM Act. Central to the DREAM Act is the option for undocumented youth to become eligible for legal residency through enlistment in the U.S. Armed Forces and, ultimately, participation in war. Yet, the militarization of the DREAM Act has been underemphasized in the visual rhetoric shaping the discourse on undocumented immigration. Instead, the DREAM Act is touted for its potential to increase educational access for undocumented youth.

Perhaps the most iconic symbol of the undocumented youth movement is the *I Support the DREAM Act/Support the DREAM Act* image. The image has provided undocumented youth and allies with a means to make visible their support for the legislation, and has since become an informal logo of undocumented youth activism. At the center of the image is an invisible figure wearing a cap and gown. The invisible graduate represents undocumented youth in schools and colleges across the U.S. who possess educational aspirations, but actively avoid deportation by employing non-disclosure strategies that prevent their detection, apprehension, and detention. The symbolic meaning of the cap and gown powerfully challenge the stereotypical media constructions of undocumented people as uneducated and parasitic. Dreamers, who have demonstrated resilience during their academic journeys, embrace the cap and gown as reminders that education is a right to which they are entitled; so much so that it has become commonplace for undocumented youth to literally wear traditional graduation ceremonial wear at DREAM Act events to perform their resistance to negative portrayals of their community.

Alongside the *I Support the DREAM Act/Support the DREAM Act* image is the *I Am Undocumented* piece, which spells out the phonetic pronunciation of the phrase. An onslaught of Tea Party and other conservative nativist actions have utilized protest signs to express anti-immigrant sentiment, including language discrimination targeted at migrants. Ironically, many of the signs have displayed gross spelling and punctuation errors while simultaneously lambasting undocumented immigrants for their supposed inability to learn and speak the English language. Like the *I Support the DREAM Act/Support the DREAM Act* piece, the *I Am Undocumented* design brings attention to the undocumented community, directly acknowledges the xenophobia that characterizes the hostility directed at people who are undocumented, and does so without promotion of any specific legislation. In doing so, this piece allows one to imagine dreamers to include anyone who is out of status and possesses aspirations for a sustainable livelihood in the U.S., regardless of their eligibility for the DREAM Act.

The power of visual rhetoric is the way in which it enables diverse groups of people to consume its messages in ways relevant to the viewer, even in ways unintended by the artist. One specific example is a group of undocumented youth dubbed the "DREAM Army," who have performed military drills while wearing shirts with the design. While advocates for the DREAM Act used the image to advocate for increased college access for undocumented youth, the DREAM Army's commodification of the image centralized the militarized components of the policy. More specifically, under the DREAM Act, undocumented

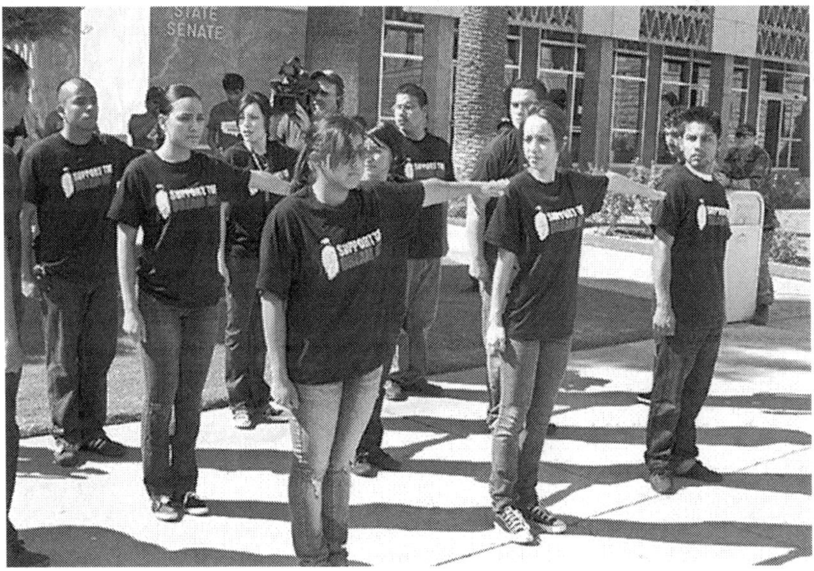

"DREAM Army." Image by Ray Hernandez.

youth could become eligible for legal permanent residency upon successful military enlistment. Military proponents have duly noted the reality that the DREAM Act would serve as a recruitment strategy for the U.S. Armed Forces. Thus, while a small minority of undocumented youth will be able to pursue higher education under the DREAM Act, for others, their pathway to attaining legal status in the U.S. is dependent on participation in the state military apparatus—a nightmare not only for the communities of color who lose members to enlistment domestically, but also those who are subject to American military terrorism globally.

CHAPTER 11

Claiming Malibu

Indian Diasporic Dancing Bodies Aligning Geographies across Time and Space

PRIYA SRINIVASAN

THE WORD *MALIBU* CONJURES UP TV SHOWS like *Baywatch* and *Malibu*, and iconic products such as the Malibu Barbie. Images of tanned, blond-haired, blue-eyed, white people—muscular males and lithe, large-breasted bikini-clad females—abound in our imagination, inextricably linked to the crystalline waters of the coast, sand, surf, and hills. So, when we hear the words *the Malibu Hindu Temple*, we are propelled into new geographic imaginaries and the linking of differently raced and ethnic bodies that may also lay claim to the Malibu land space—that is, images of Indian/American bodies that might be brown skinned, brown eyed, or black haired; bodies clad in saris and dhotis praying to Hindu deities. In this chapter, I examine the performance of Bharata Natyam by Indian American bodies as they lay claim to Malibu. Also known as the Chumash town of Humaliwo, Malibu is known to have been located on a high point next to Malibu Lagoon and is part of the state park. Humaliwo was an important center of Chumash life in this region in prehistoric and early historic times. Another Chumash town known from historical records, identified as Ta'lopop, is located a few miles up Malibu Canyon from the lagoon; it is partially within Malibu Creek State Park.[1]

I read this claiming of Malibu as new "Hindu Indian" terrain by Indian American bodies as a political act that moves against the U.S. state's hegemonic imperatives of denaturalizing the Asian body but shies away from any radical claims to citizenship or professions of political solidarity with Native American issues over sovereignty rights. I refer to the denaturalization of Indians and other Asians in the 1924 Act. The Hindu temples in North America are examples of cultural citizenship, but Indian dancing bodies' cultural practices are not pure resistance or pure commodities.[2] A reading of this binary fails to address the messy intersections. I address these messy intersections in this short essay through the spaces opened up by the ambivalence that characterizes the process of citizenship.

I was looking at some Bharata Natyam performances on YouTube when my attention was grabbed by a caption that read "Malibu Srinivasa dance." I was quite taken with this title because Indian classical dance, like many other classical arts of that region, is dedicated toward the divine, and Srinivasa is a popular deity that many dancers gravitate toward. The Srinivasa temple that is most often referred to is in the state of Andhra Pradesh in South India, known as Tirupathi. The deity Srinivasa, also known as Venkateshwara/Govinda/Vithala, happens to be my family deity and my family name.

In the Malibu temple, when the dancer invoked the famed god Srinivasa, the Lord of the Seven Hills, she described the topography of the land both from a bird's-eye view and from a devotee's perspective while climbing the seven hills to reach the Lord. This Indian/American body was laying claim to the land in the nation space, calling into being vast geographies across time and space to animate diasporic consciousness and nostalgic longing for the nation. In effect, the dancer also brings the audience to these spaces through the device of transportation embedded in the dance form itself. *Transportation* refers to the imagined worlds and peoples that are created in the act of dancing. The dancer, through her body, hand gestures, and facial expressions, conveys the meaning of the song text that is rendered by a musician. Usually, the text of the song in Bharata Natyam refers to a deity; sometimes the text also gives clues about where the deity is housed—that is, where the deity's temple is located, what the temple looks like, whether there are any identifying features of the temple, and local legends and miracles that accompany the deity. The dancer uses the lyrics in the song to elaborate details about the deity using its geography. The audience is then clued in very quickly as to which deity at which site is being referred to in the dance piece. Once the audience knows which deity is being performed, then the knowledgeable spectator will "fill in the blanks" in his/her own mind and subsequently wait for the dancer's interpretation of the deity to "fact check" details; they can then engage more fully when the improvisation takes place.

However, in this YouTube video, when the lyrics repeated, as they do in most dance items, I nevertheless found myself startled: *America vasa jaya govinda, America vasa jaya govinda* or Victory to Govinda, who lives in America.[3] I realized immediately that this was not the usual piece about the Srinivasa temple deity in South India. Rather, the song was in praise of Sri Venkateswara Temple in Malibu, California. Another set of lyrics read *America vasa jaya govinda, Malibu Hills nilaya radhe govinda, sri guru jaya guru, vithala govinda,* which means "Victory to Govinda who lives in America; Govinda who with Radha resides in Malibu Hills. Victory to Govinda, Vithala, the sacred Teacher." The dancer danced this piece as she would any other, but, strikingly, this was the first Indian dance performance in the U.S. laying claim to U.S. land and space. What was particularly intriguing was the claiming of U.S. space from the site of the Hindu temple. This seems to be a dual process of Hinduizing the American sacred space and staking a political claim of land through the bodily movement of the dancer.

As Assisi argues, Hindu Americans have begun to cultivate the strains within their own religious tradition that foster a sense of the sacred earth through myth, ritual, ceremonies, and spirit power that I argue also reflects Native American cultural practices. Indeed, Hindu Americans would not be doing this if they did not realize the land was sacred in some intrinsic way, something Native Americans have known for thousands of years. Indian Americans are locating, establishing, and embellishing sacred spaces in America by Hindu ritual rites of co-mingling the waters of the Ganga and the Kaveri with the Mississippi and Rio Grande, and by invoking holy Indian rivers in the local waters. Indians have made the land of the Americas ritually sacred in at least four ways: 1) composing songs and pious Sanskrit prayers extolling the American state where the temples are located; 2) identifying America as a specific *dvipa,* or island, as noted in the Hindu *Puranas;* 3) physically consecrating the land with waters from sacred Indian and American rivers; and 4) literally recreating the physical landscape of certain holy places in India, as in Pittsburgh or Barsana Dham, Texas. Thus, as Narayanan discerns, a process by which land or shrines held sacred by indigenous people are coopted by Hindus, and the sacrality is rearticulated with Hindu motifs.[4] Martin Manalansan has argued that, for immigrants, "rituals provide the terrain in which the consciousness of communal boundaries is heightened, thereby confirming and strengthening individual location and positionality as well as social identity."[5] For transmigrants whose identities are not rooted or territorialized within a specific place, rituals become the signs at the crossroads. These rituals, however, can be read in multiple ways.

Laying claim to the land is also a laying claim to American cultural citizenship and capital accumulation. This is of particular significance in light of early twentieth-century anti-Asian immigration policies that rendered Indians and other Asians ineligible for political citizenship and denaturalized American citizens of Asian origin. It was only after 1965 that Indians re-entered the U.S. in large numbers, mainly as professionals rather than as the laborers and unskilled migrants in the late nineteenth and early twentieth centuries. But the new immigrants and their descendants have an aporia about their earlier counterparts, one separated by time and class differences. What this dancer's body and music text does is lay claim to the land and signals of an emerging Hindu cosmology transplanted into America; there are now more than 1,500 Hindu places of worship in North America. It helps Indian Americans experience the life force of the land, enabling them to see the land of their adoption as a distinct being deserving of respect and something that they belong to, and that it is not necessarily the nation space they need to return to in order to feel at "home." In this ideal multicultural scenario, immigrants claim land and establish their citizenship rights in their new home. However, Elaine Kim, in her classic essay, signals ambivalence as she provides a complex interpretation of Asian Americans' claim to Americanness:

> So much writing by Asian Americans is focused on the theme of claiming an American, as opposed to Asian, identity that we may begin to wonder if this constitutes accommodation, a collective colonized spirit—the fervent wish to "hide our ancestry," which is impossible for us anyway, to relinquish our marginality, and to lose ourselves in an intense identification with the hegemonic culture. Or is it in fact a celebration of our marginality and a profound expression of protest against being defined by domination?[6]

The ambivalence between identification and marginality is exposed in this performance. The dancer is making a claim not only to the divine but to a diasporic citizenship that acknowledges the history of the land they live on. But the importance of dance is that the body imagines and represents the past while still in the present. It also requires the audience to be transported across space and time. Dance happens in the absolute present, simultaneously invoking the past and another space. The Indian dancing body in diaspora invokes ancient and ritual spaces through the kinesthetic traces that reside in the form, but it also invokes contemporary spaces and lays claim to them, even if this is not a radical undoing but a continuation of citizenship based on property ownership.

And therein lies the danger. I would argue here that we cannot simply delink colonialism from settler colonialism and rethink migrant claims to land as different to colonial claims of land. Nandita Sharma rightly argues that temporary migrant workers who have no land or citizenship rights (in Canada, for example) are being used as part of the neoliberal restructuring of the labor market, and that it is important to delink these migrant histories from histories of colonialism. This is certainly true. But I argue that we need to rethink this in the case of permanent migrants who claim land much as colonial settlers have done.

We would then be ignoring the act of claiming land itself as a violent and capitalist act. If Hinduism in its manifestation through Indian dance in the U.S. diaspora is attempting to control land through sacral geography, then there is a dark side to this performance. These are the tensions around the building of U.S. Hindu temples, the so-called Hinduization of North American land. Indian American claiming of American land is not a radical undoing, but a continuation of citizenship, based on property ownership, putting them on a path toward the assimilation and "whiteness" they both seek and fear. What George Lipsitz, David Roediger, and other critical race theorists suggest is that the path toward whiteness is in the claiming of certain kinds of lands by various people of color, which mimics white ownership and control of land.[7] Even though Indian immigrants might believe they are creating a minority place of worship or an alternative reimagining of land, similar to Native Americans, in essence they have followed a mainstream model of claiming the land, much like the colonial settler model. However, this is not a seamless inclusion: Muslim South Asians, for example, are denied access to this privilege in the wake of 9/11. It has become increasingly evident that Asians (Indians included) have become complicit in America's system of hierarchy by passively accepting the privileges of whiteness.[8] The post-1965 Indian immigrants are not like the pre-1928 migrants, given that the terms of whiteness itself have shifted now to include them in key and important ways.

Although in this performance the music and dance text purport to align themselves with "nature" and the Native American relationship to land, in some ways this is a dangerous move that can be understood within the frameworks of the increasingly diasporic activities of the BJP [Bharatiya Janata Party], Shiv Sena, or Hindutva (extreme right-wing Hindu political parties), which encourage Hindus all over the world to proselytize Hinduism, raise capital (political, economic, national, and cultural), and take over spaces to mark them as Hindu. Such fundamentalist moves are truly frightening and offer no political support of Native American sovereignty rights and struggles over land in the Americas. They are also frightening examples of the increasing right-wing, militant, masculine, neoliberal, capitalist-dominated forms of Hinduism that have spread both in India (for example, with the recent election win of the BJP and the installation of the controversial Narendra Modi as the prime minster of India) and among the diaspora.[9] Indian immigrants in North America, along with other immigrants, have followed in the footsteps of colonial settler movements in laying claim to land and participating in the transactions required to participate in U.S. forms of citizenship. Like other immigrants from various religious backgrounds, they have formed ethnic communities that have created religious spaces for themselves, whether that be through building temples, mosques, gurudwaras, churches, and the like, or through the act of buying and owning land. What is hidden in this dance performance is the $40 million it cost to buy the land in Malibu and build the temple, which was raised by the Hindu Society of Los Angeles.

Ironically, the dedication of this dance to the God Srinivasa in Malibu is perhaps apropos, given that this deity in Tirupati is heavily in debt to Kubera, the god of wealth. Legend has it that the God Vishnu, in his human avatar of Srinivasa, found himself insolvent and needed money quickly in order to marry his consort, the goddess Lakshmi (the goddess of wealth personified), in her human avatar as Padmavati. Apparently, the wedding costs were quite high, and Srinivasa subsequently found himself indebted to Kubera at an unfair interest rate; therefore, his temple in Tirupati continues to amass great wealth to pay his debts to Kubera (which, according to all accounts, still remain unpaid despite the vast sums of money accumulating in the temple). The temple in Malibu is also, by all accounts, quite solvent and attracts wealth, due to this insolvent Srinivasa and/or the sacred geography of Malibu itself. It is then important to ask how Indian immigrants might reimagine themselves differently vis-à-vis the land. For a possible model, we can turn to historically different Indian diasporas.

This act of re-territorializing and sacralizing land is not a new phenomenon for Indian diasporas. In Siem Reap, Cambodia, and in Jogjakarta, Indonesia, there is ample evidence of precapitalist Indian diasporas' relationship to space in ways different to those we see in the U.S. example. Inscribed in the ancient temple walls of Angkor, Banteay Srey, in the Prambanan temple in Jogja, and in the living practices of Cambodian and Javanese dancing bodies, we see how Cambodian and Javanese land was reimagined as Jamudvipa. Mount Meru was replicated in the form of local mountains, the Ganges in local rivers, and the gods themselves imitated with a difference that evolved by mingling with local deities and spirits. What we see evidence of in Cambodia, Jogja, and other Hindu temple sites around Southeast Asia is not a "claiming of land" but rather an amalgamation and syncretic development of cultural processes.

As Narayanan and others suggest, Indians who went to Southeast Asia did not arrive trying to stake claims on the land. Indian kings sent vassals to visit these lands in order to establish trade and allow citizens to travel between these geographic sites and build temples.[10] There is no evidence of wars, bloodshed, or battles over land between Hindu immigrants and locals. Rather, there is evidence of wars between locals (e.g., the Chams and the Khmer in the twelfth century, and between local kingdoms in Java in the ninth and tenth centuries) inscribed onto the walls of Angkor and Bayon (in the lower section of the temples) and onto temple wall codices and tablets in Java. The evidence points to an absorption of Hindu legends and myths, and to sacralization of land both by locals and by Indian migrants.

The performing arts in particular reflect some of these syncretic fusions of cultures even in the present day. For example, performances of the legendary tales of the Ramayana that take place on the grounds of the Prambanan temple, catering to tourists, and the Mahabharata and the Churning of the Ocean, held in the precincts of the Angkor Wat temple grounds, demonstrate the local absorption of these stories as living embodiments and political statements of cultural syncretism. What these examples in Southeast Asia suggest is that post-capital migration perhaps has no alternative but the trope of conquest and ownership. Indian immigrants follow white settler colonial models, whereas long-forgotten diasporas in Southeast Asia reveal alternative possibilities.

Indian diaspora dances urge us to consider the politics of laying claim to land. In particular, Asian immigrants have shouldered this burden in a particular way, as the constant figures of non-belonging and foreignness. The burden of belonging falls upon them, often requiring them to prove themselves as exceptional and exceeding performers of American values: individualist self-making through capitalist production, family values, model citizenship, etc. Racialization of some South Asians post-9/11, the rise of India as a superpower, and cultural performances such as "Malibu Srinivasa" leave open the recognition of unrealized connectivities and potentialities through shared beliefs in the sacred earth and the power of myths, understood within the force of contemporary politics rather than transcendent of them. However, there is ambivalence to these forms of belonging because, in the process of assimilation and trying to become "white," Indians in America may in fact be perpetrating the same kinds of violence enacted by earlier colonial settlers with this process of "claiming land."

Notes

1. Mike Sampson, "Humaliwo: Where the Surf Sounds Loudly." *California Department of Parks and Recreation.* Accessed May 2012. https://www.parks.ca.gov/?page_id=24435.
2. For more on cultural citizenship, see Lisa Lowe, *Immigrant Acts: On Asian American Cultural Politics* (Durham: Duke University Press, 1996) and Aihwa Ong, *Neoliberalism as Exception: Mutations in Citizenship and Sovereignty* (Durham: Duke University Press, 2006).
3. Francis Assisi, "The Hinduization of America," *Communalism Combat.* http://communalismcombat.blogspot.com/2005/06/hinduization-of-america-by-francis-c.html. Accessed March 27, 2017.
4. Vasudha Narayanan, "Hinduism in Southeast Asia," *Encyclopedia of Religion.* https://www.encyclopedia.com/environment/encyclopedias-almanacs-transcripts-and-maps/hinduism-southeast-asia. Accessed March 11, 2019.
5. Martin Manalansan, "Diasporic Deviants/Divas: How Filipino Gay Transmigrants 'Play with the World,'" in *Queer Diasporas,* Cindy Patton and Benigno Sanchez Eppler, eds. (Durham: Duke University Press, 2000), 183–203.
6. Elaine H. Kim, "Defining Asian American Realities Through Literature," *Cultural Critique,* no. 6 (Minneapolis: University of Minnesota Press, 1987): 88.

7. George Lipsitz, *How Racism Takes Place* (Temple University Press, 2011). David Roediger, *Working Toward Whiteness: How America's Immigrants Became White: The Strange Journey from Ellis Island to the Suburbs* (Basic Books, 2003).
8. Julia Carrie Wong, "The Complicity Cost of Racial Inclusion." Al Jazeera.com. http://america.aljazeera.com/opinions/2014/8/asian-americans-racecomplicitymodelminority.html?utm_content=opinion&utm_campaign=ajam&utm_source=twitter&utm_medium=SocialFlow. Accessed March 11, 2019.
9. Narendra Modi was the state Chief Minister of Gujarat when riots broke out in 2002 between Hindus and Muslims. According to official figures, the riots resulted in the deaths of 790 Muslims and 254 Hindus; 2,500 people were injured non-fatally, and 223 more were reported missing, "Gujarat Riot Death Toll Revealed." BBC, 11 May 2005. http://news.bbc.co.uk/2/hi/south_asia/4536199.stm. Modi, as head of state, did not respond to calls for help from Muslim-dominated areas, but sent police to support Hindu areas. His government did little to quell the violence, but instead inflamed the situation in what Pandey Gyanendra calls "state terrorism" and acts of "organized political massacres." See Pandey Gyanendra, *Routine Violence: Nations, Fragments, Histories* (Stanford, CA: Stanford University Press, 2005), pp. 187–188. The United States Department of State eventually banned Narendra Modi from traveling to the United States for his alleged role in this "pogrom."
10. Narayanan, 2005.

Chapter 12

Oh, Angelita Garcia!

Jason Magabo Perez

AUTHOR'S NOTE: The following has been excerpted from a novel-forever-in-progress. These excerpts have also made their way into two of my performance works-in-progress—*The Passion of El Hulk Hogancito* (Kularts, 2009) and *You Will Gonna Go Crazy* (Kularts, 2011).

"Anak," says Nay, her cheekbones the disconnected hemispheres of a heart. "Would you not be so very truly sad if I died?" She turns onto Mission Avenue. Her skeletal hands choke the steering wheel. "Talagang tragic, ano, anak? What would you do? What would you possibly do if I were to sleep and never ever will gonna wake? Never again. COULD YOU IMAGINE? Dying. Dying. Dead. Wala na. Like that. Dios ko! God help you, di ba, anak?"

Nay can barely see over the steering wheel. She adjusts the couch pillow underneath her. This tan interior smells of sourdough and nail polish. Nay always drives me to school in this Buick drive-by-mobile. When we hit bumps like this, potholes like that, and fractures in the road, the Buick bounces up and down as if it's traversing turbulent waters.

"Anak, what in the world would Dad do? Could you imagine the devastation? Ang lonely lonely talaga. Devastated and so very lonely. His body will gonna quit."

The sunshine is gangrenous. We pass Mega Foods, its blue grand opening pennants still up after a year. Soon after, we pass the drive-in movie theater—the Oceanside Swap Meet on the weekends. The edges of the giant screens are blackening. And the half-paved driveway leading to the entrance is crowded with brown laborers, sunburned, looking like Father, awaiting today's work.

"Anak, do you have nice classmates? Are they raised well? What do they do? Mabait ba? O hindi? How are they, anak?"

"Oh," I say, slouching in my seat, barely able to see over the dashboard myself. "Uh, um, quiet, nice, talkative, mean." I continue to list adjectives so the prying stops: "Hyper, sad, stupid, able, mean, ugly, stupid, really mean, lonely, running, pretty, poor, White, chalky, Mexican, Samoan, White, Mexican."

"Wala kang Pilipino friends?"

Recess is all about warfare, the impermanency of friendship, the arithmetic of mad-dogging. Mad-dogging so hard . . . you feel your skeleton dust.

"No," I say, "not yet."

Red light.

San Diego Avenue.

Fuck. This intersection.

Turn right and you enter el barrio de Los Locos De La Luna. Across the street is the indoor swap meet. Straight ahead: more palm trees, the I-5, the Oceanside Pier and the Pacific Ocean. Directly to the right, in the bicycle lane, stand los peewees, hooligans who have nothing better to do than ditch and flash signs at passing traffic. These nascent eses—in their shaved heads, creased Dickies and Cortezes—risk repetitive strain in order to spell with their fingers the acronyms of the most elaborately named gangs. It is their God-given purpose to assure that Rancho De La Valle One Bed One Bath Two Bed Two Bath and Quaint Yet Luxurious Studio Apartment Homes Posse does not go unnoticed in this cruel cruel world.

Green light. Nay steps on the gas, but the Buick stutters, belches, gulps, pants, coughs, and dies midway through the intersection. Helixes of smoke escape the hood.

"I-help mo," says Nay as she swings open the door.

Los peewees pay us no mind. Not even the slightest bit of mockery.

Through the windshield, through the sliver between the hood and the engine bay, I see Nay hover over smoke. Barehanded, Nay tightens bolts and clamps, bangs on the carburetor, and checks fluid levels. Nay has mastered the breakdown.[1]

"Sige," she says, "I-try mo na."

I scoot across the bench, the pleather dikit-dikit on the backs of my thighs. I wiggle the key slightly out of the ignition as I turn it, the way Nay taught me, and the engine chugs. I turn it again and thanks be to the Lord the engine roars!

Nay shuts the hood and returns.

"Anak," she says as she continues toward school, "Do not be a fearful, okay? Bakit ang embarrassed mo, ha? Humiliation is not real. Those boys are nothing but sadness, ano? Puro sadness. No school. No job. They do not know poverty. My God, anak, they are just a kid."

Nay, I wish to remind her, they look like Tomás. Just like Tomás. Same shaved head. Same hard stare to remind you of your smallness. What then of Nay's own son? What then of my own scary brother?

"If you think about such troubles," says Nay, "the troubles of the world, you will gonna CRY AND CRY. And if you will gonna cry and cry, your face will gonna stay like that forever."

"Really?"

"And then, you will gonna go crazy, anak, very very crazy."

Nay's hair is short, permed, and dyed the blackest black. I wonder if wisdom grows right there in the curls. And if so, might she be less and less wise and less and less sane and less and less alive after each and every haircut?

Perhaps this Buick should stay dead forever and ever, so we wouldn't have to keep driving off, again and again, toward the troubles of the world.

❖❖❖

Now it's not true that I'm trying to impress Angelita Garcia[2] at Show & Tell. That's not it at all. Everyone knows I outdo anyone. None of these chumps can step to someone who brings in shards of broken windshield that have been plucked from his paralyzed brother's back. Tell me one third-grader to do so. Tell me. I want to show Nay that I am normal, and that I don't just cry and cry all day. I want to show Nay that I'm not destined to be a jarhead—I don't want to live forever in the gutter of Camp Pendleton. I want to prove that in Señora Seth's second- and third-grade combination classroom, in all of McKinley Elementary, in all of Oceanside, I'm the smartest pupil. Not Angelita Garcia, Little Miss I Speak German, Spanish, English, and Chipmunk; Little Miss Mathematics is Boring Though I Excel at All Subjects, Especially Reading Aloud; Little Miss Too Many Friendships to Count. No, not that social butterfly seated across the room in her roja-brown Indio skin, in her pretty yellow sunflower dress, in her mustard Mary Janes. No, not that budding artista over there crayoning self-portraits, not that Frida

Kahlita, but yo, ako, I. I am the smartest. And I, Nay's bunso, show the best Show and tell the best Tell. EVER.

"This is my mother," I tell the class as Nay and I stand up front. "She's a nurse."

Señora Seth's classroom is a prison. The brick walls are white. Windowless. The carpet is balding. And the room smells of pencil shavings and milk-breath.

"Some say," I continue, "my mother murdered many many people before."[3]

"Oooooh!"

"How many?"

"Who?"

"Ahhhhh!"

"Liar."

"Really?"

"My mommy killed a thief!"

"My daddy killed himself!"

"So?" I say. "Some called Nay a SERIAL KILLER."

Señora Seth swallows her response. Poor Señora Seth, who often, like today, wears turquoise jewelry and smelly leather sandals, has no wrench to wrench us out of this moment. She smiles a huge smile at Nay, the kind that means she's signaling with her eyelashes.[4]

Nay, unfazed, straightens her scrubs and says, "Now listen, students."

Everyone shuts up.

I wonder if Nay is remembering. Nay was a convict at one point in her life. A real one. At this point, all I know is that she's been one. That's all. Every now and then, Tomás jokes around and says, Mom's a killer. Though on any given day such as this you couldn't possibly believe so because Nay, the lovely nurse in that lovely blue blusa, composes herself like the smartest person alive.

"Now, students," Nay continues. "Never ponder the troubles of this world, okay? You will gonna go very truly crazy. Trust me."

The rest of Show & Tell, as predicted, shall not go down in history. This day, however, Angelita Garcia shall.

❖❖❖

Before Nay leaves for work, I tour her around the classroom.

"That one," giggles Nay, pointing to Angelita Garcia. "Talagang dramatic, di ba?"

Just yesterday, Angelita Garcia's hair was long and straight and black and nice. Now it's a crimped Koosh ball, short with highlights the color of dead grass. If I knew short hair to be a radical statement of femininity, I could dig it. But I don't know, so I don't dig. Now Angelita Garcia's hair makes even more visible those pearly white teeth and that perfectly aligned bite. Nay claims I inherited my obvious overbite from her family.

Nay asks me about Angelita Garcia's parents.

"Hard laborers," I laugh. "They put her haircut on layaway."

Nay seems offended. Both the black suit I'm wearing and the bedsheets used for her blusa were purchased on layaway. In fact, she even purchased my socks and briefs on layaway. Layaway, I'll come to learn, is not a laughing matter. Layaway, I'll come to learn, is not necessary for every family.

I show Nay my desk. Unlike the flip-open desks of others, full of dried mealworms, lima beans, repeatedly chewed gum and baggies of Kool-Aid powder, mine is minimalist: three neatly folded pieces of cardboard. I set them up as if I were taking a test. I demonstrate that I keep my head close to the paper, as close as Father keeps his lips to the plate. And I whisper, "They know I have answers."

Andy Kim interrupts.

"Hello," he says to Nay, his big fat head the shape of a rugby ball, his skin peachy yellow. "Miss Mug-uh-BOO!"

Stupid kids like Andy the Korean Bully Kim never say "missus" because they're confused about the *r* in the abbreviation.

"Hello," Nay replies. "Are you my Hasón's best friend?"

"Nay!"

"No way in H-E-double hockey stick," says Andy Kim, grinning in disgust. "What the H-E-double hockey stick is *neigh?*"

Yesterday, Andy Kim laughed at my middle name: Magabo.

"What kinda name is Mug-uh-boo?" he giggled as he handed back my spelling test. "A ghost's name?"[5]

"The kind of name," I said under my breath, "for the kind of person. That gets perfect scores. Fathead Korean."

"Fuck you, WETBACK CHINK NIGGER BITCH!"

Little Does Andy the Korean Bully Kim know that Nay has been called a SLANT-EYED BITCH. For had Andy the Korean Bully Kim known that Nay had been called a SLANT-EYED BITCH, Andy the Korean Bully Kim might've never called me a WETBACK CHINK NIGGER BITCH. But Andy the Korean Bully Kim has no way of knowing that Nay has been called SLANT-EYED BITCH. So, Andy the Korean Bully Kim proceeds to call me a WETBACK CHINK NIGGER BITCH. I let Andy the Korean Bully Kim call me a WETBACK CHINK NIGGER BITCH. I let the bully bully me. I let him conflate histories because he, like I, must get used to being named.

What I should do is yank the bangs of his bowl-cut. Or suplex him! But today isn't about bravado; today is about my genius. My Outstanding Citizenship. Ignoring Andy the Korean Bully Kim and the limp collar of his polo, I seat Nay at my desk.

Señora Seth is indeed impassioned, yet a failure of a pedagogue. She rarely structures lessons. Instead, she urges us to learn as we please. Thus, up front, beatboxing his little heart out, is Ronny Wallace, the light-skinned Gary Coleman,[6] the only one able to pull off an authentic Gumby Cut and pink pleated parachute pants. He speeds up his bah boom bap clack. Though still perplexed about rap and about my brothers' sudden transition from Pink Floyd to Public Enemy, I join Ronny Wallace. As I hum metal melodies, I cannot for the asthma in me keep up. Ronny Wallace and I stare at each other. My wheezing sounds like a kazoo. Before returning to our desks, Ronny Wallace and I, certain that he will still come out as cool as ever and that I will forever house a lifetime's worth of shame, fade our noise abruptly. Nay, and only Nay, applauds.

Class usually turns out like this: never in my favor. Whenever we popcorn read, I read so slowly that others finish sentences for me. And I mispronounce words like *a lot*. I wish every vowel to be even longer. Then I could pedal my bicycle far away, along the vowel, into the vowel, through the vowel, to someplace where I wouldn't need a voice.

Miss Angelita Garcia, on the other hand, reads so rapidly and so theatrically it's as if this language can't wait to burst out of her. She probably ridicules me behind my back.

Last week, in mid-mispronunciation, I sprinted to the restroom and relieved myself too soon. Señora Seth believed me when I told her the water fountain had malfunctioned. Later that day, Patricio, the same brother who mocks me for moving my lips when I read to myself, asked me if I pissed my pants, to which Nay replied, No, the hallway was flooded. Angelita Garcia claimed the same had happened to her and then said to me: Don't worry, it's normal.

Now, as I lose more and more points with Nay, Angelita Garcia decides to perform the grand finale of Nay's visit. Angelita Garcia has changed into gold ballerina slippers. Ronny Wallace, Andy Kim, and the other boys and girls wrapped around Angelita Garcia's precious little finger use desks to build a stage. Angelita Garcia tiptoes onto a chair and then onto the stage.

"I study ballet," she says, her arms forming a C resting on its back.

"The Mexican hat dance?" says Andy Kim. "Alright, Angelita Taqueria Garcia!"

Señora Seth shushes Andy Kim.

I tug at Nay's blusa but she keeps her attention on Angelita Garcia.

And suddenly . . .

Just like that!

Angelita Garcia spins and spins and spins and spins, executing the first set of pirouettes I've ever witnessed in my entire life. So delicate. So balanced. Her yellow dress flares out.

She's like a coin spun by God!

A blur . . . then her little self again . . . then a blur . . . self . . . blur . . . again . . . again . . . again.

She curtsies, her hair-sprayed perm perfectly in place. The class cheers, hollering learned noises like the rolled r's of a machinegun. While I offer a mere golf clap, Nay gives a standing ovation.

"Anak," says Nay. "Time to go to work."

Offbeat, I keep my head down, unclip my tie and start to usher Nay to the door.

"Matalas ang utak mo," says Nay. "You're smart, anak."

Before I can thank Nay, before I can assure her that her bunso is brilliant, that I don't just cry all day, Angelita Garcia skips over to us and up to Nay.

"Hi-ya! I'm Angelita Garcia." She extends her furry arm to Nay. "No middle name."

"You're an excellent ballerina," says Nay, shaking Angelita Garcia's hand.

"Hasón's a talented musician," replies Angelita Garcia.

Everyday at recess, Angelita Garcia destroys me at tetherball. She's shorter than me. Skinnier than me. But she consistently and effortlessly powers the ball past me. Even in flats she has more hops than I do. I never even touch the ball unless it's accidentally with my face or the back of my head. And she's always so annoyingly sweet and says, I just got lucky. You have great footwork.

Tetherball has nothing to do with my feet.

"Work na," I mumble as I urge Nay away from Angelita Garcia and toward the door.

"Wait," I say. "Wait, Nay."

I point to my last chance—my Women's History Month drawing:

Through the beautiful brown sky fly several birds, various-sized black McDonald's M's.[7] And staring out into the Pasig River, with a mountainous nose and harsh dots for eyes, stands The Rachel Carson, the nature writer. Because Rachel Carson is known for exposing the dangers of pesticides, the Pasig River is full of Jesus fish. Suffering. A lot. And Rachel Carson's skin is light orange not because of cancerous chemicals but because even white-people complexion is difficult to capture with crayons. Señora Seth awarded this Second Place.[8] First Place, of course, was honored to Angelita Garcia's rendition of Frida Kahlo. I didn't even choose Rachel Carson. I wanted to portray Nay. Nay is a woman. Nay has lived historically. But when Señora Seth asked me what contributions Nay had made to the advancement of women, I simply answered: She's a good mother.

This wasn't enough.

"Ang ganda ganda," Nay now says, pushing in the clear thumbtacks and continuing on her way out.

"One more," I whisper, and stop Nay one last time. "One more one more."

This will do it. Hanging just beside the drawings is a neon red poster, the brightest sheet in all of the room. It is the Who's Who in Reading & Writing chart. We all signed our own names. I point to my signature, the neatest. Others lack control of their penmanship; some of their letters appear to be collapsing, some letters bleed into each other, and, like my recently immigrated relatives cramped in a tiny studio apartment, some letters crowd and suffocate each other.

The fact that I've earned the most green and gold stars—87 total—certifies me as the most avid reader and the most prolific writer. I submit my reading logs, signed and dated by Father, more frequently than anyone, even Miss All-Star Angelita Garcia herself, who has received a mere 63 stars.

Angelita Garcia finds us at the door and yaps on. "Hasón must be extra intelligent!" She grabs my right hand to show Nay how dark the side of it has become from smeared pencil lead. "You write hard," says Angelita Garcia, and with her thumbnail outlines the bump on my middle finger.

I retract my hand. Nay snickers. My heart beats once. Twice. Thrice. My ankles and soles now warm and prickly. Oh no, I think, oh fuck. Nay must know that I ask Father to sign my reading logs because he never pays attention when it comes to school. Nay must know I'm cheating. Nay knows I watch television and ride my bicycle and do not read and do not write and do not pray the Holy Rosary.

Damn!

The ballerina will win again. She'll discover that I'm nothing more than a counterfeit intellectual. Then she'll call Father a liar and call Nay a serial killer and then Angelita Garcia will join the bandwagon of Andy Kims and laugh and laugh at every little thing I do, every little thing that I am. Then I'll cry. And cry.

"Aalis na ako, anak," Nay says, and kisses the top of my head. She turns to Angelita Garcia and says, "Very nice to meet you, hija."

"You too," agrees Angelita Garcia, her smile now wider than ever.

I remain in the hallway until Nay disappears.

"You know what?" says Angelita Garcia, joining me.

I turn around. "What?"

Is she going to dance? Is she going to sing me into oblivion? I wait. I wait for her to talk trash. I wait for her to breathe mess, to take back her pleasantness and remind me that I soiled my black Gotcha shorts. I'm a mumbler of polysyllabic words. She most definitely has deduced that I am the most cheatingest cheater to ever cheat before.

She'll expose me. She: Número Uno. At Everything. Perhaps even at knowing me.

Staring at her mouth, I anticipate Angelita Garcia to dart her tongue out, to slap me, pinch my eyelid, wet-willy me, or to laugh and laugh until I cry cry cry. But this ballerina has something else to say, a something I'll surely chase to hear again the rest of my life. And I hope to marry an Angelita Garcia, one who will utter these marvelous words in the exact same marvelous way, with her long eyelashes fluttering, her smile glimmering, that red red tongue, those rolled r's, accented vowels, and all: "Tu mamá," she says. "Your mommy, Hasón Pérez . . . ¡Qué bonita! ¡Qué bonita! Your mamá is so so beautiful."

so so beautiful: an auto/biography of sorts[9]

I was a small kid before and I play and
I like to be a nurse and I get those dragonfly
You know that one?

And I get my needle and inject them
with water / My sister says:
Why do you do that?
Because I want to be a nurse
One of these days I will gonna be one
They're so NEAT—their
white clothes uniform shoes cap and all those
I think they don't die
because they're so nice / and so CLEAN
They don't die
because they're helping people
You have to send me to school: I told Tatay
One thing is: the only way
I can see America
is to be a nurse
Tatay said:
NO / you can't go because they killed those nurse in CHICAGO
That was Speck[10] in that time
When I leave home to come here
Nanay and Tatay is CRYING AND CRYING
Tatay said: If you find a nice guy / marry him / you're getting old
When I arrive America it's too far
It's another world
Hindi maganda ang America
I'm lonely / I have no friends / I work nights
Then I meet your Dad
Everyone said: You have a partner now
for the Valentine's / it's a dance in the hospital
WHO IS THAT?
Your dad said: O, you're going? Then we're all going?
We dance and dance
And later on / then I know him
he calls me / he come to the house
We were boyfriends for six months
We go out / We take the train
Then he said:
If you want me then I'll stay
If you don't marry me / I go to Japan
with my brother
If I stay, we'll continue / If not

then
we don't know
That time he work in St. Francis in the laundry department
He said: if you like me, then we just get married
If not / then maybe
I'm not coming back / I go home after Japan
Okay, I said, then WHEN?
It was a big wedding
Our invitation is
MADE IN THE PHILIPPINES
We had the reception in a Chinese Restaurant
THAT WAS A NICE LOVE STORY
And then—
Time goes on and on and then—
WHY DID THOSE THING HAPPEN?
God / I thought America was really a milk and honey
I was so depressed
Here I am
provinciana / POOR as mud
I come for greener pasture
then those thing happen
We DID NOT DO those crime
okay hold / okay hold / na / okay
Let me tell you what happen
What REALLY happen
I work in Ann Arbor VA
in Michigan / in ICU
okay / okay
Every time there's code
in the hospital
an ICU nurse
has to come to bring the CUT-
DOWN
TRAY / OF / COURSE
we gonna do that because that's our job, di ba?
In that time in whatever floor
THERE'S A CODE!
How come it's all the time? Something
is happening, di ba?
How come they're all DYING?

maybe it's anesthesia in ER maybe
it's too hot maybe no air-con
Then one night
on August fifteen nineteen seventy-five the date
we have three code in ICU
THREE!
One after the other
One stop breathing
We don't know if it's heart or respiratory or what
It's CODE BLUE
Then we're not done with this one—
and there's ANOTHER
coding HERE!
O GOD! COULD YOU IMAGINE?
That night / we got it settled
After work / we were so so tired
and then—
They said they wanted to talk to me downstairs
WHO?
the F B I
I'm afraid / because that's FBI!
We're just a stranger here
We don't speak the language
How can we express our self?
How can we explain
what we want to say if we don't know how to say?
Those FBI always ask and ask:
Did you administer that medicine?
I said: NO
Just say it was your friend / the other Filipino nurse
No / She didn't do anything
This goes on / and on / and then
one day June sixteen nineteen seventy-six the date
I was working morning
Something fishy / like I have hunch
something happening
I was walking / in the street and—
two big men was all of a sudden holding me:
Leonora Perez, YOU ARE UNDER ARREST.
I didn't do anything. What crime? I didn't do any crime.

Follow us to the car or we will drag you.
We arrested your friend, too.
You-don't-even-read-me-my-rights.
Then they cover / my handcuff / with my sweater
I don't know it's CRAZY those FBI
Dad / he wait for me in the train
And suddenly I'm in TV all-over-the-place
I want to let the world to know / WHY
did those thing HAPPEN?
We're INNOCENT
We're being discriminated
Even if I am / just IMMIGRANT
Even if I am just / STRANGER here
I'm a human being, di ba?

Notes

1. At the age of seven, our narrator has yet to understand the particularities of sadness.
2. Angelita Garcia is absolutely and materially nonfictional. Should Angelita Garcia be reading this by some stroke of a fictional or nonfictional God, the nonfictional Angelita Garcia must know that our ~~author~~ narrator, our little fictional narrator, whose name is Hasón, which is not what Jason Magabo Perez's father used to call him, simply and innocently wonders.
3. In 1976, two recently immigrated Filipina nurses, Leonora Perez and Filipina Narciso, were framed by the FBI for murder at the Ann Arbor Veterans Hospital in Michigan. Following the arrest, the federal government fabricated a costly, racially unjust case full of false testimonies and shady investigation, which led to the wrongful conviction and imprisonment of the two nurses. Eventually, at the appeal of the defense, the federal government dropped its charges and the nurses were freed. To this day, the FBI has never apologized or admitted wrongdoing, and the case has never been solved. *U.S. v. Narciso-Perez* is testament to the brutal underside of the American Dream, and serves a textbook example of state-sponsored, anti-immigrant racism and sexism, and a vestige of U.S. imperialism that remains largely unexamined. One of the nurses, Leonora Perez, happens to be our narrator's mother. FUCK THE FEDERAL BUREAU OF INVESTIGATION, says our narrator. And author!
4. This should not be misread as another white liberal lady teacher not really giving a flying fuck about poor flightless brown people. Instead,

this should serve as empirical proof that kindhearted white liberal lady teachers, who are often terribly self-conscious about their self-proclaimed sympathy for the marginalized, often silence themselves so as not to silence or step on the toes of the marginalized, especially the little brown toes of little brown women such as our little narrator's little marginalized mother.

5. This one, o Korean Kasama, still hurts our little narrator's little feelings. Especially the invisibility.
6. May the great, underrated, and underestimated Gary Coleman (1968–2010) rest in peace.
7. Yes, at such a tender age, our narrator is already an adept semiotician.
8. This masterpiece also won second place at a real-life museum that honors all that white feminists adore. Like the work of Frida K.
9. This abridged biography is largely based on actual nonfictional interviews with Leonora Magabo Perez. The interviews were conducted by her youngest son, our author, Jason Magabo Perez, from April 2010 to May 2010. As she read her prison diaries aloud, Leonora Magabo Perez recollected her past. Our author has taken poetic license in editing the transcripts from the interview. This abridged auto/biography is merely an abridged, preliminary experiment in oral history. Whether you read this as nonfiction or fiction, trust that our author's sustained commitment to saying FUCK YOU to the Federal Bureau of Investigation is absolutely and without hesitation nonfictional.
10. Richard Speck was a REAL and REALLY GUILTY mass murderer white motherfucker who brutally murdered eight nursing students in Chicago in 1966. Among the victims were young nurses from the Philippines. For a well-written account and analysis of the cases of both *Speck* and *Narciso-Perez* please refer to Chapter 5 in Catherine Ceniza Choy, *Empire of Care: Nursing and Migration in Filipino American History* (Duke University Press, 2003).

CHAPTER 13

Moving Tradition

Alleluia Panis and Kularts

JOYCE LU

I FIRST HEARD OF ALLELUIA PANIS DANCE THEATER and Kularts when I was the office manager at Kearny Street Workshop (KSW) in the early 1990s. At this time, KSW was not yet a nonprofit organization and was housed above the San Francisco Wholesale Flower Market. Poet and printmaker Nancy Hom was the executive director, and we regularly produced events featuring artists such as Al Robles, Jaime Jacinto, Canyon Sam, and Genny Lim—those who were present at the inception of KSW, when the establishment of Ethnic Studies departments at San Francisco State University and the University of California at Berkeley, and the fate of the International Hotel galvanized the community. After hours, poet Presco Tabios might wander into the office and inhabit the makeshift shelter he'd constructed in the back of the office with random pieces of furniture. The office of Farallon Films's Steven Okazaki was next door. This scene was the reason I came to live in the Bay Area after graduating from college in Southern California. I wanted to connect with the birthplace of the Asian American movement and with other Asian American artists.

The mailing list of KSW was basically an inventory of the evolution of Asian American arts. I probably sent several mailings to Alleluia Panis Dance Theater before I actually saw the company perform the piece *Diwata* in 1995 at Theater Artaud. I remember being blown away because I had never seen such a thing before: an ensemble of powerful Asian women presenting dance that was passionate, technically flawless, original, and dynamic, and that addressed themes that were relevant to me. I literally felt like "Yes. This is what we've been waiting for. Yes."

I started to follow Panis's work regularly and finally, in 2002 when she was offering free dance workshops at Bindlestiff Theater, I signed myself up. At this point, Panis was also the artistic and executive director of Kularts, the premier presenter of contemporary and tribal Pilipino arts in the United States. She informed the dance workshop participants about the Kularts Tribal Tour that would be happening that summer. I was midway through the Ph.D. program in Performance Studies at UC Berkeley and decided to use my summer stipend to join. I traveled to Mindanao to explore the indigenous cultures there with Panis and two other women: activist and healthcare worker Mylene Cahambing and musician and director of Mahal, Evelie Posch. After my return, I found myself participating in more Kularts activities—organizing an event that brought the indigenous T'boli of Cotabato together with Pomo Native Americans; volunteering in the holiday season Parol Lantern Festival; serving on the advisory board; performing in Anthem Salgado's piece "Brown and Black and Blue" in the 2007 *Post-Modern American Pilipino Performance Project;* and stage managing the Project another year.

Why did I keep following Panis around? For one, she is a self-proclaimed "movement innovator." When she used this term with me, she was referring specifically to her dance and choreography. Yet all arts flow from her organization, along with a steady stream of both up-and-coming as well as more established artists. So I want to suggest that she also innovates in the larger sense of creating new forms of Asian American, and even more specifically, American Pilipino political movement. For Panis, the arts are central to social justice. Her ethics and aesthetics are grounded in and guided by a global anti-colonial consciousness that fuels a prolific body of ever-innovative artwork that models to me what Asian American arts should do. How has she kept this venture going for thirty years? What drives her?

Panis's work, she will tell you, first and foremost, comes from, reflects, manages, and heals the complicated position of Filipinos in America. "It's emotionally very complex," she explains,

> living with this long history of colonization, and then facing discrimination in the country of the people who raped and pillaged your ancestors; living with the sense that these multiple colonizations have produced a mixture of blood that renders a

> non-culture. All our lives, our parents have been fed that we don't have an original idea, right? That there's no real Filipino people.

Yet despite the difficulties that these conditions present, Panis is also very clear that she does not want to iterate any kind of victim mentality: "Even in the meanest and most devastating aspects [of colonization], my people, my ancestors made the best of it. We would not be who we are now without those experiences." Panis's strategy is to use the arts and education, and the arts *as* education, in the larger project of decolonization.

Since the Tribal Tour I attended in 2002, forty-five people have gone with Panis on subsequent, almost annual, trips to Mindanao. For years, Mindanao has been on the U.S. Department travel warning "due to continued terrorist threats, insurgent activities and kidnappings." Even many Manila-based Filipinos subscribe to the notion that this region is a dangerous jungle full of bandits running amok. Despite this, the island is host to over 100 theatre groups, many of which—like Kularts—are actively engaged in wielding the performing arts as a tool for resisting the homogenizing and eradicating forces of capitalist colonialist modernization. Here, indigenous traditions are both preserved and evolving in a way that is relevant to these communities now. For American Pilipinos, to encounter such a landscape is affirming. Panis explains:

> You go to Mindanao and you realize holy shit, this is some ancient stuff! . . . we have history; we're creative; we've lived this long; we're survivors; we thrive. There's something about that that is so empowering. That's what the Tribal Tour is about. It opens up a whole way of thinking, and the colonized mind set that's been retained for generations starts to break up in the individual; it starts to crumble in some ways. At least that's my hope.

Although I thought for a long time that I was on the first Kularts Tribal Tour, it turns out that I was actually on the third. Kularts was established as a presenting and educational arts organization in 1995. Previous to that, it existed as a performance ensemble, the Kulintang Arts Ensemble (KAE), whose mission was to preserve and develop the arts of the Philippines. KAE was supported by Kulintang Arts, Inc., which was founded by Panis, along with Robert L. Henry and Marcella

Pabros-Clark, in 1984. The original Tribal Tour took place when the ten-member music and dance company KAE performed in the Philippines, in Manila and at the Baguio Arts Festival in 1989. Panis explains,

> We were doing all this Kulintang stuff and [we'd] never been to Mindanao. So, I said "Okay, let's go." I plotted the trip based on where Philippine Airlines flew. I knew nothing. We just went. It was like, "Bring your instruments cuz since we don't speak the language, we'll have to communicate and demonstrate our good intentions the artist's way . . . by speaking the cultural language . . . by playing music . . . by dancing."

It worked. The musicians had been studying in San Francisco with kulintang master musician Danongan "Danny" Kalanduyan and vocalist Musiban Guiabar. When they arrived in Cotabato, Mindanao, the local people did not believe that they were Filipino nor that they were artists who knew Mindanaoan arts. When the group members asked about where they could purchase instruments, the locals assumed that they were Indonesian or Malaysian and that they were looking for trinkets to hang on the wall as decorative pieces. Finally, the KAE musicians had to pull out their own *agung tamlang* (bamboo gongs) and start to *saronai* (practice or play kulintang). Only then did the store owners finally start to take out their inventory. The musicians played the gongs they were presented with, and the locals immediately recognized their compositions as coming from Dulawan, the birthplace of Kalanduyan. This connection through the arts was so profound that the group returned to Mindanao in 1991.

"It was such an amazing experience," recounts Panis. "So I thought, 'Oh this would be great if we could actually bring people here,' but I actually did not start doing it again until your trip, ten years later."

Recognizing that most people will not be able to attend a Tribal Tour, Kularts also presents performing groups from the Philippines as part of its programming. This strategy is pursued with the intent of bringing the source culture to American Pilipinos, encouraging exchange and maintenance of a continuum between Filipinos in the U.S. and in the homeland. Yet this venture is not without complication. For example, in 2007, the organization invited, for the first time in the U.S., seven virtuoso Ifugao tribal artists, ages 24 to 62, to do a month-long residency in the Bay Area. This residency included lectures, demonstrations, workshops, and a performance at the Zeum Theater.

After watching this performance, poet and scholar Barbara Jane Reyes expressed on her blog feeling "painfully self-conscious of my position as an audience member, viewing staged rituals by a tribal group similar to the Bontoc Igorots," who were put on display at the St. Louis World's Fair in 1904. Reyes also, however, acknowledges the difference between the 1904 exhibition that so many American Pilipino artists including herself have critiqued, grieved, and tried to re-write in their artworks, and Kularts's approach. The 1904 exhibition of "native" peoples, although it was also advertised as being educational, was really a racist strategy for juxtaposing the "primitive" with the relative "development" and "progress" of the Western world.

In Panis's introduction to the performance, she emphasized that "the folks you're going to see tonight are guests; not necessarily performers as we Americans look at performance." And while this presentation also included a representation, as did the World's Fair, of the *himong*, Panis also prefaced it in detail, describing the ritual as a way of carrying out tribal law:

> Boundary disputes often cause conflict between clans . . . violent death is seen as a destruction of the peaceful flow of energy. The Ifugao believe the sun god takes the soul of the murdered to the sky world, and then living relatives have to do a ritual to get the murdered soul free to join other ancestors . . . If justice is not served, the soul of the dead relative will haunt living relatives in dreams, or cause other unrest . . . As preparation, the priest goes into the forest and asks spirits for guidance, and the call of the ido bird must be heard before it can be performed . . .

In this way, Panis framed the ritual as part of the Ifugao's reverence to maintaining balance between the human world, the natural environment, and the spirit world. The ritual here is conceived of simultaneously as a pre-colonial, anti-colonial, and possibly postcolonial intervention in modern Eurocentric world views. So, in the end, Reyes was able to conclude that "what is important here in this performance, I believe, is not only the consent of the Ifugao to perform the himong, but . . . also that they are the ones who've determined which rituals they would demonstrate and how . . ."

The importance of the Ifugao having control of their own representation is echoed by Panis, who is adamant "that I have ancestral connections with these people, but I am not of these people and I have no right to represent them." She is very clear that when she visits Mindanao, she is not going on a mission to learn a specific folk dance in order to recreate it in the U.S. Instead, she is looking for source movement and a conceptual base from which to create her own work. The resulting aesthetic is grounded in both the ancient Philippines and her reality as an American Pilipina, yielding the dynamism that I responded to so strongly when I saw *Diwata* in 1995. These works then enter the larger cultural continuum of global arts of the Philippine peoples.

And Panis has contributed richly to this continuum. Since 1980, she has crafted fifteen full-length dance theater works, which have been performed on main stages in the U.S., Europe, and Asia. These pieces have been supported and commissioned by agencies as prestigious as the Rockefeller Foundation and the National Endowment for the Arts.

Panis also participated in the World Arts West San Francisco Ethnic Dance Festival from 1978 to 1990. In her 2008 article "The Emperor's Old Clothes?: Reflections on Thirty Years of the Ethnic Dance Festival," Lily Kharrazi reminds us that the Festival began as "a politically charged proposition. . . . With its mission to stake out a claim for culturally specific dance." Yet it took them some time to understand the specifically Asian American approach of Panis:

> I put myself in the same category with artists like Fred Ho, Cherríe Moraga, and Jon Jang. Our formal arts training was western first, and then we went back to our ancestral cultures to gain better insight and learn more about ourselves. In this way we become better creators and better storytellers of our American experiences. Yet the years I participated in EDF [Ethnic Dance Festival], choreographers were not credited. . . . I don't know why . . . maybe the presenters thought that acknowledging the role of choreographers might lead folks to question the authenticity of the dances.

The mindset that Panis was challenging here was, again, a colonial idea that "ethnic" peoples are only connected to non-Western countries and that "traditional dance" is old, fixed, and never-changing, never-evolving; that it cannot be created by diasporic "ethnics." Panis brought this issue up to the presenters several times over several years, and eventually they did come to recognize choreographers.

In recent years, Panis has also been invited back to serve as a judge at the EDF auditions.

Panis's Western dance education began when she was attending Galileo High School in San Francisco. A friend took her to an after-school program in North Beach that was led by a former Denishawn dancer, Klarna Pinska. What Pinska offered her was notable, she says, because

> unlike other older white folks I encountered, who made me feel their pity and condescension as a poor brown immigrant girl, Klarna treated me like I was just one of the girls in her after-school dance project. She showed me a different America. She introduced me to the world of cappuccinos, cannolis and opera-singing-waiters at the Caffé Trieste, beat poetry at the City Lights Bookstore, art at the SF Art Institute and to religious inclusiveness at the Unitarian Church on Geary [Street]. I was fascinated with stories of her life with Miss Ruth [St. Denis] and the modern dancers she trained with in the Denishawn School like Martha Graham, Charles Weidman, Jack Cole. She talked of the impact of war on her Jewish family who left Europe, during I think, World War I. She wasn't preachy, and, somehow, I became interested and began attending talks at the Unitarian Church to learn more about the Vietnam War. In fact, I was pretty surprised to run into Klarna at one of those moratorium marches . . . this old lady with arthritis and everything, walking for peace.

Panis went on to also study with Alonzo King, Finis Jhung, Aaron Osborne, and Nontzizi Cayou. Ed Mock also influenced her deeply by

> encouraging us to tell stories our way . . . that what we can best offer the world as artist is our particular view of the world. He really encouraged expanding our education in all kinds of dance and theater to gain greater facility . . . to learn a diversity of dance techniques meant we are better able to tell our stories.

The spaces that allowed for Panis to really explore her own stories through dance were the spaces that emerged from the collective movement of artists of color in the 1970s and 1980s. For example, Panis worked with the Asian American Dance Collective, June Watanabe, Unbound Spirit, Halifu Osumare, Janice Mirikitani, and Jill Togawa.

Her work with the Filipino American dance company, Bagong Diwa Dance Company, however, is the work Panis describes as being most "dear to my heart, because it was the beginning of my choreographic career." She participated in this group from its inception in 1974 to 1982. Inspired by the Alvin Ailey American Dance Theater, Bagong Diwa was ethnically diverse in composition, but its focus was on work in the Pilipino American experience. Panis participated in Bagong Diwa while she was also working for the San Francisco Opera ballet, teaching at different dance studios in the city, and doing other projects—"cobbling teaching gigs and all kinds of stuff to make a living," she explains. The space that Bagong Diwa provided for her is the space she marks as being seminal in helping her to find herself as a young artist: "understanding that I can dance for and in other peoples' work, and I can create something from my own experience, as well."

When Panis left Bagong Diwa in 1982 in order to embark on a solo career, members of the San Francisco Kulintang Ensemble, later known as Kalilang, led by Robert Kikuchi-Yngojo, approached her to help them develop their dance so they could get into EDF, which they did successfully do.

In 1985, Panis, along with Marcella Pabros-Clark and Robert L. Henry, founded Kulintang Arts, Incorporated. Founding members included musicians Dana Nuñez, Frank Holder, Joey Maligalig, and Musiban Guaibar, and dancers Frances Cachapero and June Mesina Qoulette, with Danongan Kalanduyan as resident master artist. When KAE's artists began to experience burnout, they all got together with community advisors and, through dialogue, decided the best thing to do, rather than close the organization, would be to transform into a presenting entity, Kularts. This wise decision has had the result of benefiting countless artists of Philippine descent ever since. What Kularts offers these artists is a very precious kind of mentorship, the same kind of mentorship that Panis feels grateful to have received from Pinska and Mock.

Part of what contributes to the sustainability of Kularts is Panis's distinct leadership style: "I want to understand peoples' strengths and their way of working," she says, "and then allow them to run with it. I'm not into micro-managing people. I want people to find their special talent and cultivate it to the fullest with discipline and joy."

I recently witnessed Panis in action at a rehearsal for *Maség,* a dance theater piece that brings together composer Florante Aguilar and choreographer Jay Loyola, who was a member of the Bayanihan Dance Company for seven years. The idea for this project came to Panis when she was reading about Palawan and learned of a particular island, Culion, which the Americans designated a leper colony in the early 1900s. Taking inspiration from William Shakespeare's *The Tempest*, she and her collaborators crafted a story that takes place on an imagined typhoon-battered island in the pre-colonial Philippines circa the 1400s. It addresses current issues facing Filipinos, such as dictatorship, exile, and immigration:

> The Prospero character, in our story, is [a] political leader, unjustly exiled, but like his enemies, he uses his power to subjugate the island people. Since the early 1900s, many people have left the Philippines for various reasons: economic, political as well as traumatic family life. It's highly unusual for Pilipinos to go back to live in the Philippines. I am interested in the question of how do we go home?

At this particular rehearsal, dance captain June Arellano, who also plays the Prospero character, is setting a dance on several of the performers. *Maség* features a cast of fourteen dancers from various Bay Area modern and folkloric dance companies, who are undertaking this project along with their main modes of employment, which include nursing and illustration. Some are students and some are parents. Panis makes a note that the choreography is looking very stereotypically "traditional" in that the dance prettily demonstrates the uses of a *salakot* in the tropics. The movement hearkens to festive dances, but in this story, she reminds Arellano, "we need to see these people in the middle of a raging typhoon." He considers this, and then creates something new in which the performers have more intention, more emotion. Now the dance has meaning that serves the context of the overall piece. Loyola looks on and approves. This is how the team works together to evolve Philippine tradition. Panis adds,

> In choosing to create *Maség* inspired by a western classic is to say that Philippine dance can tell any story. It serves our goal of creating and increasing the number of Filipino American works. My visits and immersion in Mindanaoan tribal cultures helped me gain a greater understanding of my own Tagalog/Bisaya/Kapampangan tribal heritage. I began to see within my

> own colonized culture, how the core values of indigenous ways have been and continue to be re-created in innovative ways.

Kularts itself and each new work, like *Maség,* that it produces are testaments to the creativity of the people of the Philippines. Panis's tireless efforts to improve the lives of her people keep inspiration flowing between indigenous and diasporic artists. This flow manifests in work that is never static, always responding to the present moment.

Chapter 14

Tips for Bus Riding in Los Angeles (excerpted from *Going Green the Wong Way*)

Kristina Wong

Going Green the Wong Way made its world premiere at Arsht Center for the Performing Arts November 2010 in Miami, Florida. It was produced by Mad Cat Theater Company and directed by their artistic director, Paul Tei.

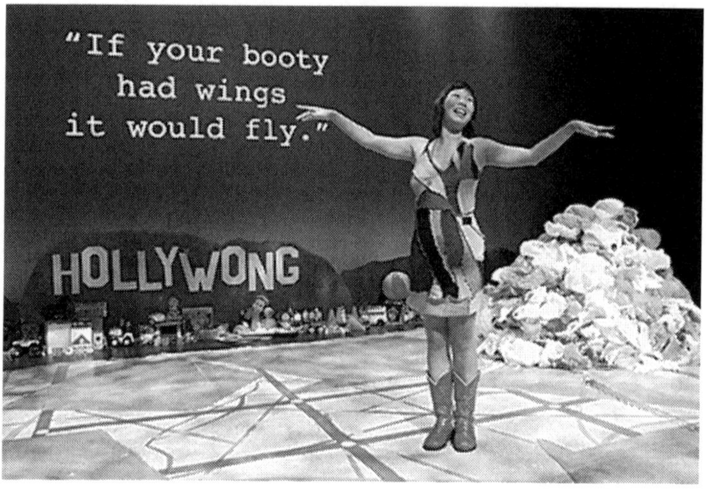

Scene from *Going Green the Wong Way*. Photo by Eli Peck.

Kristina stands in front of a screen with a slide that reads "Tips for Bus Riding in Los Angeles."
The slide changes to read "Los Angeles Bus Rider Tip #1: For days when you are on the bus all day, pack snacks to eat."

KRISTINA
When you stop driving, you can't just stop at home for lunch. In fact, you may leave your door and not come home. Very important when you are going to be a bus rider to pack snacks, because you don't want to give in to impulse buying. It's very important, though, to pack snacks low in fiber. Not high in fiber.

Slide: Picture of a colon.

I'm not sure who at the MTA decided velour would be the easiest-to-clean textile with which to line the bus seats.

Slide: Velour MTA bus seat with its messy geometric pattern.

I will say that this design does a good job at camouflage.

Slide: Same velour bus seat covered in poop.

Like I said, leave the bananas at home!

Slide: "Los Angeles Bus Rider Tip #2: Use digital technology to your advantage."

Another tip. Use digital technology to your advantage. Be a twenty-first-century hitchhiker.

Slide: A screenshot of a Facebook exchange. Kristina's top post reads "Need a ride from Silverlake and Berkeley to 3rd and La Brea. Like now. Need a carpool buddy?" Responses below from one responder who says, "I can be there in 20 minutes."

Here's an exchange I put up on Facebook. And within half an hour, I got a ride. And booked this commercial! Now, it doesn't always work.

Slide: A screenshot of a Facebook post: "I need a ride from sweetzer/santa monica to silverlake. Hurry! It's 3am!" There are no responses to this post.

Sometimes your 3000 Facebook friends just aren't awake. Which leads me to tip #3.

Slide: "Los Angeles Bus Rider Tip #3: The Wisdom of Bus People."

The bus is also a great place to pick up spiritual learnings. I'd like to share some wisdom I've picked up from my journeying about the city. This first bit of wisdom came late one night when I was waiting at the Vermont and Wilshire stop. There was a man so impassioned that he was calling this out, proclaiming it to the sky. And even now, the words ring out in my memory—

Slide: "If your booty had wings, it would fly."

It reminds me so much of the poetry of Dr. Maya Angelou.

This next bit of wisdom came from an older Latino man at the 704 stop at Santa Monica and Vermont. We were getting onto the bus together. He looked at me, pointed right at my face, and, as if the Aztecs had sent a message from above, right into his heart, he uttered just one phrase, inspired by my face.

Slide: "Chinatown"

I don't know if it was a warrior spirit that connected that sacred phrase to my face. I don't know.

This final bit of wisdom came from an impassioned conversation between a black man and a white woman aboard the bus. They had just met, but they immediately entered a discussion so personal and political, so passionate, that their voices carried loudly through the bus. As if to tell everyone, "Surrender, surrender to the wisdom." Here it is—

Slide: "Stupid fat-ass white bitch, don't you ever step to a black king like me. I got some powerful lawyers on my side. I'll call them right now. Bitch-ass, motherfucking bitch."

. . .and I don't think even Walt Whitman could string together such poetry as this. I can only imagine that if I were asked to give a commencement speech again, I would offer this. Class of 2010, if it's one thing I can leave you with, it's this!

Kristina indicates the slide again.

Slide changes: "Los Angeles Bus Rider Tip #4: Enjoy the random acts of kindness you'll witness."

Here's Bus Tip #4. The bus gives you a chance to get close to other people and witness human nature in a way you've never seen before. If you can get over the whole fear-of-rape thing, riding the bus lets you see slices of life you've never seen before.

Slide: Praying mantis on a woman's back. She is seated on the bus.

Here's a story I want to share with you. I was riding the 704 Rapid home one night, and this man comes on the bus with a praying mantis on his shoulder like a pirate with a parrot. I ask him about it, and he hadn't realized it had caught a ride with him, and so the man swats it off him and it lands on this woman's shoulder.

Slide: Praying mantis seemingly posing on the back of a bus seat.

Then the praying mantis stops to pose for all of us. So imagine everyone gathered around taking pictures of this insect. Then we were like, Well, what do we do? Because what is there to do next when you don't know what to do with nature in an urban setting? We should kill it, right? Because if we don't, someone else will.

Slide: Praying mantis in the gentle clutch of a woman's fist.

So this same woman I showed you earlier took the praying mantis and kept it safe in her hands, cupping it and protecting it from getting killed or having to live out its short life forever on the bus. And when she exited the bus, she took the praying mantis out with her. It was such a sweet and caring act of kindness towards another living creature, to make the effort to return him to nature . . .

Slide: The very urban corner of Santa Monica and Normandie Blvd. Picture shows a liquor store and a $5.99 clothing store.

. . .Nature in this case being the corner of Santa Monica and Normandie. Where he probably went shopping at the $5.99 pants store and bought a phone card to Guatemala.

Slide: "Rider Tip #5: Strategies for Isolation"

I am still dealing with a lot of issues regarding feeling isolated, especially because I work at home. And days go by before I can see people. Sometimes taking the bus is too much work. People ask, "How are you going to go carless and date?" No fear, horny carless warriors, for yours will now be a life of . . .

Slide: "INCALL ONLY POLICY! No car! No bus! No problem!"

Incall only! No car! No bus! No problem! And in your moments of isolation, why not enjoy the solitude? Have a drink alone. And after said drink, reach out to old friends in the middle of the night via text message.

Slide of drunk text: "Make out with me now dammit."

Say, "Hello old friend. How are you?"

Slide of drunk text: "I want you to read your dissertation aloud to me while you pound me."

How are things with work? Are you meeting your career goals?

Slide of drunk text: "I know you had enough cum to double the population of Korea."

Just reach out. And know that you don't have to be alone.

Slide: "Los Angeles Bus Rider Tip #6: Use Carless Discrimination to your advantage"

Final tip: There are so many things you can get out of now that you don't have a car. When someone says, "Hey Kristina, I need help moving. It will only take all weekend."

Slide: "Sorry, I would, but I don't have a car" with accompanying photo of Kristina at bus stop shrugging her shoulders.

"Sorry, I would, but I don't have a car."

If someone says, "Hey, Kristina, I wanted to know if you and some friends might want to come over for a little get-together. We'll be serving some light hors d'oeuvres. I'll be making a little presentation that will only take 90 minutes of your time and could possibly change your life forever."

Slide: "Sorry, I would, but I don't have a car" with different accompanying photo of Kristina at bus stop shrugging her shoulders.

"Sorry, I would, but I don't have a car."

Water filters, vitamin supplements, prepaid legal services . . . These are all code words to look for.

If someone says, "Hey, Kristina, would you like to have Sunday brunch? There's this place where all the celebrities go . . . It's the Sunday brunch served at . . ."

Slide: Picture of the Church of Scientology International Celebrity Center with "The Church of Scientology International Celebrity Center" caption.

. . .the Church of Scientology International Celebrity Center! ACK!

Slide: "Sorry, I would, but I don't have a car" with different accompanying photo of Kristina at bus stop shrugging her shoulders.

"Sorry, I would, but I don't have a car."

You see, there are so many things you can get out of.

Slide: "Kristina, do you mind doing the dishes?"

Sorry, I would, but I don't have a car.

Slide: "Sorry, I would, but I don't have a car" with different accompanying photo of Kristina at bus stop shrugging her shoulders.

Other exceptions to using Carless Discrimination to your advantage.

Slide: List unfolds as Kristina dictates these items.

Invitation to a first-time all-improv theater troupe's show or any kind of "open mic" situation.

Landmark Forum "Graduation."

In any of these situations, you are allowed to get rid of your car just so that you can say—

Slide: "Sorry, I would, but I don't have a car" with different accompanying photo of Kristina at bus stop shrugging her shoulders.

Sorry, I would, but I don't have a car!

Slide: Gas station with prices marked "Arm, Leg, First Born."

In conclusion. I'd like to say that I've been at this carless game for two years. And in that time, I've saved approximately $8,000 each year. I've put that money towards the home I own now—

Slide: Kristina as a new homeowner in an empty loft.

Towards alcohol—

Slide: Kristina drinking alcohol.

Towards alcohol—

Slide: Kristina drinking more alcohol, more drunk.

And towards renewing my subscription to the *Korean Times*![1]

Slides: Twelve shots of happy children from different ethnic backgrounds.

But more importantly, I feel like I have a sense of hope. I'm part of a small but important movement towards restoring this planet for our children, and our children's children. I hope I have you asking yourself, "What else can I be doing to make this planet better? Can I just try to remember to bring my cloth bags to the store? Why not curb my carbon footprint by not having another . . . child?"

Note

1. There is no picture punchline that goes with this. This is a reference to an earlier part in the show where I reference a pseudo-scary admirer who had placed ads in the *Korean Times* hoping to meet me, after a picture of me ran in the *LA Times* with my vegetable oil–run car that would later catch on fire on the freeway. I realize it makes no sense as a joke here, especially as this is an excerpt out of context.

Chapter 15

Reels

Larry Padua

Frame #1

Once, in the middle of the night, under a full moon's watch, I took my father's car and drove to the far end of the park. I slowly took off all my clothes and hung them on a tree. I lay down on the grass under an evergreen with low branches, waved away anyone who ventured too close, and watched the moon move across the sky. I was a horny adolescent trying to find lyricism in public sex. I grabbed for the moon and without touching myself, I came.

Frame #2

The last time I was here on top of this hill, I was a 27-year-old trying not to stare too hard at the teenager nervously jogging through. I was in LA for a visit and had not returned to my haunts for several years. I was interested in checking things out. Although the terrain remained the same, the views had changed. In certain sections, like the bird sanctuary, where there used to be a sea of pale bodies with specks of color, brown and black boys and men had taken over. Most of them were proudly displaying their wares to each other. The road connecting the southern end of the park (the observatory side) to the northern end (Travel Town) was closed. "Due to Fire Danger," the signs warned. Motor vehicles were not allowed to drive up this road, making this the section of the park least frequented by families and, therefore, the busiest cruising area. This road is where I watched a young man spread his legs against the back window of his car and fuck himself with a dildo. Perhaps the most telling sign of the changing times was in the litter. Mixed in with the ground cover of fallen leaves and broken branches from eucalyptus and conifers were spent condoms, their wrappers, and those tiny lube containers created by someone who saw the need and fulfilled it.

Frame #3

I hold a prism between you and these pages. I rely on memory to reconstruct these stories, but my memory is tricky and random. I can't, for example, tell you the dates of my relationships, but I can tell you the length of time I've ever spent with anyone. Neither can I describe the features of men I've been with, but I can tell you all the names I've been given. And, although I can't claim Wilt Chamberlain numbers in 23 years of having sex, I can't count how many men I've been with. Most of them have been nameless. Sometimes, I didn't even see their faces.

Frame #4

The first time cruising through, I was so scared of being seen by someone I knew that I sped from Ferndell to the observatory, zoomed through the Hollywood sign vista, coasted down to Crystal Springs, and ended up out of breath at the Riverside Tennis Courts in a matter of minutes. The next time, I was no less afraid. Again, I quickly pedaled through, but this time surreptitiously glancing at cars parked down the entire length of the road, some with doors slightly ajar to show men jacking off or men getting sucked off. After a few weeks, I actually slowed down and took the time to watch from the safety of the road as young men in tight corduroy OP shorts and blue Vans tennis shoes, and older men in jeans with crotches sanded to highlight substantial bulges, disappeared into a grotto of trees. Some men rushed, while others casually strolled in, all occasionally looking back. I kept returning almost every weekend, never daring to go further than a few yards from the mouth of the cave of trees, always trying to convince myself to move in just a little bit closer. On the tenth visit, I nervously followed a shirtless young man with shoulder-length black hair into the bushes.

Frame #5

He pushes his sunburnt torso against mine. His lips and tongue reach out for my neck, graze there for a minute, then slowly move up to my ear. He thrusts his hard dick against my thigh; his hands roam against my back as if searching for answers to hidden meanings. He asks me how old I am and I lie, "Sixteen." I don't know why. He tells me he just turned 18. His lips slide back down to my neck, jump to my left nipple, and glide down to my belly button. All the while, his hands explore my backside. When he finally takes my dick in his mouth, I shoot.

Frame #6

Afterwards, he asks me, "What are you anyway? You're too dark to be Chinese or Mexican, but your hair's not thick so you can't be black."

Frame #7

Martin and I sit together on a bench overlooking the observatory. He tells me of the first time he ever came to Griffith Park. A drunken white man had blocked his path, and without warning, threw his arms around Martin to give him a bear hug. Startled, Martin pushed him and asked what he was doing. The man then demanded that Martin turn around. Martin reached into his pants pocket, pulled out his switchblade, and aimed it at the man's neck.

"You better take off, or I'ma cut you."

He was my first park friend, my mentor and bodyguard, this young man with a lumbering, awkward body. We met in August of '79, before he was to start tenth grade at Lincoln High. I was a year younger. He was running down a dirt path, freaked out by the rattlesnake he had just seen, and ran into me. I must have been knocked back six feet. He remained standing. Although he initially assumed I was a Satanas, and I assumed he was 18th Street, we had an easy truce and became fast friends. We set up times to meet at the bench, and later on, after learning how to drive, cruised together through the park and the streets of LA in borrowed cars. We also started going to the bars and clubs together when I was in the tenth grade, our entree into the LA club scene facilitated by the universal IDs, pot, and cocaine.

I have not seen Martin since the day after my high school graduation party. By then, he was living in Austin, Texas, working construction with his uncle. He had come back to LA to celebrate with me. After he went back, our letters, postcards, and phone calls to each other slowly dwindled. Almost two years after he initially left for Texas, our communication stopped altogether. We did not have a falling out. It's just that time and distance evaporate intimacy.

Frame #8

I grew up in Silverlake, first in an apartment on Hyperion Avenue south of Sunset, then in a house on Benton Way, north of Sunset. Across from our apartment lived two gay men whose blinds always seemed to be open. Next to them lived a young married couple with their newborn son. The husband used to sit in front of the TV after dinner, most times in nothing but his wifebeater and underwear. Sometimes, as he lounged on the recliner, one of his hands would play absently with the wiry hairs on his belly, while his other hand would slip in between the waistband of his shorts to cup, fondle, or make adjustments in his crotch. I spent countless hours in my room with the lights off, lying on my bed with a blanket wrapped around me (in case one of my brothers or sister walked in). I would watch both of these apartments and masturbate to glimpses of furry crotches and, if I was lucky, fully nude men lounging.

Frame #9

I don't think my dick was ever soft between Junior High and High School. I attended King Jr. High, which stood between The Frog Pond, a bathhouse, and the Silver Dollar Saloon. Outside the gates of the school, I once found a stack of gay porn hidden behind a bush. Every night for several weeks afterwards, I would return to look for more. Though I never found any more, these early evening treks turned into an exploration of my neighborhood. Occasionally, I hid in shrubs or trees outside someone's house, and would simply watch as the inhabitant(s) lived through their routines.

I created a mental map of where the gay men lived, and where the single, straight men lived (alone or in packs). I also took notice of the young men who lived with just their mothers. I'm not really sure why. Perhaps, as a momma's boy myself, I identified with them, these tough-acting adolescents whose hearts reached out only to, and whose hearts could only be reached by, their mothers. They made my own heart ache.

Frame #10

At 14, I lost my virginity to someone old enough to be my father in the backyard of The Frog Pond. I had just finished a three-mile run and was walking to cool down. He approached, greeted me, then said, "Do you want to get sucked?" I think I mumbled my reply. Inside the gate, he knelt in front of me and took my penis in his mouth. I had dreamed about this moment, fantasized about it (although the man/boy in my fantasies was never older than 18). And though I was familiar with the pleasures of jacking off, I did not expect this feeling of rawness, the feeling that all of my nerve endings had somehow become concentrated on my dick head. The nerves were radiating across my stomach, around the top of my head, to the tips of my digits. As I shot my load into his throat, my breath seemed to get stuck in my own throat, and for a few seconds, I forgot how to breathe. I ultimately leaned against the fence, barely able to move, while the man stroked my legs and buried his nose between my balls, inhaling and exhaling deeply. After a few minutes, I thanked him, pulled up my shorts, and ran home feeling guilty and dirty, high and liberated at the same time.

Frame #11

Up the street from King, the Vista Theater showed double billings of the latest gay porn movies with intriguing titles like *One Thousand and One Inches* and *Packed Jockstraps*. Martin made friends with one of the cashiers, who would sneak us in once in a while. We'd sit at opposite ends of the theater, to jack off or get sucked off by men. Today, when I watch porn, with its virtually didactic position on condom sex and strict adherence to shaved bodies, I wonder whatever happened to the hairy, one-named porn stars of the '70s—those men who made movies before bodily fluids became anathema.

Frame #12

Yes, I was barebacking before the term was even coined. (Although *barebacking* might not be the proper term, since, in the age of AIDS, it is seen by some as an immoral act, by others as an act of resistance and expression of freedom, and by still others as a mere lapse of judgment. But one can also argue that buttfucking is also burdened by these notions. The obvious difference is that barebacking is framed in industrial society's ironic love of experiencing "the natural.") The transition from skin-to-skin sex to sex with latex was quite momentous. As gay boys and men with the "sexual revolution" still fresh in our minds, we had to re-conceptualize the condom, from a prophylactic/contraceptive (obviously used by straight people) to a necessary lifesaver. Before 1982, condoms were not generally marketed as effective protection against STDs. Additionally, for me and for a lot of young people, the difficulty was in my/our embarrassment at having to buy condoms and negotiating condom use with partners.

Frame #13

At the corner of Santa Monica and Sunset, just up the street from where the original A Different Light bookstore would open, men lined up after the bars closed, while cars circled the block. I remember waking up in the middle of the night and sneaking out of the house to walk to Sunset. In the beginning, I was too shy and had taken to heart the childhood warning about getting into a stranger's car.

Frame #14

Some truths are embedded within prisms, within layers. Within.

Frame #15

An internet search of all public sex venues in LA, excluding colleges, gyms, clubs, bookstores, street cruising, rest areas, stand-alone public bathrooms, hotels, office buildings, malls, libraries, and sports arenas (in short, bush sex), reveals nearly 100 places. Back when I was coming up, I knew of five parks. Two were in West Hollywood—this was before incorporation, when no one lived in West Hollywood, but in "Beverly Hills adjacent." Two were in Hollywood. Of course, there was Griffith Park, immortalized in countless publications and oral histories, and mythologized in public lore.

Here is where I learned, practiced, and perfected what a friend calls my "Spidey sense"—an unerring ability to sniff out public sex arenas.

I found out about Griffith Park sex by accident. In the summer of 1979, I attended a cello clinic at Immaculate Heart College. During a break, my friend Alejandra and I took a walk to Ferndell. She noticed him first—the man openly staring at my ass. This was also the moment when I realized that my ass had magic powers (as Cisco, my second boyfriend would later say, my ass could turn a bottom boy into a top).

Two years earlier, I had come out to myself and to some of my friends. 1977 was not a particularly easy time for me. I was adjusting to life in the United States, while at the same time dealing with my awakening (homo)sexuality. True to my bookworm reputation, I read all the books relating to homosexuality at the Cahuenga branch library, including 1960s psychological treatises on "aberrant" sexual behaviors. John Rechy's memoir(s)/novels, from *City of Night* to *Rushes,* also figured prominently in my early inquiries. What really kept me going back to the library, at least until I finally started having sex, was the Sunshine Press literature, which published interviews with prominent gay authors and anthologies, among them *Orgasms of Light,* a collection of poetry, short fiction, and graphics. All of these books (even the psychology texts) taught me all I needed to know about man-to-man sex, and also informed my love of research and literature.

I returned to the park by myself the following weekend.

Frame #16

Los Angeles sings to me. I hear cacophonous symphonies in the way freeways divide neighborhoods. I am enraptured by palm trees fighting their way up to the sky; to chaparral brambling down hillsides. The city, a dry riverbed of concrete and struggling vegetation, courses through me. It's an arid shield against hopelessness; a beacon for a realized future. I revel in this new energy that has come to define the city—the tongues and hues that bring back that biblical tower, with no god to damn us. Los Angeles grabs me by the waist, by the throat, spins me around, while I dance to its versatile rhythms. I dip the fog, which isn't quite fog, that covers the basin and dampens the energy of the solar-powered people. I move to the beat of high-rises and Skid Row. But most of all, I two-step to the pulse of the earth that grows daily beneath me. I feel its measured up-thrust, the gentle, almost imperceptible movement, like a new blade of grass pushing its way through fertile soil. These mountains girding the vast expanse will one day be the tallest in the world, and snow falling on the Andes, blizzards blanketing Everest, will feel like tropical rain in comparison to the tempest. But sometimes, Los Angeles swallows me and I wallow in the depth of tears the city sheds for countless unrealized dreams.

No, not of becoming A Somebody, but dreams that come with the promise of the name.

Frame #17

I haven't met many angels. One, though, came into my life, with broken wings, lustrous black hair that framed his face, and flawless brown skin. He said he was Cuban, born in Florida, and raised in Guam. (I have always been, and will continue to be, attracted to island men—I feel a connection in our land knowledge of the finite and water wisdom of endless possibilities.) With a father in the military, his family moved often. With a younger brother who never left him alone, he spent most times outside the house. We met by the tree decorated with used Christmas-tree air fresheners and talked to each other beyond the too-quick groping that resulted in a too-quick climax. We saw each other in and out of the park for the next year, and managed to slow down enough to become comfortable with each other's island brands, until his family once again had to move. Every week for six months thereafter, I received a hand-made postcard. I still have them, these angels with clipped wings clutching stomachs as if in pain, or falling from cliffs. Then one day, the postcards stopped coming and poems I sent were returned unopened. I stopped frequenting the parks soon after. There were too many reminders of his presence—the olive branch by the reservoir was still halfway broken, our blue contribution still hung on the Christmas tree, and the skunk odor, which had become aphrodisiac, lingered. According to Martin, I had broken the prime directive to "Never fall in love with trade." He had just finished reading *City of Night* and (mis)quoted incessantly from it. But why not? In my 16-year-old mind, that was one of the reasons to go to bars and parks: to look for someone to fall for, a man who could be attentive and strong, creative and intelligent, sexy, worldly, and easily delighted by simplicity.

I like to imagine that he's marooned somewhere on some island, unable to make contact. In my mind, I see him still as a young man, unchanged by the passing of time. His name still fits, still feels right curled on my tongue. And sometimes, I make my way to the ocean to implore the shark god and entreat the southerlies to carry my wishes with them, drop them off to germinate and grow somewhere along their travels.

Chapter 16

Vacuuming Dreams

Lucy MSP Burns

My newly-reunited-yet-strangers-to-each-other family piled up in two Ford station wagons. We made only one stop during our long drive away from Los Angeles, to where, we didn't know yet.

Exit I-5 to Highway 99 North, to Highway 65 South.

On Highway 65, gone were the green trees with pointy tops and pine needles. The smell of America disappeared. Land for miles, some stretches with cows grazing, some with rows of vines.

"Grape picking season starts now," said the uncle who was driving. Just at the lunch hour, we passed groves of citrus trees where clumps of workers sought out shade during their meal break. The same uncle explained that the T-shirt that covered the picker's head and neck, all but the eyes, was for protection. I wanted to say that this was not unfamiliar to us, since farmers in the Philippines do the same for minor relief from the sun.

Eventually, we arrived in the small town in San Joaquin Valley called Poplar.

My uncle said, "Five streets going north–south, three avenues going east–west. Can't get lost here."

I had no idea what he meant. He drove us around once, then headed back to the main street before the turn-off to show us the post office where we would pick up our mail. Next to it was a general store.

"There," pointing with his lips, "you can buy milk and eggs."

Right onto Poplar Avenue, right on Road 191, left on Ave 146, and left on Imperial Road.

Imperial Road. I repeat this silently, along with names of previous streets we have lived on—Jones Street, Fendler Street, Elicaño Street. The car slowed down; dust stirred then settled. A small neon-orange house came into our view. My father got out of the car to open the gate. This house, made of wood, was the most orange house I had ever seen. It was the brightest house on that street, in that town, and the next town over, and most likely in the entire world. I stared at this new house in America, feeling stirrings of shame. We left for this?

Six hours prior, in LAX, our life was under interrogation from the immigration officer: "So you are from the Philippines? Do you have *chee-chaaaa-ron*? Did you pack *hop-i-ang be-boy*?" he asked in his nasal American accent. We used to pinch our noses while speaking English to mimic how we thought Americans sounded.

My brother, sister, and I exchanged looks and snickers as the officer's voice got louder when he mispronounced *chicharon* and *baboy*, Tagalog words for pork rinds and pork.

"No," I replied. I shook my head for emphasis in case he did not understand my accent.

They made us empty our bags anyway. Our entire life belongings, mostly clothes and shoes, were littered onto the conveyor belt. A blue Levis button-up shirt, a pair of tapered dark-blue jeans, a never-been-worn Triumph training bra, one blue pleated skirt that was my school uniform, and an unopened pack of five Soen panties. These belongings were folded neatly, placed carefully to squeeze out any additional weight over seventy pounds.

The officer rummaged through these belongings with his gloved hands, then uttered "Clear." He moved on to the next arrivals in line.

I began picking up my things, trying to contain the all-too-familiar humiliation my twelve-year old body had known. This feeling was to have been left behind twelve hours before. Months of choosing, folding, and packing items that would sum up who we were when we left Olongapo City were reduced to minutes as we hurriedly collected our possessions and shoved them back into our bags.

A month later, on a scorching May day, the hottest on record for the town of Poplar, my two-year-old sister and I were sitting out on the porch. She had been running in and out of the house. I managed to have her be still by pointing at a tumbleweed slowly moving across the road. We followed its roll with our eyes until our gazes landed on a suited-figure: smoothly pressed gray American blazer and slacks, a white shirt, and a striped tie. He stopped in front of our gate.

"Hello," he said as I led my sister back into the house. "Are your parents home?" he asked as the screen door was closing behind me. I was hoping he'd leave, but he remained there, standing calmly with a smile, asking me once more if my parents were home. "May I come in?" he continued.

Just then, my father appeared. "Good afternoon, sir," my father said, gently steering my sister aside to open the door. Only then did the man unlatch the gate.

"What can I do for you?" my father asked. To my surprise, he ushered the stranger into the house and offered him a seat on the couch.

The white man introduced himself to us. He began, "I would like to talk to you about an investment, the Kirby home care system. I would like to show you a complete vacuum unit that will last so long it will feel like a member of your family." He handed a brochure to my father, and another one to my mother. Paused long enough for my parents to browse through the glossy handouts. Returning to his presentation, he continued, "Kirbys are American-made vacuum cleaners. Inventor Jim Kirby developed his first vacuum model in 1906. The Kirby Company has enhanced and improved its American-made vacuum designs ever since." He added, "You should know that we pioneered in-home demonstrations. This is so we can introduce the Kirby home care system to potential buyers like you. Our goal is to give you the opportunity to see and try the Kirby vacuum cleaner here in your home, before you make any purchasing decisions."

The rest of his speech emphasized the technological capacities of this cleaning machine, as well as personal salesmanship and the value of knowing from whom you bought what will be the family's most-prized possession. Kirby vacuums—serving up the American dream in its all-powerful suctioning capacity.

Mr. Kirby-vacuum-seller, as we would remember him, proceeded with the demonstration, which started with assembling the vacuum. We watched him locking parts together like he was performing a magic trick, the highlight of which was placing a small, square, thin cloth on top of the carpet, covering an area 10 inches by 10 inches. He turned on the vacuum for a few seconds, turned it back off, then lifted it. Left on the thin cloth was a mound of dirt, a little hill of sand, soil, and other small particles, some with mobile legs.

Inside my head, I heard myself shriek, but the audible sound in the room came from my mother's horrified "*Punyeta! Ang dumi!*"

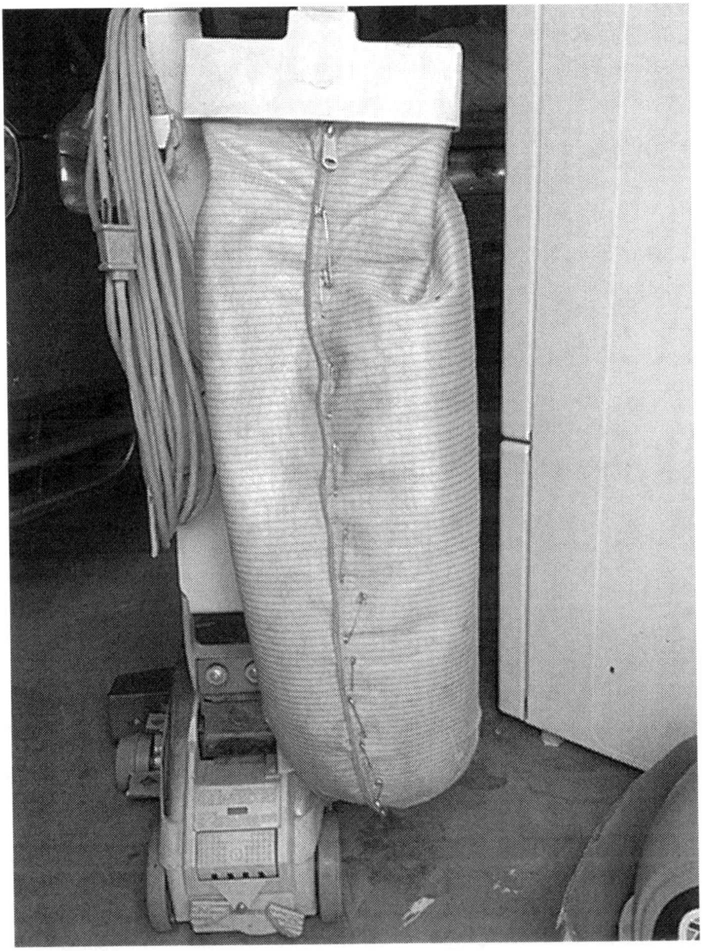

Vacuum with Safety Pins. Photo by Lucy Burns.

A sound of surprise, covering shame. My father let out his usual joyful laugh, while my youngest sister walked up to the mound and squatted next to it, preparing to grab a handful of dirt. I quickly picked her up. The white man's magic trick was successful. We were sucked in, the down payment was made, contracts were signed.

Today, aside from the safety pins holding together the vacuum bag and minor rips on its electrical cord, our Kirby vacuum's wear-and-tear hardly reveals the age of this three-decades-old machine. It remains impressive as a dirt-sucking technology.

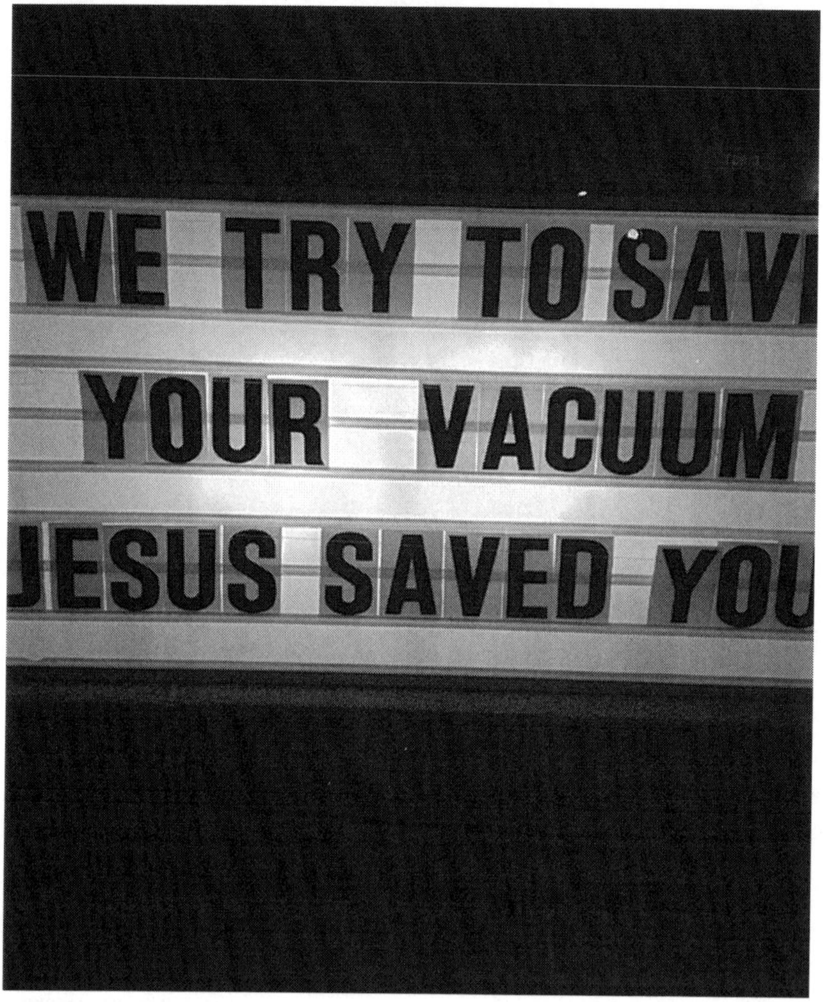

Kirby Saves. Photo by Lucy Burns.

Chapter 17

L.A. Dreaming in Taipei

SanSan Kwan

One twilit evening in Taipei in 2000, I was walking along one of the narrow, sidewalk-less streets. The area was quiet until I heard the sound of a moped approaching from behind. I stepped further to the side of the street when suddenly the moped driver swerved beside me, reached out an arm, and squeezed my backside.

In 2008, now living in Los Angeles, I saw Cheng-Chieh Yu's dance, *Hood, Veil, Shoes,* which explores the potential for sexual violence that haunts the bustling streets of Taipei. Yu grew up in Taipei; she moved to New York in 1984 and then to Los Angeles in 2001, where she currently teaches dance and choreography at UCLA. When Yu returned to her native Taipei for six months in 2007 in order to create a work for the Taiwan's Sun Shier Dance Theatre, she was struck by the changes in city traffic. In 1984, the year she left Taipei, the city was less congested, there was no subway, and, significantly to her, women did not drive their own scooters. In 2007, the city was dominated by moped traffic and tightly packed bodies on the streets. For Yu, Taipei's subtropical heat and this new confrontation of bodies, helmeted and gloved, yet viscerally proximal, suggested an undercurrent of sexual violence. The veil of the helmet and the rain poncho protected the predatory, while the open vulnerability of the moped brought bodies into touching distance with one another.

In "Bodies-Cities," feminist theorist Elizabeth Grosz discusses the ways in which bodies and cities are constitutive and mutually defining. She first establishes that bodies are in themselves incomplete entities that require "social triggering, ordering, and long-term 'administration,'" calibrated by Foucault's "micro-technologies of power."[1] In other words, the body is made meaningful when emplaced in space and time and in relation to other bodies and objects. The city is one ingredient in the social constitution of the body: ". . . the form, structure, and norms of the city seep into and effect [sic] all the other elements that go into the constitution of corporeality and/as subjectivity." Likewise (though she devotes less time to this formulation), Grosz argues that the city is determined by its bodies.[2] Thus, bodies and cities emerge out of a two-way—though not always equally balanced—process of "cobuilding."[3] Neither cities nor bodies are natural essences; rather, both are understood as producing each other.

I am interested in how a work of choreography by a diasporic Taiwanese artist living in L.A. reveals the global registers of the body-city of Taipei. In other words, to Grosz's formulation I want to add the elements of globality and diaspora. What is the body-city in a global metropolis peopled by diasporic citizens? The multiple migrations and returns that characterize the diasporic body mean that these bodies carry layers of somatic experience—of past and current places, homelands, and new lands and places in between. These layers, not really settled one on top of another but rather enmeshed at once, are both shaped by and work to shape the cities through which the diasporic body travels. This article is about the ways that the diasporic body and the global city are engaged in a process of cobuilding. Because it constitutes and is constituted by bodies marked by migrations, the global body-city cannot be reduced to a single time-space; it reaches out to—and is also introjected by—a multitude of other global bodies-cities: Taipei in/as Los Angeles and vice versa. What is more, choreography, as an art of bodies in motion through time and space, offers a rich site through which to better understand not only Grosz's idea of the body-city, but the extended idea of the *globalized* body-city as a shifting nexus of multiple bodies-cities.

In particular, this chapter explores the ways that one global body-city, Los Angeles, can be imaginatively projected/introjected into another, Taipei. I investigate how stage choreography demonstrates the intertwining of these two global bodies-cities. Thus, in Yu's *Hood, Veil, Shoes,* beneath a notion of sexual threat in Taipei also runs an idea not of Taipei but of Los Angeles—dreams of Los Angeles haunting expressions of Taipei. A network of past/present, here/there corporeal experiences are revealed as one choreographic expression in this work.

Honoring this shifting landscape/timescape, I began this chapter with a personal anecdote about an experience of Taipei. I now want to transition to some thoughts about Los Angeles, to eventually come back around to Taipei. In L.A., I focus specifically on the Chinese "ethnoburb" of San Gabriel Valley, a site that is clearly part of a global nexus of Chinese bodies-cities that includes Taipei.

Chinese Los Angeles: Automobility and the Shopping Mall

I am driving in my car down Valley Boulevard. In my car, the radio and the air conditioning on, I follow the straight lines of the boulevard. The Southern California sun is glaring so I keep a slight squint to my eyes as I watch the road in front of me. When I have the chance, I flick my eyes briefly to either side to catch glimpses of store signs in the strip malls that line the street: Chinese printers, bakers, insurance companies, banks, preschools, restaurants, realtors, medical offices, auto repair shops, and more mix with the occasional Vietnamese noodle shop, Thai restaurant, and Mexican taco stand. A major east–west corridor through the San Gabriel Valley, Valley Boulevard extends from the eastern edge of the city of Los Angeles and pierces through the center of the valley before it veers south through El Monte. It is the spinal cord linking all the Chinese cities of the area: Alhambra, Monterey Park, San Gabriel, and Rosemead, with San Marino, Arcadia, and Temple City just to its north.

My hand grasps the steering wheel, making occasional minute adjustments. One foot presses lightly on the pedal. As the "car-driver"[4] *I move forward at a constant speed, though in my contained space I am hardly aware of my own velocity. Other cars pass by me or move with me, but I don't feel them kinesthetically. The rhythm of which I am a part feels constant and monotonous, shifts being too slight to register much beyond my body's distal points: neck, wrist, ankle, or eyeballs. When necessary, I move my foot to the brake pedal and press, and my torso lurches slightly forward. As the car comes to a stop, my body, save for my right foot on the brake, relaxes somewhat and I look around me at what is outside. None of the movement I see—cross traffic and people walking through parking lots—affects my own body inside the car. Detached from the space around me, I feel in suspension, glancing continually up at the stoplight, compelled to continue the drive forward.*

As of 2003, Los Angeles County boasted an Asian population of 1.3 million, the largest concentration of Asians in a single county nationwide, according to the Asian Pacific American Legal Center

(APALC).[5] Of these 1.3 million, the majority are Chinese (about 400,000) (APALC). And, to tighten the focus, within Los Angeles County, San Gabriel Valley is home to the United States' largest Chinese community, nearly a quarter of a million people.[6] Wei Li has termed San Gabriel Valley an *ethnoburb:* a suburb whose population is dominated by a particular ethnic group, for example the Chinese in San Gabriel Valley, the Armenians in Glendale, or the Vietnamese in Westminster. The ethnoburb of San Gabriel Valley emerged beginning in the 1960s along with a more general trend in American suburbanization, but also more particularly as the Chinese population in Los Angeles began to increase[7] and conditions in L.A.'s downtown Chinatown became congested. Over the last four decades the area has expanded geographically, diversified economically and ethnically (accommodating upper-, middle- and working-class Chinese from China, Taiwan, Hong Kong, and Southeast Asia), and strengthened its socioeconomic ties both to Los Angeles and to the Greater Chinese global circuit.[8]

Los Angeles is a fascinating city in which to study urban motion. Encompassing an increasingly vast territory of urban sprawl connected by hundreds of miles of congested freeways, Los Angeles is both representative and superlative of the contemporary American, car-dependent city. The dominance of the automobile fosters the development of ethnoburbs like San Gabriel Valley where real estate parcels are more spread out and divisions between residential and commercial space are more delineated. Important for the purposes of this investigation is also the fact that automobility has a profound impact on the body's experience of movement in Los Angeles. Automobility is the dominant experience of Los Angeles as a global body-city.

Nigel Taylor writes that our experience of the modern city is inseparable from our experience of traffic, not only as drivers and passengers, but also as pedestrians or other people not traveling inside a motor vehicle. And our experience of traffic, he goes on to explain, is simultaneously hyperactive and tedious. While the intense speed enabled by the automobile requires continuous and active vigilance by anyone on or near the road, at the same time, the frequent congestion and thus the confinement in slow-moving vehicles that are a result of too much traffic leads to a numbing of the senses. Richard Sennett adds that the disengagement from space that results from being inside a car has a narcotic effect: "Navigating the geography of modern society requires very little physical effort, hence engagement; indeed, as roads become straightened and regularized, the voyager need account less and less for the people and the buildings on the street in order to move, making minute motions in an ever less complex environment."[9] Furthermore, the technical requirements of automobility (broadened roads, highways that exclude the pedestrian, massive signage, and street lights) have bulldozed through urban civil spaces and dispersed places across ever greater spaces. The resulting urban sprawl has in turn made transportation via automobile ever more necessary and the construction of more and longer highways increasingly imperative. Public space, thus, becomes subordinated to the demands of speed.

Mimi Sheller and John Urry, while acknowledging the impact that "automobilized time-space" has had on the city, also argue that freedom of mobility is a condition of the democratic ideal. This paradox whereby civility is both destroyed and championed by the car is a function of our democratic society:

> Both processes, urbanization and automobilization are *together* characteristic of modernity and of the culture of cities. Meeting places require that people get to them. Mobility cannot simply be conceived as the enemy of *civitas;* however much we may despair of vehicular traffic and busy roads, the auto-freedom of movement is part of what can constitute democratic life.[10]

We all demand the mobility, the flexibility, and even the privacy that the automobile enables. While many critics argue that the ascendance of the car and roads that are built solely for automobile travel has led to increasing disengagement from civil society, in fact, automobilization might be seen to extend civic spaces, multiply them, and make them more diverse and more accessible. A plurality of civil societies are made possible as more and more space becomes civilianized by roads and "more and more social actors have demanded the rights of personal mobility."[11] Of course, what Sheller and Urry do not acknowledge is that automobility is not always available to all, and thus an increasingly spatially dispersed city might also make sites of sociality less accessible rather than more—particularly for those without the means to get to them. Nevertheless, their ideas about how diverse and multiple centers of civic engagement arise as a result of car infrastructure is certainly relevant to the ethnoburb of San Gabriel Valley.

In contrast to a dense, mixed-use ethnic space like New York's Chinatown, an ethnoburb is characterized by the separation of territorialities that are the result of automobility. In an ethnoburb, as in suburbs generally, landscapes of consumption are detached from spaces of manufacturing or labor and residential areas are disconnected from civic or commercial localities. One shuttles the distances between home, work, and leisure via the car.

If driving in my car, removed from the space around me, I am kinesthetically numbed, then what is my experience of the various places in the city that I access from my car? Sheller and Urry suggest that places such as the modern shopping center with its vast parking lot constitute one of the dispersed loci of sociality both allowed and necessitated by car culture. Civic spaces arise at intersections of the paths of automobility and thereby become places of connection for peoples separated across long distances. Because the geography of auto space has un-tied territorialities of home, work, and leisure so that they are no longer integrated in one dense space, people are forced to travel significant distances to specified sites of sociality spaced along pathways of urban flow. Fragmentation of these different time-spaces allows for a kind of diversification. Malls, then, serve as a social and cultural convergence point for populations scattered throughout the suburbs of the city.

After about 20 minutes of driving along Valley Boulevard, I come upon a concentration of large mall complexes occupying both sides of the street. This area between New Avenue and Del Mar Avenue serves as a major focus point for the Chinese cities in San Gabriel Valley. Situated at the midpoint along Valley Boulevard, it is dominated by a multiple-story Hilton Hotel, three bi-level strip malls, and the San Gabriel Square shopping center. San Gabriel Square, in turn, is anchored by the vast Asian supermarket, 99 Ranch.

I park my car in the sprawling lot and get out. After sitting in the car feeling tense and confined it is good to stretch my legs into a stride and to feel the air on my skin. The bright sun lends a feeling of warmth and ease. I first make a tour of the whole of the mall moving through its outdoor corridors and pathways. Though there are others walking by me, I do not feel beleaguered by them, and we make no physical contact. They move in equal pace with me, neither hurried nor sluggish. Their paths and mine are not tightly directed, but more meandering. I move into and out of shade and bright sunshine. Store windows beckon, store doors are open. People sit at tables outside the tea shop drinking, chatting on the phone, playing chess, their torsos shifted sideways, legs extended. A grandmother sits on the edge of a fountain while a child explores the water.

Indoors, the restaurants feel more fast-paced. The waiters, busboys, and receptionists move more directly, more quickly. There is more bodily encounter in the spaces between the tables and more person-to-person engagement of people across the table from one another. It is louder. Faces and gestures are more animated. The proximity between bodies is more palpable. At one table I spot some family friends. Like many of the dispersed Los Angeles Chinese who come in from along extended freeways to San Gabriel Square, they have come here from a suburb one hour away to eat lunch and to stock up on Chinese groceries at 99 Ranch.

What is the overall feeling of movement here, and what does it tell me about L.A. as a body-city? Movement in Los Angeles is conditioned by the automobile, and this means that moving bodies in L.A. are produced in part through sites made possible by car culture; that is, at the mall. The kinesthetics in San Gabriel Square are circuitous, unhurried, unhindered, and, compared to the minute, confined, repetitive movements of driving a car, they are more stimulating. Of course, malls are planned spaces with limited egress and directed pathways meant to encourage consumption, so we must be reminded that bodily freedom here is still compromised. The spaces through which one can move are regularized. Corridors and aisles are wide, but they are still corridors and aisles directed toward shopping. Nevertheless, as opposed to the dulling kinesthetics of the car, there is more physical improvisation and interaction in the mall. The car culture of Los Angeles necessitates the fragmentation of time-spaces into separate spheres for automobility versus walking, shopping versus working, and so forth. San Gabriel Square, then, is a walking space surrounded by a network of roads for cars. It is a designated place for slowing down where leisure is encouraged because more time spent means more purchases made.

Though San Gabriel Square is a mall along the model of so many other malls whose design is meant to create a landscape of consumption, it is also a place of civic connection for the diverse Chinese populations scattered in suburbs across Los Angeles. Automobilization makes possible different civic spaces that give access to different populations. The sprawl that has replaced more centralized geographies of urban space is a result of the democratization of mobility allowed by car culture. And this democratization has given rise to a dispersed plurality of socialities. Of course, when Sheller and Urry refer to "democratization," they mean a democratization of space—a scattering of multiple sites of civic engagement as opposed to a hierarchizing of space between a center and a periphery.[12] If these sites are designed for consumption and built around automobility, however, then they are not fully democratic, but only available to those with vehicle access and the economic means for consumption.[13] Still, we might argue that in Los Angeles the Chinese shopping mall, a product both of car culture and of global capitalism, serves for many of the Chinese in Los Angeles as a space for identification, cultural exchange, leisure, and sociality, in addition to a site through which these diasporic Chinese might connect themselves to other Greater Chinese urban glocalities.

Cross Tracings

I grew up in Los Angeles. I am familiar with the experience of connecting to a Greater China imaginary by driving to a Chinese mall. When I was a child, my family would drive the hour up to Monterey Park in order to eat dim sum on the weekends, meet family friends, buy groceries and the Chinese language newspaper, or go to the Chinese tailor. Even now I travel up the 710 freeway to San Gabriel Valley in order to fulfill a craving for a bowl of Chinese noodles at one of the strip mall restaurants along Valley Boulevard.

In order to return to the question of how diaspora marks the body—and how the body can mark diaspora—let me pair my kinesthetic analysis of L.A. with a choreography of Taipei. *Hood, Veil, Shoes* is a work that inflects one urban time-space with the somatic experiences of another.

The dance opens with a video projected onto the entire back scrim of the stage. The image is of a busy intersection in nighttime Taipei. Filmed from a raised vantage point, the sped-up image shows the headlights of cars and mopeds waiting at a light and the red and white lights of other vehicles streaming across the intersection. The light changes and the vectors of motion switch. Set to a delicate rhythmic score, the video is a beautiful, harmonic choreography of twinkling lights and streaming flows. Dancers gradually appear from the wings wearing street clothes and, for some, the face masks that moped drivers in Taipei use to filter the vehicle fumes that assault them on the streets. They prance lightly across the stage, suggesting various kinds of movers traversing urban space.

Slowly, as the video goes to black, the scene transitions into another in which the pace slows and pairs of dancers take turns pulling at each other's faces in slow motion and then abruptly releasing, or twisting an arm, or pulling at hair. In between, they dip and sway their hips in blank-faced yet come-hither fashion. This is the first instance in which Yu introduces the trope of sexual violence. Other scenes in the dance extend this idea of physical violation. The title of the piece refers to the Little Red Riding Hood tale, and dancers alternate wearing a red moped helmet, a granny wig, and a wolf mask, along with red stilettos, to highlight the sexual threat implied in the tale. The gruff and threatening voice of the wolf talking to the innocent voice of Red Riding Hood serves as the soundtrack to some of these scenes.

Another scene mimics models on a catwalk, strutting and posing in the red heels with alternating menace and seduction. Still another features women in billowy crimson pants lying on their backs, legs up in the air, feet in the stilettos. Viewed as a whole piece, suggestions of blood, bound feet, masks, hoods, and sharp implements emerge as recurring masochistic tropes. At the same time, there are more lovely videos of the city—the tops of skyscrapers that appear to float among clouds, an image of a Taipei intersection that gradually becomes covered by water[14]—that seem to work in counterpoint to Yu's idea of Taipei as a site of sexual violence.

During a talkback after the performance I saw in 2008 at UCLA, Yu discussed the shock of her recent return to Taipei. In reply, the director of Sun Shier, the dance company that commissioned her piece, responded with bemusement that Yu's was an outsider's perspective of Taipei. The perceived threat of violence and the new phenomenon of women drivers was not something a local would take note of, she said.

As I mention above, Yu is a diasporic Taiwanese now living in Los Angeles. In a profile of her by the Los Angeles Department of Cultural Affairs she states that she is inspired by "the Asian diaspora dance communities of Monterey Park and neighboring San Gabriel Valley cities" (Los Angeles Dept. of Cultural Affairs). Of Los Angeles she has said, "For me, Los Angeles has been a place where you can reflect more, unlike New York or Taiwan, where I'm always going, going, going." For Yu, Los Angeles is a relaxed place, a place where she has room to contemplate.

As I argue above, the kinetic quality that best characterizes Los Angeles, unlike Taipei, is automobility. The dominance of the car in Los Angeles means that for immigrant communities a sense of collective belonging is built not on the streets of the city, where bodies in their steel boxes are isolated from other bodies, but at sites of sociality where one parks one's car and gathers on foot. That is, at the mall. Here diasporic Chinese encounter one another in a landscape meant to please the senses and thereby encourage buying. If Yu is inspired by her experiences maneuvering in her car through the Chinese ethnoburbs of San Gabriel Valley, then it follows that a return to Taipei's crowded streets, where people come into more physical contact with one another—walking on the sidewalk-less streets, jostling on the subway platforms, knee to knee on mopeds at the intersections, both men and women in the driver's seats—would be a jolting experience. Yu's impressions of the city of her youth are indelibly colored by the changes across the twenty-plus years and thousands of miles that are now between her and that city.

Urban space marks the body. Diaspora marks the body. The diasporic body in turn marks urban space: global bodies-cities. Often when we talk about the diasporic experience, we focus on the ways that "where you're from" haunts "where you're at."[15] This is certainly evidenced by Yu's reflection: "I suppose that living here [in L.A.] has made me more focused on looking back into myself, into who I really am" (Josephs). But Yu's choreographic response to her return to Taipei also suggests how the diasporic experience can work in the other direction. As global migrations increasingly involve bodies crisscrossing to *and fro,* forth *and back,* transnational Chinese are now multiply marked by the various nodes on their circuits of migration. Our bodies are palimpsests of the numerous kinetic encounters we carry.

At the conclusion of *Hood, Veil, Shoes,* Yu projects onto the scrim an image of her dancers in street clothes standing on a sidewalk in Taipei. She has said that she wanted to incorporate into her dance the somatic experiences of her dancers, who came into the studio each day with the soot of their travels across the city (interview). Yu's work, in the way that it imagines Taipei through an experience of Los Angeles, one Chinese urban space traced through another Chinese urban space, reminds me that in an era of globalization, cities and bodies cannot be studied in isolation. Global bodies-cities are complicated textures of belonging, motion, travel, passage, and flow. Like dancing bodies, global bodies-cities are entangled, interlaced, multiply enmeshed, and always in motion.

Notes

1. See Elizabeth Grosz, "Bodies-Cities" in *Feminist Theory and the Body: A Reader,* Janet Price and Margrit Shildrick, eds. (New York: Routledge, 1999), 243. See also Michel Foucault, *Discipline and Punish: The Birth of the Prison.* Trans. Alan Sheridan (New York: Vintage Books, 1977).
2. Grosz, "Bodies-Cities," 248–249.

3. Grosz, "Bodies-Cities," 258.
4. See Mimi Sheller and John Urry, "The New Mobilities Paradigm," Special Issue of *Environment and Planning A*, "Materialities and Mobilities" 38 (2006): 207–226. As they write, "The driver's body is itself fragmented and disciplined to the machine, with eyes, ears, hands and feet all trained to respond instantaneously, while the desire to stretch, to change position, or to look around must be suppressed. The car becomes an extension of the driver's body, creating new urban subjectivities" (211).
5. Asian Pacific American Legal Center. *The Diverse Faces of Asian and Pacific Islanders in California: Asian & Pacific Islander Demographic Profile*, 2005. Online at https://www.advancingjustice-la.org/system/files/ENTERED_DiverseFace_CA_2005.pdf.
6. Charles Perry and Linda Burum. "Real Fireworks," *Los Angeles Times*, January 26, 2005.
7. The 1965 U.S. Immigration Act, political uncertainty in China and Taiwan, and later the 1997 Hong Kong handover, along with increasingly wealthy Chinese from Southeast Asia, fueled the increase in the Chinese population in Los Angeles. See Wei Li, "Building Ethnoburbia: The Emergence and Manifestation of the Chinese Ethnoburb in Los Angeles' San Gabriel Valley," *Journal of Asian American Studies* 2.1 (1999): 1–28.
8. See Wei Li, "Building Ethnoburbia."
9. Richard Sennett, *Flesh and Stone: The Body and the City in Western Civilization* (New York: W. W. Norton & Company, 1996), 18.
10. Sheller and Urry, "The New Mobilities Paradigm," 207.
11. Sheller and Urry, "The New Mobilities Paradigm," 207.
12. Sheller and Urry, "The New Mobilities Paradigm."
13. See Staeheli and Mitchell for a discussion of how shopping malls are replacing town squares and thus how they muffle political activism in favor of civility. Lynn A. Staeheli and Don Mitchell, "USA's Destiny? Regulating Space and Creating Community in American Shopping Malls," *Urban Studies* 43.5/6 (May 2006): 977–992.
14. Yu has said that she thinks of Taipei as a city submerged by water. Personal interview with the author (May 10, 2010).
15. See Paul Gilroy, "It Ain't Where You're from, It's Where You're At . . . The Dialectics of Diasporic Identification," *Third Text* (Winter 1990–1991): 3–16.

CHAPTER 18

Poems

MAI DER VANG

Original Bones

I wonder the earliest days
When I had a written language

Before 1952 when missionaries
In Laos wrote one for me

Before 1959 when a phantom script
Came to the *mother of writing*

Before 1986 when I drew
The letters of mai der

I showed up in southern china
A few millennia back
Uncooked people
Led to war

As a child I once looked up
From a farm in fresno's valley

So much deeper the engine echoes
In my kicking eardrum

Grayer now my eyelids
Gnarl into clouds

There was a time
The mountain came to surrender
Pressed itself down as my page

Beyond the Backyard

Light passing through
geometry of chain-link gate.
Wig of barbed wire.
All, I might see.

We pay our rent
to the mechanic next door.
He's industry too.

Someday,
I will forgive dirt floor
alleys with dumpsters everyone used.

Forgive forklifts
crawling in the lumberyard.

Forgive acoustic winds
lashing open the back door.
Anchor let go.

I will climb on the ledge
to peer over,
beggar my eyes
to a view.

Rusted sedan, wire zipline
to stapled roof, retired
shopping cart missing wheel.

My parents fled for this.

Crash Calling

Do not linger here that is not your brick,

Nor cling to the elbow of a passing car.

The median will trap you during day,

Clip your eyes to hunger as you forage

Along these thin and splintered roads.

Come to the calico kitchen

Where a grandchild grows and waits

For you to string his wrecked balloon.

He will drop the thread, every time again,

Until you hear the wishing in his chest.

He will bury the morning dove dying
Inside your shoe. Still, there are secrets

You preserve: tarnished coins folded

In a worn blue cloth.

Late Harvest

It started with the apricots
Turning all copper hues on the orchard floor.
The farmer had no one to pick them.

Then oranges.
And the tomatoes.

Someone has tilted the land.

A star flashes
As if it needs help.
Other times it is a loose tooth

In the open mouth of the galaxy.

There are no laborers.
The crates, empty.

Stare long enough at the fields,
The parched horizon,
And you will see, from its lifting,
A kind of smalt fog.

CHAPTER 19

"Parents' Fairytale"

Excerpt from *Self (The Remix)*

ROBERT FARID KARIMI

SELF (THE REMIX) IS A SPOKEN-WORD, hip-hop play that mixes together stories, movement, and music to tell the tale of an American child of Iranian and Guatemalan immigrants growing up in California in the 1970s and 1980s in the shadow of the Iranian Hostage Crisis. Karimi, accompanied by a soundscape created by DJ D Double, tells a "remixed" autobiographical tale of a boy struggling to learn about manhood, nationhood, and neighborhood with the voices and music of his environment helping him along. It was first presented at the United States of Asian America Festival at San Francisco's API Cultural Center in 2003. Karimi has also performed this show at Minneapolis's Intermedia Arts (2011), San Diego's Mo'olelo Performing Arts Company (2010), and Philadelphia's Asian Arts Initiative (2010).

SCENE 3—Parents' Fairytale

DJ cuts out previous song and plays "Star Wars Theme." The thunderous beginning cuts Karimi off abruptly, and he transforms into a grandiose storyteller, matching the thunder of the music in his delivery.

KARIMI: Long ago in a land far far far away *(Karimi stretches out words)* called Iran

lived a man named MOoooooHAaaMMED!

(Karimi waves for DJ to cut off music.)

Wait a minute. Wait. Wait. It's not so futuristic, really. It's more like a fairy tale, sort of, but with airplanes.

(DJ plays airplane sound effect and then softly fades up Shahzeydi-Tajvidi. Karimi crosses to downstage left.)

KARIMI: *(in storyteller voice)* Long ago in a land far far far away called Iran—

DJ: Let me hear you say Iran!

(Karimi stretches fingertips to give an image to the word "Iran," so the audience knows to repeat after him. He encourages them until they say "Iran.")

—lived an industrious man named—

(DJ fades in "Popcorn" by Hot Butter as Karimi transforms into Father.)

FATHER: Mohammed Ebrahim Karimi Rouzbehani.

I dreamed of leaving the Enchanted Land of Iran, so I went to night school and worked every day for Iran Air and finally saved enough money

(Father pirouettes to down center.)

to buy a one-way ticket and take a plane

(DJ adds airplane sound.)

from that far far far away land of Iran

(DJ cuts out Iranian music as Father continues to cross stage.)

and landed in

(Airplane sound skids.)

Germany.

("Popcorn" stops.)

But they didn't like my kind of people there

so I took another plane *(more plane sound effects)* and landed *(plane sound skids)* in a land of fruit trees and abundance *(DJ plays "Galaxy" by War)* called Union City, California—

where

I

(Father positions himself as maintenance man cleaning the stage)

worked and worked and worked

(Father pauses as DJ begins to sample "Minimum Wage" by They Might Be Giants.)

living out my American Dream

by cleaning up the shit left from automobile assembly lines

to assembly lines to assembly lines.

(DJ fades out "Minimum Wage" as Father becomes Karimi and approaches audience.)

DJ: BOO! HISS!! *(Encourages audience to join in.)* BOO! HISSS.

(Karimi crouches.)

KARIMI: Meanwhile

in another land far far away

(DJ plays "Luna de Miel en Rio Dulce" by Marimba Chapinlandia.)

named Guatemala.

DJ: Let me hear you say "Guatemala."

(Motions for audience to repeat, praises them with "Good, good," before resuming narration voice.)

KARIMI: lived an independent girl
named

(Karimi slides upstage center to become Mother)

MOTHER: Laura Albertina Comparini Tellez.
I dreamed of having my own office job and a tiny little family
but instead
an uncle named Sam offered me a green card so I could go to his house and work for him.

(DJ fades out "Luna de Miel . . .")

I accepted
And took a plane

(DJ adds airplane sound.)

from that far far away land of Guatemala and landed in

(Airplane sound skids. DJ starts Union City music, then stops so audience can respond. DJ and Mother continue after audience response.)

Union City, California as well.

(Mother kneels and mimes scrubbing the floor).

I worked and worked and worked for my uncle,

(DJ plays "Minimum Wage" sample.)

who made me clean his house, take care of his children, and even wash his dirty underwear.

("Minimum Wage" fades out as Mother becomes Karimi crossing to down center.)

DJ: BOO! HISS! *(DJ gets audience to repeat with him.)* BOO! HISS!

(DJ plays "Luna de Miel . . .")

MOTHER: I also went to English school
where Mohammed also was.

(Mother winks at audience, and DJ crossfades to "Popcorn." Mother becomes Father.)

FATHER: Where Eric also was.
Your mother had long black hair.
And blue eyes and light skin—
which made her stand out in her family of Indios,
but caught my attention:
I strolled on by her desk in the English school
to utilize my improved English skills.
I said:

(DJ plays "True" by Spandau Ballet.)

(Father unbuttons all the buttons of his shirt to expose his chest hair. He puts up his collar and gets into pimp daddy position for courting purposes. He checks his breath and strolls to downstage center.)

Did you know that both of our countries were the first two to be infiltrated by the CIA?

(DJ holds the record. Then scratches to signify Mother's anger. Father realizes his error and tries to rectify it as DJ backspins 80s modern rock slow jam and plays it from the beginning.)

FATHER: "Would you like to join me for dinner?"

(DJ fades out "True" and plays "Luna del Miel . . ." as Father transforms into Mother.)

MOTHER: I saw your father's Tom Jones, Engelbert Humperdinck, James Caan bush of chest hair. I accepted. I said, "He must be Latino."

(DJ cuts out "Luna del Miel . . ." and immediately plays "Popcorn" for character change.)

FATHER: I took your mother to the park, dinner, everywhere,
and we knew it was love.
But your mother was unsure, so she went to the neighborhood priest.

(DJ cuts from "Popcorn" to "Our Father" as Mother kneels at pew center stage. DJ adds "Luna del Miel . . ." to the mix.)

MOTHER: I love Mohammed, Padre. But he is Muslim. I do not want to go to hell for love. What does the church think?

(DJ plays "Gregorian Chant" as Mother changes position and becomes a priest taking confession.)

PRIEST: Laura, as long as we can convert him—
like we converted the Indians—
and he attends Catechism classes before the marriage,
it shall be OK in the eyes of the Lord.

(DJ fades out "Gregorian Chant" and fades up "Popcorn" as Father crosses to downstage center.)

FATHER: So, on Iranian New Year's Day, Norooz.

(DJ cuts "Popcorn" and plays "Luna del Miel . . .")

MOTHER: the first day of spring,

(All music fades out.)

PRIEST: Ladies and Gentlemen, I present to you the new couple, Mr. & Mrs. Laura and Moham, I mean Eric . . .

(DJ plays intro to "Creator" by Pete Rock and C. L. Smooth.)

MOTHER: And after 17 months,

on the one-year anniversary of the death
of slain Chicano journalist Ruben Salazar,

FATHER: and the 13th birthday of Michael Jackson,

(Father becomes Karimi, who runs all the way upstage, then bursts through the birth canal of light.)

I
was born.
in a tiny Union City hospital at 4:20 P.M.
Named Robert. Farid. Karimi.

(DJ plays echoed "Popcorn" on top of other music.)

FATHER: I didn't want "Roberto" because I wanted him to be an American, so I named my son, Robert. Robert.

(DJ cuts "Popcorn" and plays echoed "Luna de Miel . . .")

MOTHER: I wanted Robert to not forget where he came from SO I named him Farid . . . Robert Farid . . . Robert Farid.

KARIMI: RFK. Robert F. Kennedy. The slain Kennedy my parents thought would be president of these United States.

(All music fades out. DJ fades in "2001: A Space Odyssey" as Karimi walks stage right.)

And we were a team. Going everywhere together. Mom and Dad both working. Me.

(Karimi positions body as if he is a little boy being pulled by adult babysitters.)

Going from babysitter to babysitter to babysitter. The model American family. A nuclear family.
(Sings) "A man and a woman had a little baby,
they were three, and that's a magic number."

(Karimi gets water and approaches audience as DJ plays "Tell Me When to Go" by E-40.)

KARIMI: Now, the idea of an Iranian-Guatemalan combination may sound delicious.

But it doesn't always make for a good marriage.

Four years later, my parents divorced. And they always fought about the littlest things. Like who had to pay for the groceries. Laura, you should pay for the orange juice. Mo, it's your turn. Ay madre dios. Don't speak Spanish! Speak English!

Scene 6—Ted Koppel becomes famous

(Lights crossfade to DSR. DJ plays typewriter.)

KARIMI: *(Pauses as he crosses to downstage center.)*
It was 1979
when Pan American flight 429
from Guatemala City
touched down to Union City, CA.

(Karimi makes motion with body, then DJ plays War / Union City *theme, then switches back to typewriter.)*

KARIMI: The year changed
from timeline to Nightline, and
Ted Koppel became famous
with these words: *(Typewriter sound ends.)*

(Karimi becomes Ted Koppel.)

TED KOPPEL: Day 1 of the Iranian Hostage Crisis.

(Ted Koppel becomes Karimi, who crouches upstage.)

KARIMI: The day I became . . .

Scene 7—Church ladies and drunk man talk about Iranians at a party

(Lights change. DJ plays intro to "Spanish Harlem" by Ben E. King.)

CHURCH LADY 1: Poor Robertito. Que malo a tener un padre asi.

(DJ loops "Spanish Harlem" intro.)

CHURCH LADY 2: Ay, poor Laura. I just watched that made-for-TV movie. His father might steal him away. You know how they are.

(DJ loops "Spanish Harlem" intro.)

CHURCH LADY 3: Oh, no. He is half Muslim. That means Robertito is half devil.

(DJ crashes in "Mi Viejo San Juan" by Trio Los Panchos.)

DRUNK MAN: Pinche Irani. Who invited you? We all know what you pendejos want. Dejame! No, leave me alone! I don't give a shit if he is 8 years old. This little nieto of Ayatollah Cabron tiene que hear this!

(Lights change; Drunk Man slowly becomes 8-year-old Robertito reacting to Drunk Man USR in harsh light of the cross like a deer caught in headlights. DJ plays only sound of heartbeat.)

Scene 9—Catholic Boy Not Pictured

(All lights up. Karimi moves to upstage center, grabs water and approaches audience.)

KARIMI: How many people have heard of the Iranian Hostage Crisis? If you've heard about it, applaud.

(Ad-lib options for response: "Not that loudly; it's not something to applaud for," or "Wow. We have a young crowd.")

The Iranian Hostage Crisis lasted 444 days.

The only historical event to be counted like this.

Do you know where you were on day 76? What about day 141?

I know where I was on day 33.

I was in St. Bede's Catholic School. In the third grade.

Saying the Pledge of Allegiance.

(Bell rings. Karimi becomes Robertito, who frantically goes upstage, removes top shirt to reveal Catholic Boy uniform and hurries to Pledge Special UCL.)

ROBERTITO (at 8 years old):
I pledge allegiance to
Our Father, who art in Heaven,
the United States of America,
and to the Kingdom, for which it stands,
one nation, under God,
on Earth as it is in Heaven,
invisible,
with liberty and justice for all.
(Pauses to take a breath.)
Amen.

(Robertito makes the sign of the cross and kisses thumb. DJ plays "Charlie Brown's Theme." Lights change.)

ROBERTITO (at 8 years old):

On this day. Day 33. Our prayers were said quickly because a photographer from the *Catholic Voice*, our archdiocese newspaper, was coming to take our picture. Because one of my classmates is a niece of an Iranian hostage. And we were going to send a class picture to him in Iran.

Monsignor Francis and Miss and the photographer were constantly looking at me. And I knew why.

(pause) Because, I was the smallest in the class, and I was always in the front. So they were just making sure I followed all the dress code rules.

(Robertito tucks in shirt)

I did.

Then, the photographer went all the way to the back, Monsignor Francis went all the way to the side, and Miss came up to us and said:

(Robertito becomes Miss Third Grade Teacher trying to get everyone's attention in Charlie Brown Teacher's Voice that's incomprehensible. Gets very frustrated that her class is not listening, then erupts.)

MISS THIRD GRADE TEACHER:

David Lawrence Dimaano! Thank you. *(DJ scratches in response.)* That will be five Hail Marys, Mr. Dimaano! *(DJ scratches in response.)* Six! And a Rosary. *(And if audience laughs, ad-lib: "No laughing. Jesus doesn't love a devil's helper.")*

(Miss Third Grade Teacher approaches audience.)

OK, everyone.*(Improv getting audience to prepare themselves for the class picture. After teacher is satisfied, then smiles at audience.)* Big smile for Jesus.

(Smiles back at audience.)

And Robert. Robert, honey. *(DJ scratches in response.)* Could you do Miss a favor, and move a little to the right?

(DJ plays "I Can't Go for That" by Hall and Oates; Miss follows the path of the young Robertito, going stage left until he is out of the light, then sound out.)

MISS THIRD GRADE TEACHER (continued):

A little bit more. And more. And more. And more. Now, one more big step for Jesus. Perfect.

(Lights flash as a camera flash, on audience. At the same time, click of camera is heard. Lights out. Miss Third Grade Teacher becomes Robertito in the darkness.)

ROBERTITO (at 8 years old): No fair. Miss, you said everyone else was going to be part of the picture. Miss? When do I get my turn? When's my turn? Miss? Jesus? Jesus.

Scene 11—Porque Bailo Como Un Negrito

(As he rises, Robertito becomes Karimi.)

KARIMI:

It was Nineteen Seventy-Nine
And I had to go
I had to escape
to *(walks to center left and stops as lights change)*
La India Bonita
que bonita

(Lights all up in bright, celebratory colors. DJ plays "Si Dios Me Quita La Vida" by Javier Solis as Karimi rises in exultation, happy to be free of the pain.)

KARIMI:

La restaurante where my cousin used to work
where Mexicanas y Guatemaltecas struggled
with manteca on their hands
and worked and worked and worked *(Slight pause as DJ mixes in quick sample of "Minimum Wage.")*
for the price of chips & salsa.

(Pause)

I walked in.

(Karimi becomes Robertito at 8 years old). Lights crossfade to the restaurant look (2/3 of stage). (All music out.)

and all eyes were on me.

ROBERTITO (at 8 years old): But I ignored them.
("Si Dios . . ." remix returns.)

and I looked at the

velvet Chihuahuas the velvet Chihuahuas, the velvet Chihuahuas on the wall.

ROBERTITO (at 8 years old):

Tortilla, hominy y chicharron smell *(inhales)*

hit my nose.

as my 8-year-old eyes turned to the corner of the store

that always caught my attention . . . *(Cross to down right.)*

El jukebox:

con Javier Solis, Jose Feliciano Lighting Fire

and the Trammps, con un fuego, a disco inferno.

(DJ fades out "Si Dios . . .")

I picked A514,

But B137, McFadden & Whitehead came on instead

I heard my cousin Sera

in the back

doing her sing-hum rendition:

(DJ plays "Ain't No Stoppin' Us Now" by McFadden & Whitehead. Robertito dances upstage right-center and becomes his cousin Sera, who holds a tray and sings to the upstage customers in the restaurant.)

SERA: *(singing)* Ain't No Stoppin' Us Now
Hmm Hmmm Humm
Ain't No Stoppin' Us Now
Hmm Humm hummm.

(While she sings, she notices Robertito in the restaurant near the jukebox, and approaches him.)

Robertito! Don't listen to them. Ven aqui. Ven aqui . . . No preocupes. Don't worry about those cerotes. *(to the customers)* That's right, I called you cerotes. *(To Robertito)* Come here. Sientate. Que quieres? I make your favorite tacos with extra cheese. And if those cerotes give you any trouble, I will . . . *(Shakes fighting fists at audience.)*

(DJ repeats the chorus, as Sera sings and spins upstage center.)

SERA: *(singing)* Ain't No Stoppin' Us Now
Hmm Hmmm Humm
Ain't No Stoppin' Us Now
Hmm Humm hummm.

(Sera dances around the Mexican restaurant until she bumps into imaginary Big Bigote Man, upstage right. DJ glides needle across record as Sera falls and then becomes Big Bigote Man. DJ plays heartbeat.)

BIG BIGOTE MAN: Ching . . . Pendejo . . . bruta! My brand new white guayabera! *(touches moustaches and simmers, then explodes)* It's all you! Your fault! You! You're the one that put on that music. You Irani! Terrorista! You!

(Big Bigote Man lunges after imaginary Robertito. DJ plays heartbeat sounds. Robertito runs to downstage right jukebox.)

ROBERTITO (at 8 years old):
(in slow motion) I ran. (Speech to normal speed) I ran to the jukebox
and held onto it tight.

(Robertito hugs imaginary jukebox downstage right.)

ROBERTITO (at 8 years old):
To save me from the anger,
the screams, the pain.

(DJ fades in "Boogie Oogie" by A Taste of Honey.)

my music filled the restaurant with an all-encompassing groove.
I moved my feet.

(Robertito shuffles left, right.)

My body.

(Robertito does "Stayin' Alive" dance)

Making moves I didn't even comprehend.

(Robertito does Prince eyes and growls DR at jukebox)

My eyes focused on the jukebox glass.
But I could hear the words of the people behind me.

(DJ cuts off music; Robertito slides to center-center and becomes Church Lady 1)

CHURCH LADY 1: Ay que lindo.

(Church Lady 1 slides to upstage left and becomes Big Bigote Man)

BIG BIGOTE MAN: Porque Bailas Como Un Negrito!

(Big Bigote Man spins forward and becomes Sera)

SERA: Aha. I told you que he's not Mexican!
He's Guatemalteco!

(DJ continues "Boogie Oogie"; Sera becomes Robertito, who stomps on all of the previous characters locations with an up-rocky-type disco dance.)

ROBERTITO:

Pero a que me importa! I boogied in my wonderland Doin' my cousin Fernando's hustle with all my 8-year-old muscle.	*(Robertito does Fernando's hustle)*
Shakin' my groove thang and I was only concentrated on the infinite number of Moves.	*Robertito shakes hips;* *moves with jazzy flowy happy hands;*
I was feelin' free freedom to the funk. I guess they thought I was going to break out with a Frankie Smith in the middle of their carne asada or menudo platters.	*DJ cuts out record;* *Breaks out to audience and speaks to them;*
Give me a ho if you got that funky bus fare HO! HO! The double dutch bus coming down the street.	*Robertito lunges to UC and sings;* *If audience does not do "Ho!" with him, DJ cuts record, and rebukes and teaches audience how to "Ho!" and repeat; music resumes.*
Moving my chuck taylors. Dancing to the beat. BOOM!	*Robertito lunges to DR to the point in front of jukebox, and then . . .* *Falls to ground; Music out.*

ROBERTITO: My prima Sera came by and gave me a bump
that moved my 44-lb ass off its axis
and down to the ground.
She did some funky thang she called the body language
to show that she could still turn the beat around.
But as I got up.
To my surprise . . . *(Robertito rises).*

(DJ plays "Don't Stop till You Get Enough"/ "Rock with You/Burn This Disco" instrumental mix as Robertito dances with joy. He dances upstage and becomes Karimi.)

KARIMI: Michael Jackson!
was the son who dreamed with wax wings
when his father screamed to beware of the sun.
Michael made his wings into solar panels
to harness its energy
can you feel the force?
it's gotta lotta power baby . . .
no one can stop me . . . woo!

Robertito picks up dancing while DJ mixes, making fun of the people who are trying to stop him in the restaurant. He embodies freedom. DJ fade-slams in Iranian music to imply the impending arrival of Father, each sample of Iranian music gets bigger, until Father stops the DJ's mix completely.

CHAPTER 20

Traveling Subjects and the Subject of Travel in Vietnamese Diasporic Films

LAN DUONG

IN VIETNAMESE, THE WORDS *kỷ niệm* act as a noun (a souvenir) and a verb (to commemorate); both meanings refer to the gesture of making memory into artifact. This essay explores how the processes of *kỷ niệm* operate in Vietnamese travel films. In so doing, I centralize not the Western tourist, often presumed to be the mobile tourist *par excellence*, but rather, the Vietnamese tourist, a figure that has had little traction in tourism scholarship until recently.[1] Travel and tourism have been especially redolent in the years following normalized relations between U.S. and Việt Nam in 1994. Elsewhere, I have argued that directors such as Victor Vu, Ham Tran, and Charlie Nguyen, who hail from southern California, have chosen to make films tailored for audiences in Việt Nam.[2] And while tourism *to* Việt Nam has certainly increased in the past years due to the government's easing of visa restrictions for diasporic travelers, the country's outmigration—for migrants who study abroad, work, and travel—has also grown. In particular, parts of southern California are desirable areas for international Vietnamese students to attend community colleges (Golden West College), state colleges (California State University, Fullerton), and private universities (University of Southern California) for their undergraduate and graduate work.[3] In short, a circuitry of bodies and knowledge production has flowed between the regions of California and HồChí Minh City, a city more affectionately known as Sài Gòn by many domestic and diasporic Vietnamese.

It is precisely this affection for South Việt Nam, or Sài Gòn especially, with which this chapter is concerned. This article centers on global South–South modes of travel as a major trope in Vietnamese/diasporic films. Investigating travel as a form of memory-making, my analysis focuses on two different film texts: *Việt Kiều Về Quê Ăn Chơi [Overseas Vietnamese Go Home and Party]: Volume 2* and *Finding Phong* (2015). While the former is a Vietnamese American production of a travelogue that reimagines the country as a haven for sensual delights, the latter is a collaboratively directed documentary produced in Việt Nam about a trans woman who undergoes gender reaffirmation surgery (GRS) in Thailand. Although the films' themes and styles are different, they are similarly grounded. In documenting the encounters between self and other, the works are intensely personal and thoroughly saturated with the bodily pleasures of seeing and being seen, of being active and mobile.

Mirroring the themes of the collection in which this essay is found, the chapter queries what it means to "dream" in California and Việt Nam, examining low-budget, independent films that travel along southern routes marked by the axes of class and capital. These films are part of a growing archive constituting a "playground of collective memories," to use Svetlana Boym's words, that re/connect Californians and Vietnamese via networks of affective feeling and transnational modes of distribution.[4] Diasporic travel films like *Overseas Vietnamese Go Home and Party* emphasize a homecoming narrative specific to a Vietnamese-language market, hailing not only the nostalgic consumer, but also one of a certain class and *habitus*.[5] This consumer can cheaply stream the films online or buy hard copies in Garden Grove and San Jose, two regions where Vietnamese are most populous outside of Việt Nam. Moreover, in these densely populated Vietnamese American cities, where a vibrant, transnational Vietnamese media circulates, audiences are able to screen relatively obscure Vietnamese films such as *Finding Phong* at festivals like Viet Film Fest.

Where before travel to and from Việt Nam was exceedingly difficult because of the fraught politics dividing Vietnamese Americans and the Vietnamese state, now the rapidity with which capital, people, and culture circulate between California and Sài Gòn, and the degree to which this takes place, highlight major transformations in the "minor transnational" relations between Việt Nam and the diaspora. Cultural theorists Françoise Lionnet and Shu-mei Shih formulate a theory of "minor transnationalism," which eschews a binary model of the local and global, and which emphasizes the "awareness and recognition of the creative interventions that networks of minoritized cultures produce within and across national boundaries."[6] Borrowing from this framework, I argue that the difficult relations between the Vietnamese state and the diaspora form a major component of transnational Vietnamese politics, but in a minor key. Minor transnational relations between such groups highlight the strategies artists deploy against the narrative of Vietnamese nationalism, while illuminating the state's neoliberal forms of statecraft today. While promoting its domestic population as a mobile labor force, for example, the state now welcomes the diaspora "home" after decades of disavowing diasporic history.

What follows is a mapping of the routes that traveling subjects in film undertake, and the circuits through which films about travel continue to move. Queering and gendering the tourist's gaze, these films serve as a useful rejoinder to early colonial travelogues that glorified French travel within an exoticized Indochina and featured the native as an enduring part of the spectacle.[7] In contrast, *Overseas Vietnamese* and *Finding Phong* reorient the tourist gaze to include those who tour within a context of "minor transnationalism" and for whom *kỷ niệm* is particular to our contemporary moment. Just as importantly, these films also show how minoritized cultures in Việt Nam and the diaspora make memory (*làm kỷ niệm*) outside of the frames of the national.

Vietnamese Film Industry: Revolution and Renovation

In recent years, the Vietnamese state has put in place several pieces of legislation that permit the diasporic community to work in the country for a longer period of time, to vote, and to buy property. Overseas Vietnamese can now stay in the country for up to five years, provided they obtain a visa to live and work there. In 2008, Việt Nam amended its citizenship laws to allow diasporic individuals to hold dual citizenship. The Law of Housing, established in 2014, permits the purchasing of land by *Việt Kiều* (overseas Vietnamese) and foreigners. Finally, in 2015, overseas Vietnamese, their foreign spouses and children, were permitted to visit Việt Nam without having to apply for a visa, with foreign family members of Vietnamese citizens also benefiting from the new policy.

Following such legislation, transnational collaborations between those in southern Việt Nam and southern California are now part of the infrastructure of today's Vietnamese film industry. Many of the films that have changed the landscape of Vietnamese cinema have been directed by Vietnamese American filmmakers who hail from California, where they went to film school, began their careers, and then traveled to Sài Gòn to make movies. It is not only directors who return to Việt Nam to make films; numerous Vietnamese American actors and producers also return to Việt Nam to make a variety of commercially viable genre films, often customized for a Vietnamese market.[8]

Vietnamese American filmmakers and their work must also be regarded through the lens of refugee histories in which the relations between the state and the diaspora have been especially tense. This context puts in relief the ways that the state tries to "disappear" refugee histories, at the same time that it welcomes the diaspora back into the fold of the nation. It is clear that in the postwar years, the Vietnamese diaspora has represented a problem to the nation-state; anti-communist factions actively challenge the state's authority to rule, often critiquing the country's abuse of human rights, its appropriation of land from Việt Nam's minority communities, and state crackdowns on political and religious freedoms.

Given these developments, Vietnamese American filmmakers must maintain delicate relations with the state, avoiding subjects that are still taboo and subject to censorship, particularly those that deal with the American war, re-education, Vietnamese refugees, South Vietnamese resentment, and anti-communist feeling. These negotiations are part of the way that the business of work is executed in Việt Nam. This is particularly true in Sài Gòn, where, as Philip Taylor notes, social relations in this region have been shaped by a colonial legacy. Because of this, Sài Gòn's social structure and governance style have always been "personalistic, egalitarian, and informal" and connoted a certain "looseness, openness, and mobility associated with the rapid development of high levels of land concentration, social inequality, itinerancy, and social banditry."[9] In conjunction with the dismantling of socialist command and control policies in the late 1980s, Taylor adds, this "looseness" and "openness" remade the city into the bustling commercial center in the South that it is today.[10]

As a lively hub of commercial activity, with its long lineage of capitalistic and cultural exchange, Sài Gòn (renamed Hồ Chí Minh City after the end of the war) is *the* place of connection for many in the overseas community, with many Vietnamese diasporic travelers coming to this city to eat, shop, travel, and visit family and friends. Diasporic travel narratives capitalize on this feeling of affection and connection, organizing content and imagery to centralize the kinds of pleasures that can be had in this southern city. If, as John Urry and Jason Larsen argue, the tourist gaze "implicates both the gazer and the gazee in an ongoing and systematic set of social and physical relations," the reportage film discussed in the next section delineates a particular way of seeing and touring Việt Nam, one that realizes the affective relationship between the viewed and the viewer through a variety of filmic techniques and marketing strategies.[11]

The Camera Eye/I and the Embodied Voice in Vietnamese Diasporic Travelogues

In 2000, the Vietnamese state issued 130,000 visas (out of 150,000) for Việt Kiều from the United States. In 2003, some 360,000 Việt Kiều from all around the world visited the country.[12] Since 2007, the state has allowed overseas Vietnamese to apply for five-year visas to lengthen their stay. As scholars have noted, Việt Kiều travel to the "homeland" remains strong, bundled as it is with pleasure, nostalgia, and obligation when returnees return to work, travel, and play.[13] Such numbers paint a vibrant portrait of Việt Nam as a major destination point for diasporic travelers; they also point to the extent to which the state works with the tourist industry to accommodate the large number of returnees.

The travel film (*phim du lịch*) taps into this market by providing a filmic keepsake of the homeland. Its market viability is aided by the fact that this genre is cheaply made. Vietnamese American DVD stores in Westminster and San Jose, California, are well stocked with travel films that promote tours to Việt Nam as well as to Hong Kong, Cambodia, Laos, and other countries. These films are priced low (at $3.99/per disc) and often sold in bulk (3 for $10.00). Their low value is also signaled by the way the films are often piled in bins for customers to peruse, while the latest installments of the better-selling Vietnamese American variety show *Paris by Night* are prominently displayed at the counter and hawked by the clerks.

The cheap quality of these travel films extends to the use of stock images of female Vietnamese models featured on their covers. Depending on the sights and landmarks the DVDs promise to cover, the women wear various fashions and reveal various body parts that signify different modes of modernity and tradition. To emphasize the former, for example, the models may dress in wedding gowns, bathing suits, and/or revealing eveningwear. To signify the latter, the women wear an *aó dài* (Việt Nam's national costume for women) or ethnic minority garb. As Hjorleifur Jonsson and Nora Taylor argue, these sartorial signs tell a particular story about Việt Nam and its "internal Orientalism," which privileges Kinh women and their modernity over ethnic minority women.[14] Both styles of dress, however, as Jonsson and Taylor underline, are important ways for the Vietnamese state to promote diversity and multiculturalism within its borders.[15] As displayed on the labels of diasporic travel films, femaleness operates as a sign equivalent to images of national foods and touristic sites. As much as the foods and locales signify a sense of place, local Vietnamese women feminize, eroticize, and at times, ethnicize the country.

Travel films are also produced on the cheap. Filmed with a digital camera, the quintessential travel film is shot by (most likely) one camera technician who appears to be charged with capturing the energy and beauty of the site in question. Accordingly, their shots follow a particular visual grammar that is marked by slow pans, tracking shots, and zooms. They draw on the bustling energy of the urban landscape to underscore the ways in which Sài Gòn is a burlesque theater. With an emphasis on this southern city as the site of nostalgic pleasure for its viewership, Sài Gòn serves as *the* grounds for carnal pleasures in many of these travelogues. The camera eye/I of the film is explicit in allowing the viewer access to the city streets and seedy nightlife, emphasizing all the while the pleasures of seeing, eating, and consuming in the city.

An example of this filmic style is found in the series *Việt Kiều Về Quê Ăn Chơi [Overseas Vietnamese Go Home and Party]*. Composed of 28 DVDs thus far, this travel series is produced by Vina Video and Golden Entertainment, located in Anaheim, California. As signaled by its title, the series hails the returnee in marketing the return as a carnivalesque experience. The words *ăn chơi* mean to indulge in a debauched life, while *Việt Kiều Về quê* is to return to the homeland. Conjoined, the two phrases signify how an unrepressed and wild Việt Nam beckons to the diasporic visitor. Given the branding of the series, the symmetry between the theme of the films (coming home to party) and the images of the women used to sell them is clear. Women's bodies are overtly sexualized and operate as a sign for the openness and seductiveness of the city. In particular, volume 2 of the series features well-known Vietnamese model/actress Minh Thư wearing a long red gown.

Her Photoshopped image on the back of the DVD is positioned in front of Sài Gòn's high-rises and the famous Rex Hotel, a sign of colonial decadence in a prewar version of the city. Known for her "long legs" (because she starred in a popular 2004 film called *Long-Legged Girls*), Minh Thư reclines in a white, silky dress. At the apex of her crossed legs is a picture of one of the most populous thoroughfares in the city, a bustling commercial street named after Emperor Nguyễn Huệ of the Tây Sơn dynasty.

Yet the racy images on the cover do not necessarily cohere with the content, since this installment discusses rather staidly the ways that Tết, or Lunar New Year, is traditionally celebrated in the country. Tết rituals are detailed and performed on screen, enacting for the viewer a pedagogical exercise of cultural instruction and transmission. In keeping with this directive, the camera eye is often placed at eye level and alongside the locals to portray how knowledgeable the camera eye, or the "I" of the narrative, may be. A sense of immediacy and intimacy is also connoted when the camera is placed on people's motorbikes, inside their homes, and in front of their altars; the camera eye/I is both a native to and a tourist in the country, someone to whom these sights may be both familiar and unfamiliar. In these ways, the series *Overseas Việt Kiều Go Home and Party* has an earnest undertone of documentation and takes seriously its label as *phóng sự đặc biệt,* or exclusive reportage, as part of its packaging.

Guided tours such as this film offer a cityscape full of sensorial possibility. For the postmodern visitor to Sài Gòn, one who experiences it on their computer, phone, or television screen, the city is also thoroughly modern, thrumming with activity and eventhood. In contrast to Western films that chronicle the country's tragic past and its poverty, the city's contemporaneity and modernity in travel films are highly valued. While noting the devastation of the war in postwar Sài Gòn, since street names have been changed by the communist government and buildings transformed by Asian and Western corporations in the post–Đổi Mới era, war and displacement are more affectively cued by the fact of the films' making and by the question of who is making them and consuming them. More than 40 years ago, the diaspora was formed in the aftermath of war across many continents. In viewing travel films today, which have been expressly produced to make diasporic memories out of the vestiges of war, the traveler finds herself experiencing (anew and again) the pasts and presents of Sài Gòn.

Finding Phong and the Visualization of "Mess" In Post-Socialist Việt Nam

Finding Phong begins in a diaristic fashion, starting with Phong talking (and crying) into the camera because she has decided to begin her transition. The opening provides a painful entrée into Phong's life as a trans subject living in Hà Nội. As her narrative reveals, Phong is transplanted in the city after having grown up in the rural area of Quãng Ngải. Poor and alone (at least, in the opening frames of the film), she has trepidations about her transition because of the lack of support she has received from her family, some of whom uphold her decision (like her father and sister) and some of whom do not understand it (like her mother and brother). Narratively speaking, *Finding Phong* is informed by Western tropes about self-discovery and the desire to remake the body; its telos builds on spectatorial anticipation, as we witness her preparation for the surgery that awaits her in Thailand and brace ourselves for the physical change that is destined to be a part of Phong's trajectory to "find" herself in ways that speak to the film's neoliberal framing.

In addition to the scenes of Phong's self-filming, on view through her perspective is a touristic experience of Thailand. A libidinal Thailand takes center stage in her filmic imagination; here, she seeks out those who appear like her on the streets of the capital and those who will care for her at the hospital where the surgery takes place. In Bangkok, she hangs out with *kathoeys,* who she understands to be "ladyboys," and while she identifies with them, she also tries to distinguish herself from them, announcing to them and the camera that she does not identify as *kathoey* but as a transsexual. Phong's interactions with nurses in Thailand are also key: a care-giving medical staff in Thailand performs a feminized emotional labor for her on screen that dovetails with Aren Aizura's work on the medical industry in Thailand. He notes how Thailand's tourism and marketing industries exploit cultural notions of Thai femininity and culture, invoking feminized care in advertising and appealing to patients wanting GRS. In this way, Aizura argues that Thailand is often figured, especially for non-Thai patients, as a "space of magic, exotic transformation and the fulfillment of (Western) desire,"[16] emphasizing that this fantasy is always "racialized and gendered, often iconized in images of the responsive Thai women and the *kathoey*."[17] Both the figure of the caring Thai woman and the *kathoey* as socially accepted figures in Thailand constitute part of *Finding Phong*'s cast and point to an underlying exoticizing discourse in the film, one that posits how Thailand functions as the ultimate site of transformation, authenticity, and ideal femininity. Besides the film's exoticism, *Finding Phong* also offers a sensationalistic "look" at the transgender / transitioning body, culminating as it does with Phong's surgery and the focus on her pre- and post-operation body throughout.

At the same time, the film's subject of Phong's life and the subject of medical tourism are fascinatingly cross-hatched by issues of class and access that underscore some of the film's more moving passages about Việt Nam's trans community more generally. I look especially to the joyful scenes with Phong's friends to counter some of the exploitative aspects of the film. These scenes visualize and archive Vietnamese queerness on screen in ways that are powerful and embody Martin F. Manalansan's recent formulations about the "messy" lives of queer subjects. In his ethnography of queer Filipino households in New York, he writes, "mess, clutter, and muddled entanglements are the 'stuff' of queerness, historical memory, aberrant desires and the archive."[18] Similarly, the "stuff" of queerness clutters *Finding Phong* and its mise-en-scène.

Even though the movie's predominant themes revolve around binaries—of the urban/rural, male/female, and Thailand/Việt Nam—the film's compositions are not so well cleaved. Many scenes show disarray and discombobulation, with the bodies of Phong and her friends haphazardly littering them and bisecting the scenes' compositional frames. Phong's friends and acquaintances, a coterie of straight, gay, lesbian, and trans youth, also provide insight to Phong's not-so-individualistic journey to selfhood, as they provide solace, guidance, and advice for her throughout the film. Such scenes of collectivity and community nonetheless evidence the precarity of living as a queer subject in a transphobic and homophobic Việt Nam because they are still minority subjects. Placed against the state's narratives about economic success and progress, *Finding Phong* dramatizes not only the neoliberal promise of transformation but also the lived realities of minority subjects who experience firsthand the limitations of a post-socialist regime.

Finding Phong eventually found its way to southern California, where it was warmly received by a small audience at the Viet Film Fest in 2016. The Q&A panel that followed the film screening included Lê Anh Phong herself, the producers (Gerald Herman and Nicole Pham), and activist Tran Phuc from Viet Rainbow of Orange County (VROC), an organization that advocates for LGBTQ inclusivity in the

Vietnamese American community and that co-sponsored the discussion. The film later won both a Spotlight Award and an Audience Favorite Award. While small in the number of participants, the bilingual discussion among us was important in opening a community space to talk about trans issues and identities and the violence that is too often committed against trans people of color in the U.S. Overall, the predominant sentiment of the discussion was rooted in a liberal tolerance and acceptance of gender and sexual difference in the Vietnamese American community. As witness to this discussion, I note, however, that the carving out of community spaces via Viet Film Fest demonstrates how this community is truly heterogeneous in terms of ability, class, age, political ideology, gender presentation, and sexual orientation, a recognition that bears repeating in order to combat community discourses redolent with the sentimentalization of Vietnamese American tradition and family.

Perhaps not surprisingly, *Finding Phong*'s message about difference and tolerance resonated with state officials in Việt Nam, who purportedly saw the film and legislated for the allowance of gender reassignment surgeries to take place in Việt Nam in 2015, the same year that *Finding Phong* came out. It was also this year that the state legalized same-sex marriages.[19] But even as such changes index an important transformation in the state's understanding of gender and sexuality, this mantle of progressivism must be understood alongside the country's dismal record of human rights abuses and the way it continues to crack down on expressions of dissent by ethnic minorities as well as political and religious activists.[20] For while the LGBTQ community faces discrimination and abuse at every level of Vietnamese society, the state's stand on such issues promotes the country as one with liberal and progressive views. Indeed, Việt Nam was cited in some news outlets as the first among Southeast Asian countries to adopt such policies.[21] That *Finding Phong* was well-received in Việt Nam and by the Vietnamese American community underscores the power of neoliberal narratives and markets in both locations. In such cases, the promise of change and renewal through consumption and travel is understood to be an ameliorative process for the Vietnamese self.

Authentic Selfhoods and Transnational Mobility

As demonstrated by the films examined here, the workings of *kỷ niệm* are embedded in the making and receiving of Vietnamese/diasporic films about travel. Framing tourism in this way animates the Vietnamese subject's desires for an authentic selfhood as well as for transnational mobility, where the act of "dreaming" is enacted across multiple sites and functions as a way to archive both the past and the present. This essay has looked at diasporic travel films like *Overseas Vietnamese Go Home and Party* and their nostalgic and gendered forms of address. Such travel narratives, however, exercise their own emotional logic and make narrative sense to the gendered diasporic subjects to whom these texts cater. Juxtaposed with this film text is my reading of the documentary *Finding Phong*. Herein the visualization of memory is most expressive when it archives contemporary Hà Nội as the location of queer precarity. In tandem, these small, minor works constitute a larger siting of how Vietnamese transnational memory has been produced in film.

Notes

1. Thu-Huong Nguyen and Brian King make this point. They also write, "Existing theories of travel consumer behavior are predominantly Eurocentric in their presuppositions, and we would contend, not readily applicable to the consumption patterns of Asian migration" (185). Thu-Huong Nguyen and Brian King, "Migrant Communities and Tourism Consumption: The Case of the Vietnamese in Australia," in *Tourism and Migration: New Relationships between Production and Consumption*, ed. Michael Hall (Boston, London, and Dordrecht: Kluwer Academic Publishers, 2002), 221–240.
2. See Lan Duong, "Diasporic Returns and the Making of Vietnamese American Ghost Films in Việt Nam," *MELUS* 41, no. 3 (2016): 153–170.
3. See article, "Vietnam's Creaking Education System Pushes Students Overseas," in *Daily Mail.com* (January 21, 2015), https://www.dailymail.co.uk/wires/afp/article-2919749/Vietnams-creaking-education-pushes-students-overseas.html; and Rosanna Xia, "Number of International Students in U.S. Colleges at an All-Time High, and California is their Top Destination," *Los Angeles Times* (November 25, 2016), http://www.latimes.com/local/lanow/la-me-study-abroad-students-20161124-story.html. On community colleges, see Tam Huu Do, "East Meets West: The Adaptation of Vietnamese International Students to California Community Colleges," *Journal of Southeast Asian American Education and Advancement*, 2.1 (2007), 1–29. On students who attend California State Fullerton, see Jennifer Nguyen, "CSUF Creates First Vietnamese Program," *Daily Titan* (February 26, 2013), https://dailytitan.com/2013/02/new-major/. On USC's acceptance rate of international

students more generally, see Jason Song, "USC Has Second Most Foreign Students in the Nation, Again," *Los Angeles Times* (November 16, 2015), http://www.latimes.com/local/lanow/la-me-study-abroad-students-20161124-story.html.

4. Svetlana Boym, *The Future of Nostalgia* (New York: Basic Books, 2001), 67.
5. Pierre Bourdieu, *Distinction: A Social Critique of the Judgment of Taste.* Translated by Richard Nice (London, Melbourne, and Henley: Routledge & Kegan Paul, 1984), 170.
6. Françoise Lionnet and Shu-Mei Shih, "Introduction: Thinking through the Minor, Transnationally," in *Minor Transnationalism,* ed. Shu-Mei Shih and Francoise Lionnet (Durham: Duke University Press, 2005), 7.
7. See Allison Griffiths, "'To the World the World We Show: Early Travelogues as Filmed Ethnography," *Film History* 11, no. 3 (1999): 282–307, and Panivong Norindr, "Enlisting Early Cinema in the Service of 'La Grande France,'" in *Early Cinema and the National,* ed. Richard Abel, Giorgio Bertellini, and Rob King (New Barnet: John Libbey Publishing Ltd., 2008), 109–117, for critiques of nonfiction films that worked as both travel narratives and as propaganda for French colonialism.
8. See John Boudreau, "Decades After Fleeing, Vietnamese American Filmmakers Return to a Changed Country," *San Jose Mercury News* (November 24, 2012), http://www.mercurynews.com/business/ci_21965098/decades-after-fleeing-vietnamese-american-filmmakers-return-changed.
9. Philip Taylor, "Introduction: An Overture to New Ethnographic Research on Connection and Disconnection in Vietnam," in *Connected and Disconnected in Viet Nam: Remaking Social Relations in a Post-Socialist Nation,* ed. Philip Taylor (Acton: The Australian National University, 2016), 4.
10. Ibid., 4.
11. John Urry and Jonas Larsen, *The Tourist Gaze 3.0.* (London: Sage, 2011), 17.
12. Mark Sidel, *Vietnamese-American Diaspora Philanthropy to Vietnam* (Report, Harvard University, 2007), 4.
13. As Thu-Huong Nguyen and Brian King argue, there are many motivations for *Việt Kiều* travel; religion, spirituality, family, and community are the reasons why returnees go to Vietnam (174). Nguyen and King, "Migrant Communities and Tourism Consumption: The Case of the Vietnamese in Australia," in *Tourism and Migration.*
14. Hjorleifur R. Jonsson and Nora A. Taylor, "National Colors: Ethnic Minorities in Vietnamese Public Imagery," in *Re-Orienting Fashion: The Globalization of Asian Dress,* eds. Sandra Niessen, Ann Marie Leshkowich, and Carla Jones (Oxford and New York: Berg, 2003), 175.

15. Hjorleifur R. Jonsson and Nora A. Taylor, "National Colors," 171.
16. Aren Aizura, "The Romance of the Amazing Scalpel: 'Race,' Labour and Affect in Thai Gender Reassignment Clinics," in *Queer Bangkok: Twenty-First-Century Markets, Media and Rights,* ed. Peter Jackson (Aberdeen, Hong Kong: Hong Kong University Press, 2011), 137.
17. Aren Aizura, "The Romance of the Amazing Scalpel," 138.
18. Martin F. Manalansan, "The 'Stuff' of Archives: Mess, Migration, and Queer Lives," *Radical History Review* 120 (2014), 94.
19. John Boudreau and Nguyen Dieu Tu Uyen, "Gay Weddings Planned as Vietnam Marriage Law Is Repealed," *Bloomberg* (January 7, 2015), http://www.bloomberg.com/news/articles/2015–01–07/gay-weddings-planned-as-vietnam-marriage-law-is-repealed.
20. Seth Mydans, "Activists Convicted in Việt Nam Crackdown on Dissent," *The New York Times* (January 9, 2013), http://www.nytimes.com/2013/01/10/world/asia/activists-convicted-in-Việt Nam-crackdown-on-dissent.html.
21. Thomas Maresca, "Việt Nam: Flawed on Human Rights, but a Leader in Gay Rights," *The Atlantic* (April 30, 2013), https://www.theatlantic.com/international/archive/2013/04/Việt Nam-flawed-on-human-rights-but-a-leader-in-gay-rights/275413/.

Chapter 21

Photographs from Live and Online Performances

Philip Huang

In his early twenties, Philip Huang was marked as the "next big thing" in Asian American fiction. This early critical success, its highs and lows, led him to recognize the dependency artists have on institutions [such as publishers, foundations, and arts venues].

"I just got sick of this mentality artists had," explains Huang. "They were always only receiving resources, and institutions were always only giving resources. The Home Theater Festival is about putting an idea into practice, but also, it's to change people's mindset. No, we're self-generative. We create opportunities. We can do it ourselves. We can make a name for ourselves. We can do everything we want right now with nothing extra added."

This ethos led him to start, in 2011, the Dana Street Theater, a queer performance space based out of the bedroom of his rent-controlled Berkeley apartment. Shortly thereafter, Huang became one of the founders of the Home Theater Festival, an international event that, with just a website and the willing participation of friends and strangers, has taken place in over 30 countries and cities across the globe.

An agent provocateur, Huang's work has been deemed agit-prop, conceptual, comedic, and counter-protest. Huang subscribes to the philosophy that anything can be a performance as long as you have the means to document it.

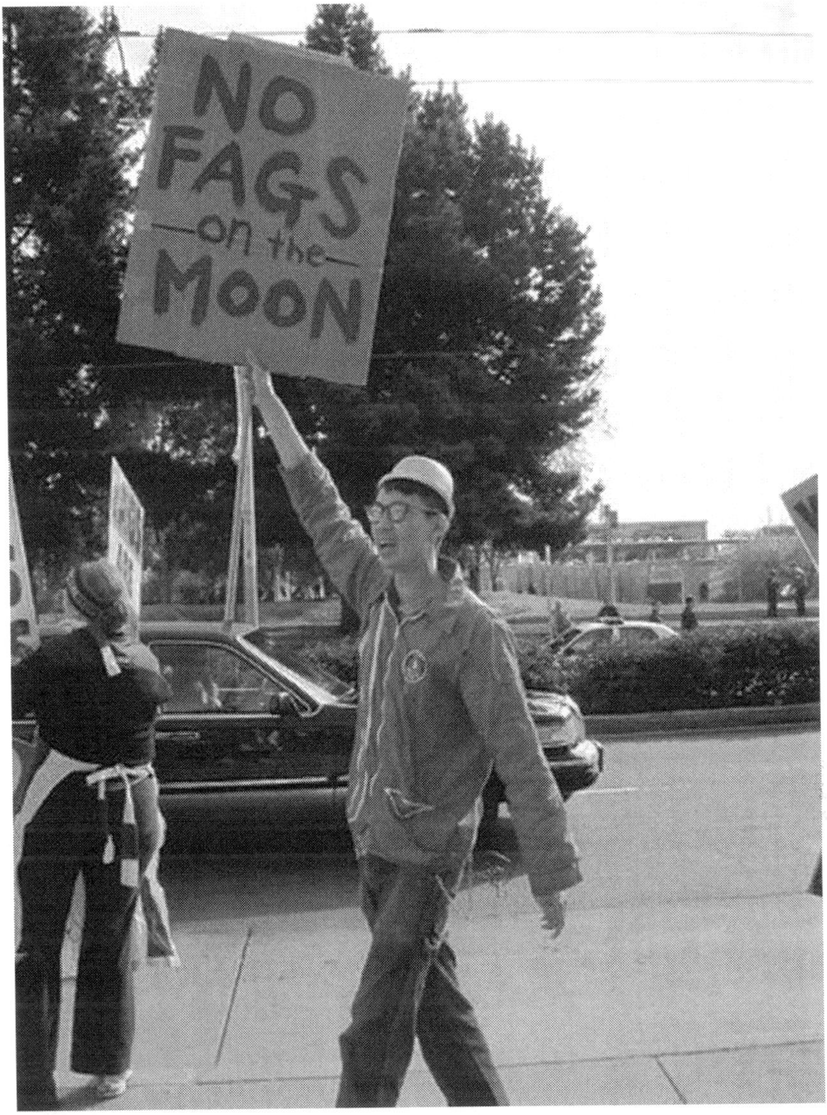

Photo from "The Lunar Homosexual Agenda" [2010 counter-protest of Westboro Church, San Francisco, CA]. Image by Philip Huang.

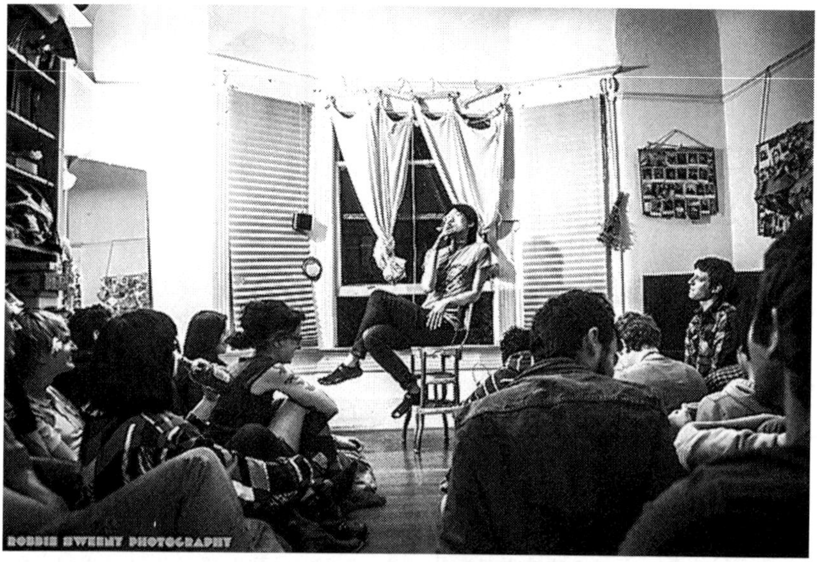

"Home Theater Festival" (2011) (Berkeley, CA). Image by Philip Huang.

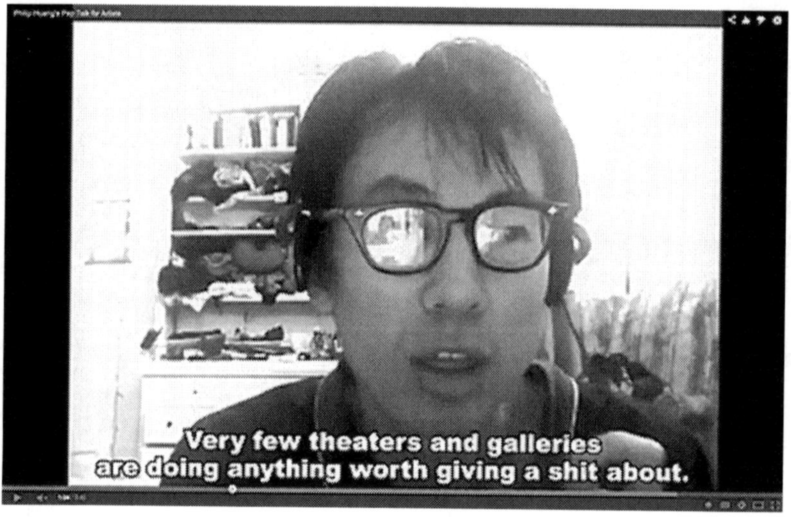

Screenshot from "Philip Huang's Pep Talk for Artists." Subtitle reads: "Very few theaters and galleries are doing anything worth giving a shit about." Image by Philip Huang.

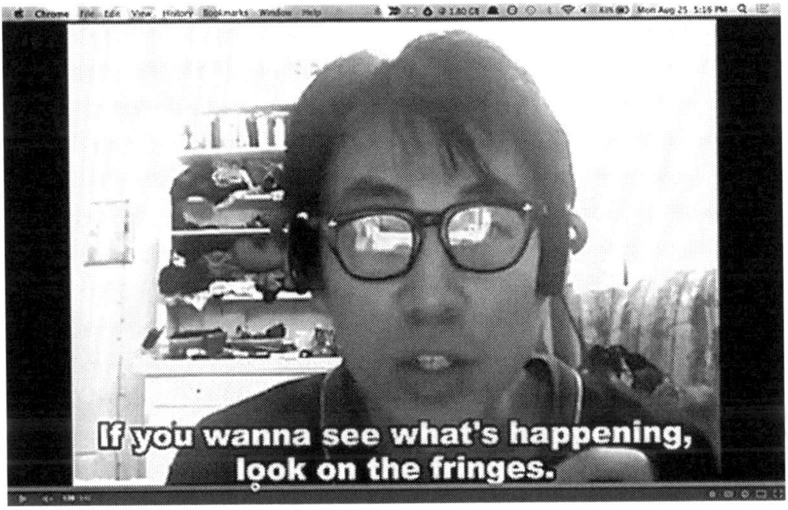

Screenshot from "Philip Huang's Pep Talk for Artists." Subtitle reads: "If you wanna see what's happening, look on the fringes." Image by Philip Huang.

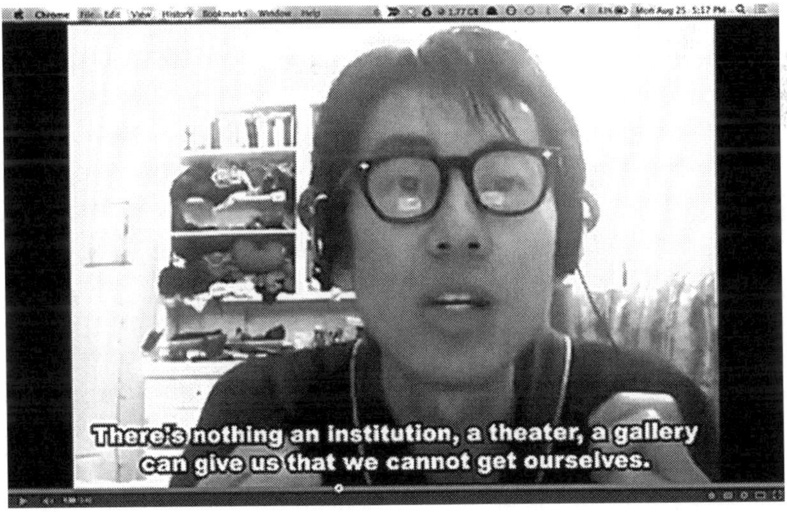

Screenshot from "Philip Huang's Pep Talk for Artists." Subtitle reads: "There's nothing an institution, a theater, a gallery can give us that we cannot get ourselves." Image by Philip Huang.

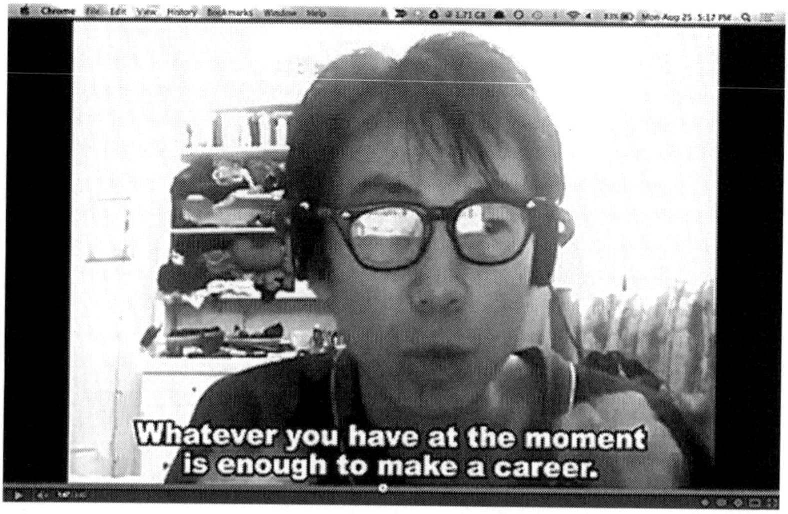

Screenshot from "Philip Huang's Pep Talk for Artists." Subtitle reads: "Whatever you have at the moment is enough to make a career." Image by Philip Huang.

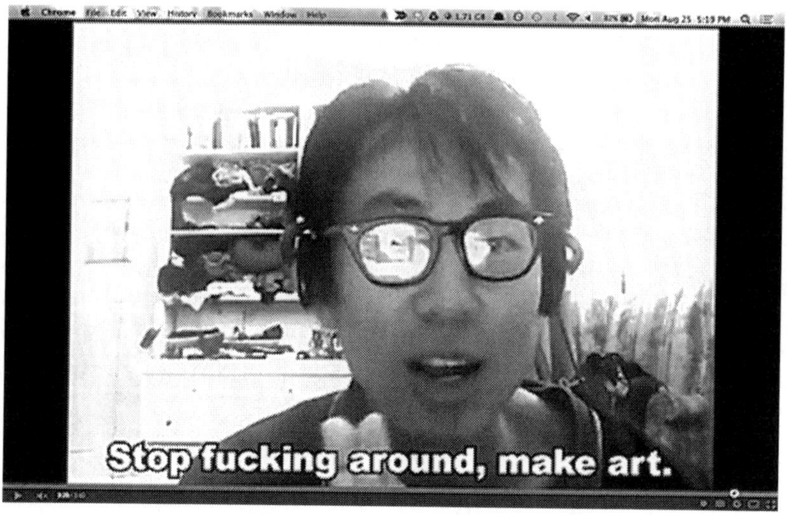

Screenshot from "Philip Huang's Pep Talk for Artists." Subtitle reads: "Stop fucking around, make art." Image by Philip Huang.

Chapter 22

Abstraction 2

Television Sitcom from DentalOptics

Karen Tei Yamashita

Episode #21: "Blockbusters"

Directed by: Mako

Summary

Story A: Heco and Okada's covert Civil Rights mission is to subvert a neighborhood real estate blockbusting scheme.

Subplot B: Heco and Okada have posed for an Asian American male nude calendar, possibly damaging their father Warren's chances for local re-election.

Subplot C: Lucy San Pablo, office administrator of DentalOptics, is fed up with the work and threatens to quit.

Characters

HECO HAMADA:	*Twin to the left. Dentist at DentalOptics and secret agent for Civil Rights. Characteristics: Pragmatic and logical, while artistic. Plays taiko and shakuhachi. Abstract painter. Verbally adept, persuasive, with wit and humor. Excels in team sports (baseball, basketball, volleyball, soccer). Drives a 400 HP Twin Turbo Supra. Interest in archeology and musicology. Although possessing imperfect language skills, charm makes him readily understood. Taekwondo and capoeira.*

OKADA HAMADA:	*Twin to the right. Optometrist at DentalOptics and secret agent for Civil Rights. Characteristics: Highly imaginative and a math genius. Plays the saxophone and keyboards. Practices sumi-e and calligraphy. Introspective, intuitive, skilled psychoanalyst. In sports, excels as an individualist (track and field, diving, archery, scuba, weightlifting). Drives a Mazda RX7. Interested in geography, ecology, and political economics. Speaks multiple languages. Judo and karate.*
NOBUKO HAMADA:	*Mother and avid community activist, energetic but overextended*
WARREN HAMADA:	*Father and activist in local politics*
LUCY SAN PABLO:	*Office administrator for DentalOptics, overqualified and extremely efficient*
AGENT CHANG:	*Civil Rights agent*
AGENT ENG:	*Civil Rights agent*
NANCY KIM:	*Reporter for radical left radio and newsprint; astute and passionate*

Time

Circa 1990s

Place

Gardena, California

<u>*CAST LIST*</u>

HECO HAMADA . . . . MICHAEL HAYAKAWA
OKADA HAMADA . . . . DAVID SHIGETA
NOBUKO HAMADA . . . . MARY KWAN
WARREN HAMADA . . . . JAMES SOO
LUCY SAN PABLO . . . . BEA SALONGA
AGENT CHANG . . . . ROBERT SHIMODA
AGENT ENG . . . . LINDA IWAMOTO
NANCY KIM . . . . LISA RHEE

WITH CAMEO APPEARANCES BY:

TRICIA TOYOTA, CONNIE CHUNG, KRISTI YAMAGUCHI, AMY TAN, MARGARET CHO, PAT MORITA, GEORGE TAKEI, JUDGE LANCE ITO, ANGELA OH, DAVID CARRADINE, AND SENATOR DANIEL INOUYE

STATION ID w/upcoming shows (1 min)

SHOW INTRO W/TITLES (1 min)

FADE IN:

1 EXT. GARDENA NEIGHBORHOOD—DAY

Pan Japanese American aspects of the neighborhood (Japanese gardens with perfect dichondra lawns and lollipop bushes, local restaurants, shops, cultural centers, Buddhist temples, and Baptist churches). Follow red RX7 Mazda into mini-mall parking lot in front of offices of DentalOptics.

Flashbacks and photo albums; inserts of 1960s Asian America and the twins growing up.

Sound of Asian American jazz fusion (oxymoron) and shakuhachi.

V.O.

In the mid-sixties, two healthy twin baby boys were born to a sansei couple in Gardena, California. The couple—known Asian American movement radicals—had made a conscientious decision to live and work in the community and chose Gardena, a small working-class city on the greater metropolitan outskirts of L.A. where an Asian American enclave continued to thrive. With faith in the power of the people, they raised and educated their boys to epitomize mentally and physically the very perfection of Asian America. Indeed, the two boys grew to be men unlike any others—mentally astute, sensitive, visionary, politically active, artistic, and physically exquisite. The only imperfection—a word denied by the

> boys and their parents—was the inconvenience of being bound to each other near the hip by a thick, fleshy ligament. Since words like "Oriental" and "Siam" were considered passé, the boys were heroically referred to as "the Asian American duo."

HECO AND OKADA emerge from sports car.

Sound of taiko.

DISSOLVE TO:

2 INT. DENTALOPTICS OFFICE—DAY

Waiting room filled with mostly Asian American patients reading the *Rafu-Shimpo, Amerasia Journal,* and assorted iconic Asian American texts. Corner game of goh. Children playing with transformers, occasionally watching video of *Chan Is Missing.*

HECO AND OKADA enter, greet patients.

LUCY SAN PABLO hands twins patient files.

Pan wall art, sumi-e and oil abstracts, and diplomas: Dental degree from USC and Optics degree from UCLA.

<u>TEASER</u> (3 min)

CUT TO:

3 INT. INNER DENTALOPTICS OFFICES—DAY

AGENT CHANG and AGENT ENG are prepped in dental and optician's chairs. CHANG is wearing a bib.

HECO AND OKADA enter in white coats.

AGENT ENG hands OKADA a small envelope. OKADA removes microfilm and places it in optics lens, enlarging it on dark wall

AGENT CHANG

Your mission, should yo—

HECO jams the dental mirror into CHANG's mouth, where he carefully scrutinizes reflected SLIDE IMAGES: the offices of Freedom Real Estate Enterprises, face of some suited white guy, tract of houses under construction, portrait photo of an African American family.

AGENT ENG

Have a look. Find out what they're up to.

OKADA switches to the eye chart's big E.

HECO

(moving his drill into CHANG's back molar)

You need to lay off the soda and sweets.

AGENT CHANG

(breaks away and wipes his mouth on the bib)

See if you can put your right and left brains together.

CUT TO:

COMMERCIAL BREAK: *Mazda* (RX7) (1 min)

ACT ONE (7 min)

FADE IN:

4 INT. DENTALOPTICS OFFICES—DAY

WARREN storms into office with a glossy calendar: *The Asian American Male Calendar 19—.*

WARREN HAMADA

What's this? Since when did you guys become pin-ups?

OKADA

When did that come out? It's not even December.

HECO

Not bad. I'm the one who's buffer. Check out the pecs!

OKADA

We're August.

WARREN

Are you crazy? What about my conservative constituency?

OKADA

How many are they?

Enter NOBUKO HAMADA in a big rush and loaded down with stuff.

NOBUKO HAMADA

I brought you obento lunch.
(hands them boxes of sushi, then notices calendar)
How cute. Reminds me of you guys as babies with your little thingies sticking out. Oh, I've gotta go. This morning was the Pioneer Project. Afternoon is the Manzanar committee.

WARREN

(groans) You know I could use some help on my committee to re-elect me.

NOBUKO dashes away.

CUT TO:

5 EXT. WHITE RESIDENTIAL NEIGHBORHOOD—DAY

HECO AND OKADA in front of house with Freedom Real Estate Enterprise "**SOLD**" sign.

OKADA

House is vacant.

HECO

Sale was by white owner directly to real estate. I checked out the status. Escrow initiated by real estate with family named Dandridge.

OKADA

Dandridges are African American.

(TWINS step into car.)

HECO

(looking out of car)

Integrating the neighborhood.

OKADA

(looking at rearview mirror)

I think we're being followed.

HECO steps on the gas, and the RX7 disappears in smoke.

FADE TO:

6 INT. DENTALOPTICS OFFICES—DAY

LUCY SAN PABLO is gathering her belongings.

HECO

You can't quit.

OKADA

We can't survive without you. You do everything.

LUCY

Right. I do everything. From scheduling to accounting, from bibbing down to adjusting nose pads. Now you want me to write a grant? For what?

HECO

We've bought the space next door. We're starting a nonprofit youth center.

OKADA

We thought you wanted to do more intelligent work. Expand your horizons.

HECO

We want a ping pong table.

LUCY

That's it.

(stomps off)

OKADA

Maybe if I ask her to marry me.

CUT TO:

COMMERCIAL BREAK: *7/11* (smiling Korean American store owners) (1 min)

ACT TWO (8 min)

DISSOLVE IN:

7 EXT. SUBURBAN HOUSING TRACT IN CONSTRUCTION—DAY

HECO AND OKADA walking around construction site of tract homes with sign: Freedom Enterprises.

HECO

It's elementary.

OKADA

One-drop rule.

HECO

Just one African American family in an all-white neighborhood to start a selling frenzy.

OKADA

(adopts some kind of white accent)

Your lily-white neighborhood is "turning." Have you thought about moving to the Valley?

HECO

White flight. They get sales coming—

OKADA

And going.

FADE TO:

8 INT. DENTALOPTICS OFFICES—DAY

HECO AND OKADA enter offices and find everything in disarray.

OKADA

And I loved Lucy.

WARREN enters.

WARREN

What a mess. You were taking advantage of Lucy. But now she's working for my re-election campaign.

DISSOLVE TO:

9 INT. APARTMENT OF AFRICAN AMERICAN FAMILY—EVENING

HECO AND OKADA are sitting in the living room with the DANDRIDGES, their children running around in the background.

MR. DANDRIDGE

The price is reasonable.

MRS. DANDRIDGE

They offered it like this: a pretty little starter house in a safe neighborhood

MR. DANDRIDGE

With a good school just blocks away.

MRS. DANDRIDGE

We're renting now. It would be a dream come true.

CUT TO:

10 EXT. OUTSIDE APARTMENT OF AFRICAN AMERICAN FAMILY—EVENING

HECO AND OKADA walk away from the apartment to street. Two masked kids, ATTACKER ONE and ATTACKER TWO, emerge in the dark and attack them. The twins act swiftly with combined taekwondo-capoeira-karate moves.

HECO

(grabbing ATTACKER 1)

Who are you?

ATTACKER ONE

A gangsta.

OKADA

(sitting on ATTACKER 2)

What?

ATTACKER TWO

Stay outta our hood.

HECO AND OKADA pull off attackers' masks to reveal white faces.

HECO

What do you call this?

OKADA

Appropriation? Inauthenticity? Parody? Stereotyping? Blackface? Cultural imperialism? Minstrelism? Cross-dressing? Exploitation? Reverse passing? Racial drag? Slumming it?

HECO

(to Attackers)

You work for Freedom.

ATTACKER ONE

Yeah, you could say that.

OKADA

Are you a neo-Nazi?

ATTACKER TWO

What's a neo-Nazi?

FADE TO:

11 INT. HAMADA LIVING ROOM—EVENING

WARREN

It's called blockbusting. Tactic is as old as the John Birchers.

NOBUKO

I'm on it. I'll start a committee.

WARREN

Okay, saved. Your mother's on it. (sighs) Lucy is driving me crazy. She's running my campaign like a doctor's office.

OKADA

How *does* one run a doctor's office?

CUT TO:

COMMERCIAL BREAK: *United Colors of Benetton* (cute multicultural kids) (1 min)

ACT THREE (4 min)

DISSOLVE IN:

12 INT. NEIGHBORHOOD MEETING—DAY

NOBUKU and DANDRIDGE FAMILY and COMMUNITY MEMBERS gathered, socializing, organizing, making placards.

NOBUKO

Eight o'clock sharp in front of Freedom Real Estate.

DISSOLVE TO:

13 EXT. FREEDOM REAL ESTATE ENTERPRISES—NEXT DAY

NEIGHBORHOOD COMMITTEE TO BUST BLOCKBUSTING (NCBB) are picketing and organizing cheers.

NANCY KIM

(with mic in front of camera)

Freedom Real Estate refuses to make any comments. However, members of the NCBB, short for Neighborhood Committee to Bust Blockbusting, have issued a strong statement against Freedom's purported tactics of discrimination and racism.

FADE TO:

14 INT. HAMADA FAMILY KITCHEN—LATER

WARREN

(with copy of *The Asian American Male Calendar*)

This thing is selling like hotcakes. Nisei Vets even bought it. (looks through the calendar) What the heck? The second edition is endorsing my re-election.

NOBUKO

Hmmm. This endorsement suggests you are *in* the calendar.

WARREN scrutinizes the calendar cover.

NOBUKO (cont'd)

You know, I think you could use a smart political organizer like me.

FADE TO:

15 INT. DENTALOPTICS OFFICES—DAY

HECO AND OKADA return to a clean and efficiently run office. LUCY is busy behind the desk.

LUCY

Politics is not my thing.

OKADA

I know how you feel. I crave a life of quiet contemplation.

HECO

Are you kidding?

(Hands LUCY the grant application.)

HECO (cont'd.)

Don't forget the ping pong table.

CREDITS (1 min)

While credits roll, in the background, HECO plays the shakuhachi, and OKADA plays the saxophone.

<u>END</u>

FADE OUT

CUT TO:

COMMERCIAL BREAK: *Yamaha* (Hiroshima Band playing) (1 min)

Station ID (1 min)

Chapter 23

Generations Within

Los Angeles 1992 and South Korean 8008

Yong Soon Min

On two shores across the Pacific, three historic events are featured in a comparative consideration that also imbricates their generational aspects. Two of these events took place in South Korea and one in the United States. Koreans, of course, are the central characters of the events that happened in South Korea, but what happened in Los Angeles in 1992 was a complex, layered event. I put all three events in relationship with one another in this essay.

In Korea (this term, for the sake of brevity, will represent South Korea, officially known as the Republic of Korea), the two events were initiated by "demos," a shorthand term that, for Koreans, stood for demonstrations or civilian actions. The first one happened in mid-May 1980 in a city in the south of Korea. The other one started in Seoul in May 2008 and lasted through June. The more recent of the two, commonly known as the Candlelight Vigils, the Candlelight Girls Protest, or the Mad Cow Protests, was in general a peaceful civil action that introduced a radically distinct protest population to Korea: young girls and housewives. It also highlighted the continued central role of *netizens,* a term that Koreans gave to the critical internet-using citizens after the 2002 election of Roh Moo-hyun as president.

On our California shores, the event started on April 29, 1992, and has continued to traumatize diasporic Koreans to this day. That event has been known by many different names, but many Koreans simply refer to the tragedy as the "L.A. riots."

Soldiers played crucial, distinctively contrasting roles in the two cities. The first group were in Gwangju, Korea, to violently fight for law and order in the name of their leader; the second were in Los Angeles, where they worked to restore order and peace after the conflagrations and the rioting. In Gwangju, the momentous event took place in 1980 and is popularly known as the Gwangju Uprising and Massacre. It is known officially as the Gwangju Democratization Movement, *o-il-pal* (오일팔), or 5.18, the first day of the uprising in May.

A decade later, in 1992, the Los Angeles calamity took place and has been termed the multicultural riots. To Koreans in America who had a significant role in the riots, this event is known as *sa-i-gu* (사이구),[1] a literal translation of the number 4.29 in the Korean language, meaning April 29.

These watershed events offer a multivalent opportunity to explore the experiences of generations of Koreans on both sides of the Pacific, both in Los Angeles (and by extension the U.S.) and in Korea. In order to probe these historic events, a discussion of my own identity in terms of generations may provide an anchored perspective with which to examine and question the multifaceted histories that unfold. As an immigrant in the U.S., I am part of the so-called 1.5 generation of Korean Americans—born in Korea but raised in the U.S. As such, I exist in the classic interstitial in-between-ness, straddling my identity as both an American and a Korean. But since I immigrated to the U.S. in 1960, at the age of seven, I also identify myself very much as an American of the Baby Boom Generation, born following World War II, commonly dated from 1946 to 1964 and in a period marked by a dramatic increase in birth rates. A prominent concept for this generation was the American Dream, facilitated by things like the GI Bill of Rights, which led to college education for many and, with it, the growth of middle-class families with housing in the suburbs.

In the early 1960s, the Cold War tensions of the Cuban Missile Crisis scared us. By the mid-1960s, the advent of color TV brought the world into our living rooms, including the traumatically vivid reports from the war in Vietnam. Conflicts flared on the home front that eventually brought that war to an end in 1975. At the same time, other cultural touchstones of our generation in the 1960s and the 1970s were the growth of a civil rights movement, which inspired the Third World movement along with the women's and gay liberation movements. In the 1980s, the conservative "payback" of Reaganomics reigned supreme, with major cuts in civil rights bills and the worst recession since the

1930s. Boomers currently face the struggle of globalized economic issues related to debt and the shortage of retirement funds. Nevertheless, it can be said that the boomers' rebellious, anti-establishment attitudes have been carried on into the present, as they age. Where at first, they stood in stark contrast to a previously more deferential society, they now contrast again with the more recent late twentieth-century apathy.

As a boomer, I remember singing "California Dreaming" as part of the "hippie" movement back in the late 1960s and the 1970s. The luxury to be romantic and muse about the weather was far from the realities of Korea during that period, a country that was still struggling to recover from the Korean War and build a future under authoritarian rule. The recent history of Korea, since the turn of the twentieth century, seems more accelerated and compressed with time, rendering it nearly impossible to compose a complete picture with confidence. It may be more in tune with a series of snapshots. Distinctions between generations prevail over continuities . . . One such generation that stands out in Korea is the 386 (삼팔육) generation, which shares a general progressive outlook with the boomers in the States. The name of this generation was coined in the 1990s, when "the 386 model" referred to the newest PC (personal computer) at the time. In reference to the 386 generation, the "3" stands for 30-something, the age they were at the time; "8" stands for the '80s, when they were in college; and "6" stands for the '60s, when this generation was born.

Playing with numbers continues to fascinate Koreans, and "8008" also tells a story that is central to my study of generations. In this case, the "80" stands for 1980, which represents the Gwangju Democratization Movement, while the latter half, "08," refers to the Candlelight Vigil, or Mad Cow Protests, which took place in 2008. Nearly thirty years apart, both events started in the month of May. The Candlelight Vigil lasted two months, growing into a huge protest of thousands of Seoulites. This was a radically different type of gathering compared to the Gwangju event. The Candlelight Vigil signaled the embodiment of a new generation, distinguishing itself from the 386 generation.

❖❖❖

> "They broke glass table tops, carried off ensembles, capped off gunshots. I could see it all from my vantage point. . . . It was incredible. I told [my wife] to close up [her clothing] shop and go home. 'Call the police and tell them we are trapped.' We hid

for three hours while people laughed and stole and rioted. That whole time, I kept thinking the police were coming." – Jay Lee, owner of a furniture store on Florence and Normandie in Los Angeles.[2]

"Around 7 p.m. [of April 29], we started to get phone calls. Someone saying that "I'm at such and such intersection, a crowd of black people are gathering in the front of my store, and they seem threatening. What would be the best thing to do?" Before long, we thought, 'Let's just go live with the phone calls.' Because we started receiving too many phone calls. And because, for the Korean people listening to the broadcast, we needed to let them know what was happening. So we put callers on live, so they could say, 'Something is happening. Be careful, be careful.'"– Richard Choi, radio newscaster for Radio Korea.[3]

Abandoned by the city police, led by Police Chief Darryl Gates, who was accused of having a "let Koreatown burn" attitude,[4] Koreans who were able and had the means defended their stores. These were the Korean men, referred to by some as vigilantes, up on the rooftops of

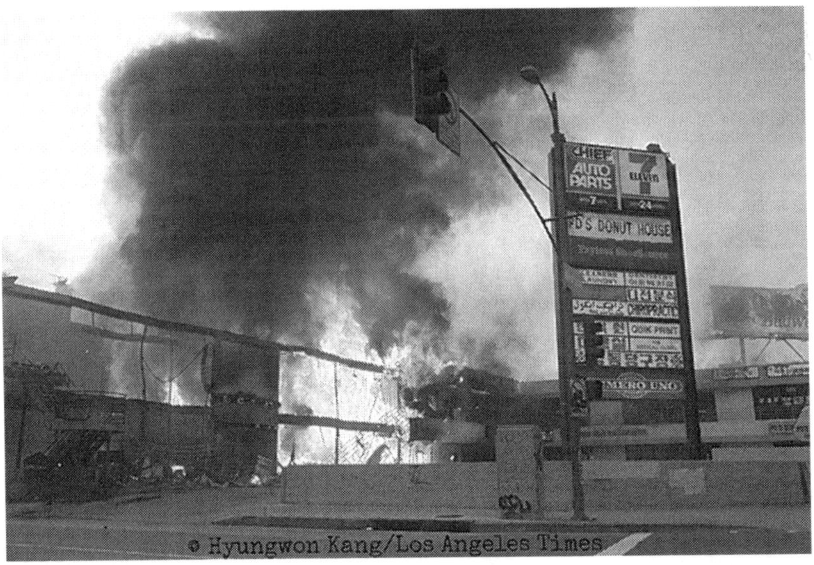

A strip mall burning on Western Avenue and Sixth Street in Koreatown. Photo by Hyungwon Kang.

the stores with guns and rifles, ready to shoot at the trespassers. Looting was widespread as the poor suddenly saw a way to help "redistribute the wealth." Surprisingly, many Latinos who had worked in relative harmony with the Koreans in the past constituted the majority of the looters, breaking into stores to take whatever they could. Destruction and damage were widespread in certain areas of Los Angeles that were primarily populated by African Americans, Latinos, and Korean Americans. The Korean toll was five killed, 2,100 businesses burned, and more than $350 million in damage—or nearly half the city's total from the riots.[5]

> "On 30 April 1992, a satellite operated by the National Oceanic and Atmospheric Administration began transmitting an image of an unusual heat source emanating from Southern California. This heat source spanned nearly thirty-three square miles and was as hot as the Mount Pinatubo eruption of 1991 in the Philippines. When researchers processed the image, they realized that what they were looking at was a picture from outer space of the second day of the Los Angeles riots. The heat source was attributed to the fact that an average of three new fires were started each minute during the three hours preceding the image."[6]

At the time of the L.A. conflagration, I had reached the end of an art residence in Maine, the farthest from California one could be in the continental U.S. I happened to catch the news coverage on TV: long aerial shots of L.A. up in flames. I heard that it had hit southern Los Angeles and Koreatown specifically, but couldn't make much sense of it. I returned to New York City the next night; it was eerily quiet, with a peculiar stillness everywhere. In L.A., the rage against the acquittal of four LAPD officers accused in the beating of African American motorist Rodney King had spread like lightning, quickly becoming a citywide riot. I was relieved that New York City was alarmed enough by the news from Los Angeles to take cautionary steps the next day; many businesses closed at midday to let off their workers early.

In an operation code-named "Operation Garden Plot," troops were called in to Los Angeles on April 30. Governor Pete Wilson had declared a state of emergency for all of L.A. County at 12:05 a.m. He dispatched a force of 2,500 soldiers from Fort Ord (located near Monterey), 1,500 Marines from Camp Pendleton, and about 8,000 federal troops from the National Guard under the command of General Marvin L. Covault.

The soldiers initially battled with gangs and looters. But, for the rest of their stay until the end of May, they had a peaceful role as they guarded firefighters and served on patrols mostly in the South Los Angeles area. Angelenos stayed home, watching on TV with the rest of the country, as Mayor Tom Bradley had declared a dusk-to-dawn curfew for the South Central area as well as closing schools and businesses. That four-day Los Angeles curfew brought to mind the midnight-to-4-a.m. curfews that I feared violating when I first visited Korea in 1979 and that had been in place for 36 years, mostly during the Park Chung Hee presidency. It was on that same trip that I had had to observe the monthly air raid drills that were also enforced during Park's administration.

While still in New York City, I was inspired by the Korean inclination to commemorate historic events by their dates to create a six-part photo series called "Defining Moments." In it, I chose the significant dates of Korean history for their connection with the personal, an embodiment of the personal-is-the-political, as it were. The series begins with an image of my naked body in the negative. A spiral originates from the belly button and is inscribed with significant dates. Additionally, the word "HEARTLAND" appears written on my chest, with "OCCUPIED" and "TERRITORY" written on my arms. Photographic images that follow in the series are those of my face and chest overlaid with journalistic images relevant to each date. The first date, "1953," represents the year the Korean War ended, illustrated by a picture of soldiers crossing rice paddies; 1953 also happens to be the year of my birth.

For the next date, *sa-i-gu* or April 19 (1960), I chose an aerial scene representing a riot initiated by students that led to the overthrow of the autocratic President Syngman Rhee. The end of the Rhee administration by the end of that year in effect triggered my family's emigration. The third date, May 19, stands for the Gwangju Uprising; it also represents my awakening of consciousness concerning the struggles for democracy in Korea. The fourth date is April 29 (4/29), which also happens to be my birthday. I chose to represent *sa-i-gu* with the front page of the *Korea Times* English weekend edition that depicted the cleanup effort in Koreatown. I wanted to emphasize that Koreans immediately rallied to heal their community and the city beyond.

On Saturday, May 2, only four days after the start of the riot, even before order in the city was completely restored, the Korean community held a march in Koreatown to call attention to their plight. Despite the fact that their businesses were targets of arsonists and looters, an estimated 30,000 people—some wearing white headbands and carrying brooms and plastic garbage bags—chanted "Peace," while many younger people carried signs demanding justice for Rodney King.[7] Many Koreans were frustrated by media misrepresentation of the shop owners only as either victims or vigilantes in the tragedy. Due to the lack of effective spokespeople, or interracial outreach, Koreans had little means of communication and no political allies.

The series ends with an image of *Baekdusan* overlaid with the word "HEARTLAND." *Baekdusan* is a beautiful volcanic mountain with a crater lake that straddles North Korea and China and represents an origin myth for Koreans. This territory has come to symbolize for many Koreans, North and South alike, the reunification of the peninsula.

When I moved to L.A. in 1993 to assume my faculty position at UC Irvine, I was ill prepared for and overwhelmed by the emotional onslaught. I started meeting Korean students who were traumatized by the riots. These students were the daughters and sons of Korean

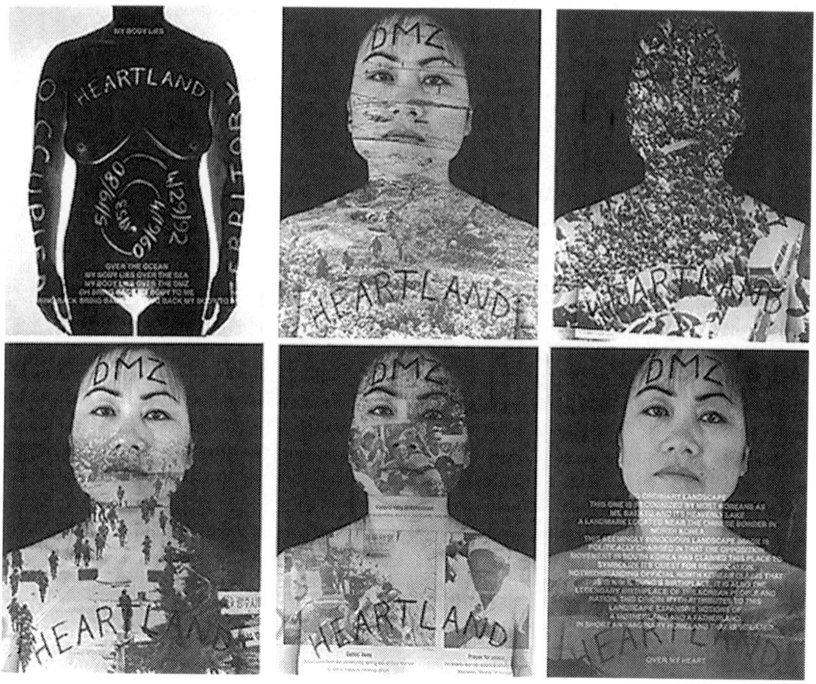

"Defining Moments" (1992). Photo by Yong Soon Min.

shop owners. For the most part, they were second- and 1.5-generation Koreans who came to see me during office hours; many broke down in tears as they spoke of the recent events. It was hard for me to gauge their class or economic status because Koreans are fairly adept at overriding their hardships in order to send their kids to school. Some had trouble making ends meet. Many students had to work for their parents while also going to school. Most talked of being alienated from their parents, who were too busy to pay them much attention. Many of these students felt guilty for feeling superior to parents who couldn't speak English very well; not surprisingly, most also experienced difficulty talking with their parents. Parents seemed to expect good grades from their children, who were often experiencing challenges that they couldn't discuss with them. If anything, students were, at best, cynical about the American Dream that their parents unquestionably subscribed to. Some joined gangs or groups that resembled gangs. They felt torn by the racial conflicts they found themselves in and were critical of their parents, who seemed harsh to them. Then *sa-i-gu* happened, and like a wake-up call, the students suddenly had their consciousness raised about their parents' lives and experiences.

Young Chung, an undergraduate student at the time of the L.A. riots, told me about his father's near-death experience on April 29.[8] His father was, like many shop owners, an immigrant who came to the U.S. in the 1980s. He worked in a half grocery store/half indoor swap meet, at 47th and Broadway. On the first day of *sa-i-gu*, his father sent Young's mother, and sister and the other workers home. He remained upstairs with a weapon to protect the business, and someone broke in and shot him five times in the stomach. He crawled downstairs and managed to find someone who called 9-1-1. Although no ambulance came, he managed to get into the back seat of a police car and was rushed to a nearby hospital.

Miraculously, he survived, but it took him two years to fully recuperate. In the meantime, he filed for bankruptcy. Like so many other Korean shopkeepers, he had no insurance on the store; ultimately, he was forced to sell their family home. He eventually opened another market in a poor part of town; as before, he resumed working over twelve hours per day, every day of the week.

Young has an older brother who, as a gang member, committed a serious felony crime and was incarcerated in 1993. Young told me that he personally suffered from guilt at having been spared so much difficulty, and that he also felt lucky to be able to stay in school in spite of all the hardships his family had gone through. His parents were happy that he had finished school and were especially proud that he is the first in the family to get a graduate degree. Education was the best gift Young could give his parents. The same dynamic exists between parents and children in Korea.

8008

In parallel with Los Angeles, violence also erupted in the city of Gwangju at the hands of Korean soldiers in May 1980. This event was precipitated by Chun Doo Hwan's maneuvering to a position of power after the assassination of the previous president, Park Chung Hee, by an officer of the National Intelligence Service, the Korean version of the CIA. Opposition raged in many Korean cities during May, protesting this move as well as Chun's imposition of martial law. In reaction to the protests, Chun sent soldiers to these cities to quell the unrest. In Gwangju, however, soldiers arrived with particularly malevolent force. From May 18 through May 21, battles were waged in Gwangju, initially between students and the soldiers, but the brutal actions of the soldiers brought enraged residents of the city on to the streets. Eventually, troops retreated to the suburbs to wait for reinforcements and prevented communication with the outside world. Contact with the Korean press was curtailed, and the only news that made it out was from foreign individuals and others who managed to escape.

In the interim, the citizens took control of the city and secured what munitions were available. On May 27th, special air force commandos and 20,000 martial law troops joined the waiting soldiers and crushed the civil militias. Many of the commandos were part of the forces that had had fierce battle experience under Chun Doo Hwan during the war in Vietnam a decade prior, and they had no qualms about quelling the opposition in Gwangju. Estimates of the death toll from the Gwangju Uprising range from over 200 to 2,000. With the Gwangju protest defeated, Chun Doo Hwan took over as an unelected president of the country, continuing authoritarian rule for seven years. The brutal defeat of the Gwangju Uprising was kept silent for many weeks. For the generation of 386, the Gwangju Democratization Movement became a central event that shook their consciousness to the core and became a driving force for their actions in the 1980s.

The Gwangju Uprising inspired diasporic activism in the U.S. Yoon Han Bong, an exiled student leader from Gwangju who was blacklisted for his leadership, started Young Koreans United (YKU), or 한청연 (Han Cheong Nyeon), initially in Los Angeles. His activism had spread to many cities in the States by the mid-1980s. I found out about this group during my New York City years and joined the group based in Jackson Heights for a couple of years, but left for a number of reasons. In the diaspora, YKU followed the *minjung* ("common people") as well as Korean student activist leadership in spirit and principles. YKU espoused *undongkown,* meaning "sphere of movement," claiming a "counterpublic sphere" that sought an alternative to existing social and cultural programs and envisioned a civil society that was emancipatory.[9] In practice, members were extremely well organized but also extremely hierarchical; this meant, for example, that while they espoused women's liberation, in reality, their practices were very patriarchal. They persevered until the early 1990s, but their stance was criticized by mainstream Korean society and the media as a form of communism. Yoon Han Bong returned to Korea in May 1993 and resumed activism until his untimely death in 2007.

In Korea, the 386 generation was viewed as a singular generation with specific, prominent features. Viewed in thumbnail, they were university students with a liberal (or more radical) political bent. Many had studied Marxism, and some leaned toward North Korea. In the 1980s, protesters were known for the militancy and strenuousness of their activism. The government depicted them as violent and dangerous. Thousands of male activists wore masks to hide their identity as well as to provide a defense against the ubiquitous tear gas; they carried steel pipes and firebombs to fight against the police. Mobilization typically depended on a systematic hierarchy of presidents of college-level councils from most Korean universities.[10]

As the first generation of Koreans to grow up in a relatively affluent society, the 386 generation did not have first-hand knowledge of the Korean War. Some had experienced a bit of poverty in childhood, but few had experienced the real destitution that their parents had. They advocated for and benefited from economic development, but they also strove for a more equal distribution of wealth. As they strove for democracy in 1987, the 386 generation played a major role in the peaceful uprising that put an end to decades of dictatorial rule. Although not all of the 386 generation were involved in activism, the legacy of the Gwangju

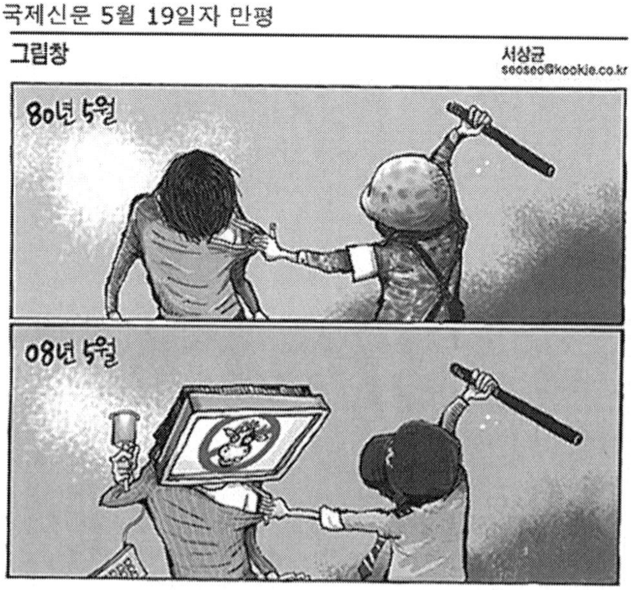

Korean Newspaper Editorial Cartoon, ©Seo Sang Kyoon. From *Kookje Daily News*, editorial cartoon, Seo Sang Kyoon, http://www.kookje.co.kr/news2011/asp/newsbody.asp?code=&key=20080516.22003212037. Accessed December 28, 2018.

event had been deeply ingrained in them. Witnessing the U.S. failure to intervene in the military repression in Gwangju, they came to believe America was responsible for the "ugly history" of national division and military dictatorship in the South.[11]

After the struggle against authoritarian rule, the 1990s represented a period of lull as Korea's first-time secular president, Kim Young Sam, came to power in 1993. In 1998, the 386 generation campaigned for and won the presidency for Kim Dae Jung, who hailed from Gwangju. However, in 1997, they witnessed a major setback with the financial crisis (better known in Korea as the IMF [International Monetary Fund] crisis), which saw many households falling into bankruptcy. Then, in 2002, the 386 generation were again largely credited with the election of Roh Moo-hyun, who represented liberal policies. However, there were some negative changes, like the growth in youth unemployment and an economic slowdown; this time, the Korean public put the blame squarely on the administration. Thus, in 2007, much to the 386 generation's dismay, neo-conservative Lee Myung Bak was elected president.

Neoliberalism was now the policy of the day; a new generation had arrived that is still in search of a name. The term *Shinsadae* was coined in the 1990s to represent the "new generation" (the literal translation), but the name has now lost much of its "new"-ness, although it is still in use by some. One name that has some traction is *ssang pal nyun* (쌍팔년); this is a slang term for the "88 generation," which refers to the 880,000 *won* ($812) per month that represents the average part-time salary. This generation faces a highly competitive job market, as youth unemployment has emerged as a core problem in Korea. Their slogan is, "It's the economy, stupid." A new generation of students values economic growth in contrast to the 386 generation's position of working to decrease the disparity in wealth.

Globalization and neoliberalism have tightened their influence over Koreans, and their effects are a part of everyday life. Under these circumstances, President Lee Myung Bak's promise to promote the resurgence of Korea's economy was eagerly anticipated by the public. However, many of his policies, such as the liberalization of education and the privatization of medical insurance and other public services, provided little benefit to the average Korean. Furthermore, his ambition to create the pan-Korea Grand Waterway was perceived to be anti-ecological and public work–based, which seemed to repeat the 1960s and 1970s style of economic development. People began to realize that the reality of the government's vision for the nation-state wasn't what they'd voted for.

But what drove people into the streets was a particularly raw deal. In April of 2008, President Lee returned from a trip to Washington, DC, with a deal that did away with any restriction on beef imports. The deal included meat and other body parts from thirty-month-old cattle, which had been banned from the U.S. food supply because of the perceived high risk of mad cow disease. Lee's administration didn't renegotiate the agreement, prioritizing economic logic and the administration's ties with the U.S. above all.

In light of this deal, on May 2, 2008, the first candlelight demonstration was initiated by teenage girls. In addition to their protest of the beef agreement, they questioned the government's educational reforms. Some members of famous entertainers' fan clubs were concerned that American beef could harm their idols. Among numerous signs in the demonstrations, a famously smart slogan was, "After I eat mad cow at school meals and die without any proper health care because of expensive private health insurance, please throw my ashes into [the] Grand Canal."[12]

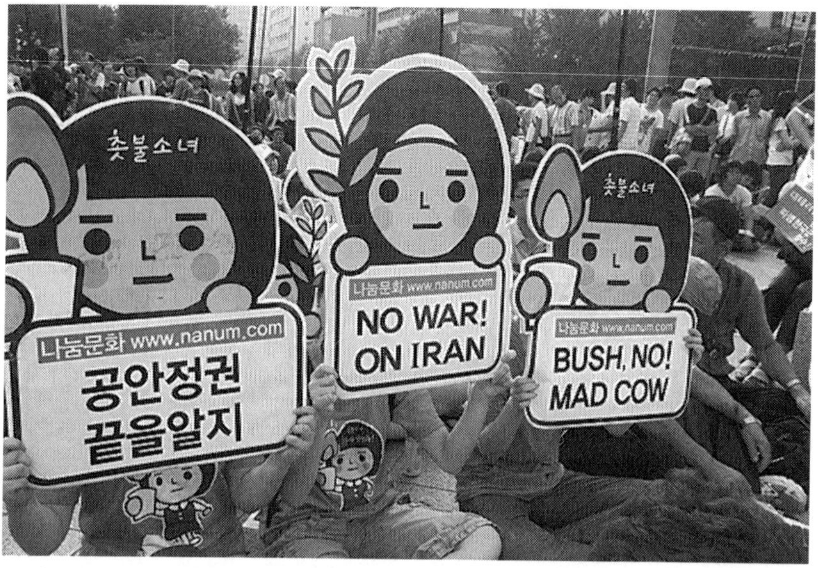

Candlelight rally at Cheonggye Square in Seoul on August 5, 2008, the day of US President George W. Bush's visit to Korea, ©NANUMMUNHWA.

Protests lasted two months and subsequent days brought out a great diversity of people, but there was a predominance of women and teenagers. One of the starkly visual differences from the conventional practices from the 386 generation days were that this protest featured women in their 20s and 30s as well as housewives with their children.

June 10 saw the largest mobilization. It was joined by an organization formed to commemorate the twenty-first anniversary of the death of Lee Han-yeol, a former Yonsei University student who had died after being hit by a canister of tear gas during pro-democracy demonstrations in June 1987. The main event, a candlelight march, estimated by the organizers to have been attended by up to one million people, began at 7 p.m., with simultaneous demonstrations held at Seoul's City Hall and along the central Sejong Avenue. The protesters went near the American embassy, but they avoided going there in order to emphasize that their protest was not anti-American like some other demonstrations.

Protesters varied enormously, but in the main, they were demanding that the government renegotiate the U.S. beef agreement and called on President Lee Myung Bak to resign. The internet played an enormous role in the success of the protest, as it was not only the main means of communication but was also instrumental in creating "agoras," online community networks devoted to discussing issues.

The fact that the protest was initiated by teenagers had several significant consequences. It induced the participation of their parents' generation. It also attracted the public's attention at the same time that it slowed the government's response. Authorities couldn't forcibly suppress the youth, and this endowed the protests with a moral stance and sustenance. Instead of the orderly slogans and traditional campaign songs of the past, teenagers sang pop songs and danced to hip-hop. The protest was unpredictable and inconsistent. In one place, a band organized a street concert. In another, people created speeches about Korea's social problems. Compared with mobilizations elsewhere, these gatherings were experimental and imaginative, ideologically open, rhizomatic in organization, nonrepresentational and undialectical in action, and infused with a healthy sense of humor and zest for life.[13]

Unlike their parents' generation, the so-called Candlelight Girls[14] had grown up in a democratized society. The 386 generation studied democracy and struggled for it harder than any generation had since the foundation of the Korean nation. However, they were more familiar with the operations of the authoritarian system. In contrast, the young Candlelight Girls may not have had clear ideas about democracy, but they responded to the concept as part of their daily life. For many teenagers, democracy was not just another political ideology or catchphrase, as was the case with conventional politics. Instead, democracy was the way in which they expected their society, the Republic of Korea, to function.

Also, unlike the 386 generation or the *undongkwon,* the Candlelighters harbored no doubts about the legitimacy of the Republic of Korea per se as their nation-state. Because presidential candidate Lee Myung Bak was democratically elected by a majority of voters in 2007, legitimacy should not have been a problem in principle. However, because the candlelight participants perceived that Lee's government did not represent the interests of the citizens or listen to their expressions of concern— heeding instead the interests of the establishment and the U.S.—they challenged its legitimacy as their state.

The streets are alive both here and there. When they erupt—whether that be in the battles waged during the L.A. riots, or the Gwangju Uprising, or the Candlelight Girls's demonstrations—they beckon the people to act. In Korea, the 386 generation and the Candlelight Girls rose to hold the future of the country in their hands. In Los Angeles, the memory of *sa-i-gu* reminds previous and new generations of how the streets represent the multitude of journeys taken and yet to be taken.

Notes

1. Elaine Kim, "Home is Where the Han Is: a Korean American Perspective on the Los Angeles Upheavals," *Social Justice,* 51–52 (summer 1993): 1–21.
2. Jay Lee, owner of a furniture store on Florence and Normandie, translated from Korean to English, in "Saigu: An Oral History," *KoreAm,* April 29, 2012, http://kore.am/april-issue-la-riots-in-our-own-words/.
3. Richard Choi, announcer for Radio Korea, which played a central role for Koreans during the L.A. Riots. Translated from Korean to English, in "Saigu: An Oral History," *KoreAm,* April 29, 2012, http://kore.am/april-issue-la-riots-in-our-own-words/.
4. Jay Kim, "L.A. Riots," *Korea Times,* September 30, 2010, http://www.koreatimes.co.kr/www/news/include/print.asp?newsIdx=73767.
5. Dennis Romero, "See a Map of Korean Businesses Targeted During L.A. Riots 20 Years Ago," *L.A. Weekly,* April 24, 2012, https://www.laweekly.com/news/see-a-map-of-korean-businesses-targeted-during-la-riots-20-years-ago-2386976.
6. Min Hyoung Song, *Strange Future: Pessimism and the 1992 Los Angeles Riots* (Durham: Duke University Press, 2005), 25.
7. Staff of the *Los Angeles Times, Understanding the Riots: Los Angeles Before and After the Rodney King Case* (Los Angeles: L.A. Times Syndicate Books, 1996), 123.
8. Author's mail exchanges with Young Chung, an artist and a gallery dealer at the Commonwealth and Council art gallery in Los Angeles. Young graduated from UCI in 1996 and earned an MFA degree from the Art Institute of Chicago in 1998.
9. Namhee Lee, *The Making of Minjung: Democracy and the Politics of Representation in South Korea* (Ithaca: Cornell University Press, 2007).
10. *Sandglass* (aka *The Hourglass,* 모래시계) was one of the highest-rated and most significant dramas in Korean television history. Twenty-four episodes aired in 1995. The series mixed politics, melodrama, and action in an unfolding story about the relationship of three friends in the midst of the political and civilian oppression of the 1970s and 1980s. The first television dramatization of the Gwangju Uprising and Massacre, interspersed with archival video footage, produced one of the most realistic and memorable moments in Korean television history. Through one of the characters, *Sandglass* also gives the audience an inside view of political organization among activists in a university.

11. Seungsook Moon, *Militarized Modernity and Gendered Citizenship in South Korea* (Durham: Duke University Press, 2005), 27.
12. Nae-Hee Kang, "The Political Situation around the Candle and Neoliberalism: the Task and Choice of the Korean Left," [in Korean] *Culture/Science* 55 (Fall 2008): 66–89, quoted in Seung-Ook Lee, Sook-Jin Kim, and Joel Wainwright, "Mad Cow Militancy: Neoliberal Hegemony and Social Resistance in South Korea," *Political Geography* (2010), https://cpb-us-w2.wpmucdn.com/u.osu.edu/dist/4/45440/files/2017/04/Lee-Wainwright-2010-Regulation-theory-Korean-capitalism-w612kw.pdf.
13. Concept derived from Seung-Ook Lee, Sook-Jin Kim, and Joel Wainwright, "Mad Cow Militancy: Neoliberal Hegemony and Social Resistance in South Korea," *Political Geography* (2010), http://citeseerx.ist.psu.edu/viewdoc/download?doi=10.1.1.461.8977&rep=rep1&type=.
14. An iconic character in the history of Korea's citizens' movement, the Candlelight Girl was developed by Nanummunhwa, a Seoul-based nonprofit social movement organization. The term "nanum munhwa" in Korean means "culture of sharing." Established in 2000, Nanummunhwa is funded solely by its 3,500 members. The founder of the organization, Park Nohae, is a Korean resistance poet who published his acclaimed collection of poems, *The Dawn of Labor*, during the military dictatorship in the 1980s in Korea.

Chapter 24

Golden States of Mind

Cambodian and Vietnamese Artistic Organizing in Southern California and Southeast Asia

Việt Lê

Jean-Luc Nancy proclaims, "Community takes place always *through* others and for others."[1] Community is often rooted in place, but takes its place not in a single space but *through* multiple spheres. I argue that cultural practices and identification, while rooted in geographic locales—a through-line, as it were—traverse borders. This real and imagined moving "through" becomes a thoroughfare—a point of access: arriving and leaving.

Upon "leaving" their homelands and arriving as refugees and immigrants, Southeast Asians have established the largest expatriate communities in Southern California: Cambodians in Long Beach and Vietnamese in Little Sài Gòn. This selection of "portraits" highlights contemporary artists with links to Việt Nam, Laos, and Cambodia, as well as organizers and art organizations with physical and psychic ties to California and Southeast Asia. The transnational flows of artistic production are examined through three "case study" interviews, which are prefaced by a short description of the artist or organization. The case studies include *Global Hybrid,* an annual exhibition held in both Long Beach, California, and Phnom Penh, Cambodia; the Vietnamese Arts & Letters Association (VAALA); and dancer and Khmer Arts Ensemble Associate Artistic Director Prumsodon Ok.

These artist-organizers are highlighted because they each have unique, sustained engagement with their chosen communities. Every artist featured is also an experienced organizer. Through their long-ranging activities, each pioneering interviewee addresses the dearth of critical and creative dialogue within and without Southeast Asia and the United States. The artist-organizers of the traveling exhibition *Global Hybrid* discuss the logistical demands of presenting art exhibitions in different countries. Ysa Lê, the executive director of VAALA, talks about meeting the needs of a local constituency and dealing with diasporic community politics in organizing cultural events such as art exhibitions and international film festivals. Dancer-organizer Prumsodon Ok discusses rebuilding after trauma, as well as bridging the gaps between the sacred and profane. Each "case study" occupies an important role in its respective community.

This collection of interviews and contextualizing information follows Moira Roth's art historical essays in which email "letters" or face-to-face interviews with artists bring critical insights.[2] Through extended participant observation and oral interviews, I engage with creative practitioners from the ground up. On the ground, the cultural producers question creative and geographic categories.

Current Asian American Studies scholarship has shifted from descriptively naming and representing Southeast Asian American experiences to a framework that takes into account transnational movements and affiliations.[3] Asian American Studies and area studies such as Southeast Asian Studies each have their own disciplinary "blind spots."[4] As Asian American Studies refocuses on transnational interactions, Southeast Asian Studies should also look beyond its national purviews to account for complex movements of culture and people.

It is no longer adequate to represent the historically marginalized. It isn't about quotas or catching up. During the heyday of 1990s multiculturalism in the United States, minority voices claimed visibility. At the edge of the twenty-first century, a spectacular explosion of high-profile international art bienniales and trienniales has largely swept identitarian politics to the side. Nonetheless national, racial, and aesthetic hierarchies still exist. How do we make sense of—and challenge—these creative and cultural centers and margins?

Echoing art historian Alice Yang's claim that contemporary Asian art histories are often marginalized, I assert that Southeast Asian and Asian American art histories are barely visible.[5] Art historian Joan Kee bemoans the "relative absence" of contemporary Southeast Asian art from museum collections, exhibitions, and most notably, university courses.[6] Instead of affinities based on the nation-state, Kee also suggests looking at contemporary Southeast Asian art through a regional lens.

This "recognition of contingency" opens up connections. This perspective also allows us to see beyond linear timelines and to think beyond center/periphery binaries.[7] As the case studies in this essay demonstrate, regional connections extend past geographic and temporal bounds. Looking at *transregional* exchanges helps us understand the contemporary moment in all of its transgressions, between and across communing borders and bodies.

Global Hybrid: Cross-Cultural Exhibitions between Phnom Penh and Long Beach (2008–Present)

Global Hybrid (GH) is an ongoing international multimedia group art exhibit that features artists with links to Cambodia and Southeast Asia. It is organized by artist/founder and Senior Curator Denise A. Scott, in collaboration with U.S.-based artist/Exhibition Coordinator Sayon Syprasoeuth, and Meta House's Art Manager/Curator Lydia Parusol (2008–2010). The exhibit is held twice a year during the summer monsoon season at Meta House; at the German Cambodian Cultural

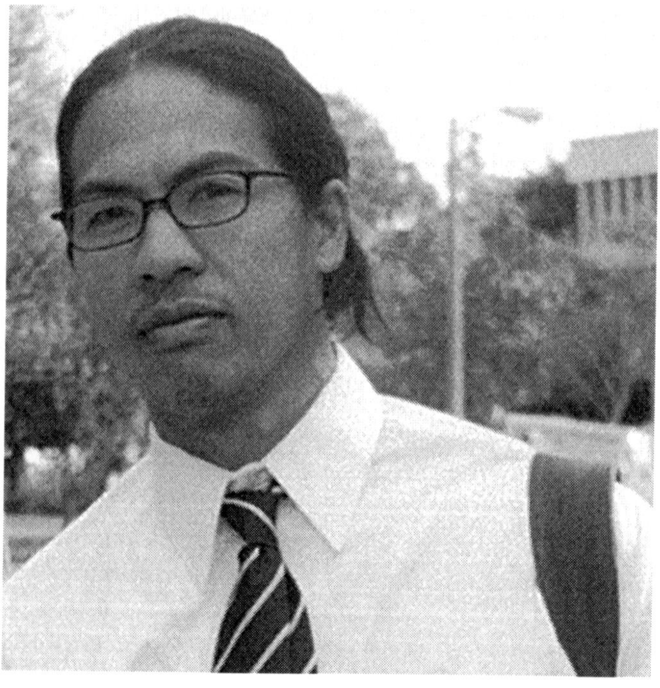

Sayon Syprasoeuth. Photo by Sayon Syprasoeuth.

Center in Phnom Penh; and during Khmer New Year (April) at various Long Beach art venues. To date, there have been seven exhibitions. In addition, *Global Hybrid*'s artist residency program invites Khmer artists to Long Beach and supports them during their stay; past residents include Battambang-based artist Kchao Touch (April 2009) and Phnom Penh-based artist Meas Sokhorn (February–May 2010).

One aim of the series of exhibitions is to address the lack of contemporary art exhibitions in the U.S. by artists connected to Southeast Asia. Another goal is to foster local and diasporic linkages. Over the last five years, according to Scott, fourteen Cambodian American artists and twenty-five Cambodian artists have been featured in *GH*. Since April 2010, *GH* has broadened its focus to include artists connected to Korea, the United States, and the Southeast Asian Mekong region, including Thailand and Việt Nam, among other countries.[8] In the United States, there are few contemporary art shows that foster exchanges between Cambodia and the United States; *Global Hybrid* is a rare example.

On February 24, 2012, in Denise Scott's airy Long Beach studio loft, I met with the U.S. collaborators, Sayon and Denise. Focusing the conversation on the logistics of putting on a traveling exhibit in two countries, these artist-organizers divulged how *GH* projects were organized, as well as the complications of working with a wide range of artists in various media and institutions. The conversation thread revealed how to negotiate the gaps between an inherited Euro-American "standard" of artistic practices and exhibition infrastructure with realities in an emerging art venue in Cambodia (e.g., no insurance or art handlers). Although the U.S.-based organizers have been indoctrinated into particular dominant Western aesthetic discourses, they are also attuned to the logistical difficulties and cultural slippages that occur when Cambodian-based artists exhibit abroad (e.g., visa issues, translation, and funding). Underlying the conversation were the unspoken—perhaps neocolonial—hierarchies of art knowledge, production, and consumption that may guide our collective efforts at mobilizing disparate communities.

Việt Lê (VL): How was *Global Hybrid* first conceived?

Denise Scott (DS): I was invited in by Carlos Silviera, an art education professor at Cal State University Long Beach, to participate in the "Art and Social Action" international exchange program to monitor students in Cambodia. This was a three-week joint venture in December 2005 with Pannasastra University students at nine NGO sites working in the arts with local youth, ages six to eighteen.

Mostly expats or visiting artists, along with perhaps only six noted Cambodian artists, dominated the art scene from 2000 to 2004, until the Visual Arts Open [VAO] in December 2005. VAO marks the first city-wide contemporary/traditional exhibition in thirty years, organized by Khmer diasporic artists Sopheap Pich, Linda Saphan and Chet Pier Seth.

After meeting several Khmer artists, who were recent graduates of the Royal University of Fine Arts [RUFA] and/or inspired by incoming international artists offering workshops and seminars, I realized that I wanted to foster greater relations between U.S. and Khmer artists. I questioned, "Who are the Cambodian American artists, since I live in Long Beach, with a population of 60,000 Khmers? How are Cambodian artists being represented in their own country and in exhibitions abroad?"

It wasn't until March 2008 that I met Sayon Syprasoeuth at his "Obsessive Compulsive" art opening at the Huntington Beach Art Center, and that I proposed a cross-cultural exhibition between U.S. and Cambodia, which marked our inaugural exhibition at Meta House in July 2008. *Global Hybrid* was adopted/branded as our signature in 2009. Its major premise was to find Cambodian American artists in the U.S., who were an isolated group of first-generation residents and artists. We advocated for their participation in *GH* and ideally to return to Cambodia for exhibition in order to facilitate a dialogue with the Khmer artists. I am proud to say that after meeting Sayon, my first Cambodian/Laos/American artist in Huntington Beach, he returned to Battambang-Sisphon after thirty years, in 2008 and 2009.

Sayon Syprasoeuth (SS): In the beginning I let Denise Scott organize and take the wheel of the show, since I didn't know which direction she wanted to take it. Once I got to see the works and the look of the show, I thought it needed some weeding out. I had expressed to Denise Scott that the works need to be stronger. I like to get people involved in participating in the arts and art making, but I don't want to sacrifice the integrity of the work and the big picture of the show and what I know to be good art—I wanted to have a first-rate contemporary art show.

VL: Sayon, as a Laotian American with ties to the U.S., Cambodia, and Laos, how do you identify as an artist and organizer? Does it vary with each location?

SS: I've lived in Cambodia, but never in Laos. Recently, I've gone back to Cambodia and I have since reconnected with it. For Laos, I know the culture and lifestyle, but not the country itself—I've started some readings on it to catch up on the history of communism [and its] takeover.

I guess I identify with the vernaculars of the people, and yes—I adjust to each location. For Cambodia I can speak a little, and for Laos I can speak fluently (at least I think so). I identify with them equally, even though I speak Laotian.

VL: Who helped fund the *GH* residency program?

DS: Another highlight and logistical issue was the residency component. We invited several Cambodian artists to come to the U.S. as part of the *GH* shows, but many of our Khmer artists are male, under thirty years of age, and do not own property; therefore, U.S. visas were difficult to obtain. Fortunately, in 2009, with the Arts in Embassy program in Phnom Penh, *GH* artists Phung Huynh, Aragna Ker, Linda Saphan, Sayon Syprasoeuth, and Kong Vollak were represented. Carol Rodley, our U.S. ambassador in PP [Phnom Penh], proudly supported our cross-cultural *GH* exhibitions and facilitated our residency program. In April 2009, Battambang-based artist Kchao Touch was our first residency artist; [he] stayed for a month in Long Beach. Meas Sokhorn did a three-month residency, starting in February 2010. The U.S. Embassy in Phnom Penh supported the plane flight, while housing, meals, and art supplies were sponsored by Denise A. Scott.

SS: We're lucky that with so many works over the years, there has been very little damage while in transit, during the show, or after de-installing. One issue in organizing shows is that if work is damaged, [we have to figure] out who has to deal with that. The space? The organizers? That's a difficult issue. Another issue is drawing up contracts with artworks loaned from various U.S. galleries.

In addition, few Cambodian artists have the money for framing and material costs, especially to construct large-scale installations. *GH* provides [this] on an as-needed basis. *GH* usually balances their exhibitions amongst painting, sculpture, installation, performance, and video art. Looping videos from artists in the U.S. and Cambodia requires PAL/NTSC [video] conversion, which can be costly in the U.S. but more manageable in Cambodia, through Meta House and/or other resources.

VL: Why are certain artists privileged over others? What helps empower artists?

DS: Education in the arts is the key. Workshops play a vital role in assisting artists in Southeast Asia, as well as residencies. A dear friend and Khmer artist, Nawath Chhan, said, "The glue

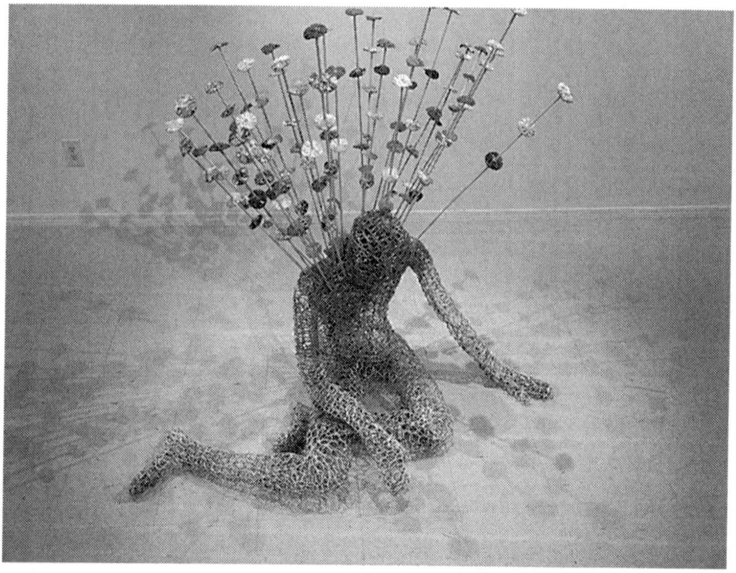

Sayon Syprasoeuth, *Birth of the Dragon Lady* (2011–2012). Mixed media. Approximate dimensions 4' x 4' 5".

was missing until I attended workshops by Sopheap Pich at Sala Arts, who introduced us to contemporary arts and aesthetics."

SS: They [international curators, organizers, museums] may hear some names and approach those artists who are most visible. It's also about networking. We try to give Southeast Asian artists greater exposure globally.

Vietnamese American Arts & Letters Association (VAALA), Westminster

Based in the heart of Little Sài Gòn, the Vietnamese American Arts & Letters Association (VAALA), a medium-sized nonprofit arts organization, has been actively serving its Southern California constituents for over twenty years. Established in 1991, the organization regularly hosts classes, art exhibitions, readings, recitals, and talks. After VAALA's current executive director, Ysa Lê, became involved in 2000, the organization expanded its activities. Highlights include the annual Children's Moon Festival Art Contest, which draws over 300 participants. Its largest project is the annual Vietnamese Film Festival (formerly the biannual Vietnamese International Film Fest [ViFF]), which showcases films from across the globe and attracts over 5,000 viewers during the festival run. On August 2, 2012, I sat down with Lê in her Orange County home for a chat about her lifelong involvement with VAALA.

The daughter of late VAALA cofounder Lê Đình Điều, current leader Ysa Lê talks about VAALA's growth and lessons learned while spearheading ViFF and other events. She also touches on Vietnamese American community and cultural politics. Among other anticommunist community protests, mainly first-generation Vietnamese Americans protested the 2009 *FOB II* art exhibit. These incidents were often sensationally portrayed within mainstream American media without fully addressing the vexed histories and complicated generational and political divides at play. Some neoliberal newspapers asked, "Do Vietnamese Americans not understand freedom of expression?" Such thinking misses the point. This interview illuminates the reasons for putting on a provocative show and reassesses its aftermath. For Lê, the arts are essential to eliciting at times difficult but important dialogue; arts organizations also provide a vital generational and cultural lifeline.

Việt Lê (VL): I know that the annual Viet Film Fest is near and dear to your heart. How has it grown? Can you talk about the international connections the festival fosters through film, including between Sài Gòn and Little Sài Gòn and other places in the Vietnamese diaspora?

Ysa Lê (YL): At that time, I already knew some filmmakers. The first [biannual] Vietnamese International Film Fest [now called Viet Film Fest] was in 2003. We expected ten films and got seventy-two submissions, including Vietnamese traditional opera VHS tapes, and television shows. We had to talk to the public about what short films are, not just full-length films.

We had a very small budget—$10,000. Lots of in-kind donations from the newspaper—mostly because of printing costs. We did a fundraiser and recitals and sought sponsorship. The turnout was a few thousand people. People were interested because we showed *Three Seasons, Green Dragon,* as well as *The Anniversary,* among other films. We showcased Victor Vu's first feature, *First Morning,* for Spotlight Night and closed the festival with the Canadian film *The Marsh* by Kim Nguyễn. There is certainly an interest in watching Vietnamese and Vietnamese diasporic stories on the big screen. We also showed Trinh T. Minh-ha's work, which is more experimental and theoretical.

For the third ViFF, we had big budget films like action blockbuster *The Rebel;* it was packed. People were amazed how Vietnamese film could move forward so fast. One of the main goals was to connect people together in different directions, from France, Canada, Australia, and even Poland and Israel and so on. We showed *Journey from the Fall* at UCLA. It was also packed, as it was like a "homecoming" for director Ham Tran, who graduated from UCLA Film School. Lan Dương [UC Riverside professor and former VAALA board member] was the head of the screening committee.

The film festival has become more popular in the community, but many people don't make the connection that VAALA is actually its parent organization. With *FOB II,* VAALA certainly became known.

VL: In light of controversial exhibits such as *FOB II* in January 2009, what are your thoughts on balancing community politics and generational divides?

YL: At a board meeting, a board member brought up that the community [had] responded negatively to a piece of art. As an art organizer, I was very concerned about how *Người Việt* reacted to Huỳnh Thư̛y Châu and her artwork.[9] We thought of different ways to discuss the issues. Someone suggested that we do an art exhibition. We thought of calling it *FOB II* [*FOB I* was curated by Tram Lê in 2002]. Trâm Lê said she needed a co-curator. We asked Lan Dương, who was also on the board, to co-curate with Trâm.

The theme of *FOB II* was *Art Speaks,* focused on the crossroads of community, politics, and arts. We'd wanted to explore censorship/self-censorship issues, freedom of artistic expression in relation to the community. We included many different angles such as "reconstructing memory" (in honoring the traumatic past that many Vietnamese refugees had to endure), contemporary politics (in the context of post-9/11), the politics of sexuality, Vietnamese American community politics, youth culture, and identity politics.

Things got worse when the protests happened in response to some artworks due to the Vietnamese American community's politics. Looking back, it was hard because each one of us has a different background and would therefore experience different pressures. We met with the [Santa Ana] city manager. He said that the city didn't have the budget to pay the police overtime to watch over the protests. We had violated the city permit, so we had to close down. VAALA Center, technically a large office space, wasn't zoned for gallery use. At the press conference we announced we had to close down the exhibition as we had violated the zoning by the city. The exhibition was only open for seven instead of ten days as planned.

Ly Tong came in disguise and destroyed Brian Đoan's framed artwork and Steven Toly's work. It was very chaotic. Looking back, *FOB II* was very important for VAALA. We learned a lot of lessons. If I had to do it again, I would probably do the same thing. We have to ask, "How much should we endure? How can we secure the longevity of the organization? What is our focus? What would be our ultimate goal of the project?" For *FOB II* our intention is arts, community and politics—we have to explore that through certain artworks even though we knew they may spark controversies and even protests. At the same time, we'd have to watch our back and recognize the difficulties [in administration] we had to go through and how much resources we had. Internally, we'd need to be on the same page.

It was one of the most successful openings ever. It was amazing on that Saturday when a lot of people came, and that second week, Assemblyman Van Tran sent that letter [urging us to remove the "offensive" artwork].[10] We, however, would not take down any artworks because that'd be self-censoring, the exact theme that *FOB II* focused on. Through the short-lived exhibition, I believe that we have been successful in opening dialogue within the community and showcasing the diversity of our community. Lessons we learned: we have to be more careful when we decide on such sensitive issues. The board members now know the possible consequences. Now we know if we have ties with certain people, we will be more affected. Certainly, at that time, some board members worked closely with the community, so they'd feel more pressure. There's a lot of anticommunist pressure in the community. I'm so glad my mom, brother, and grandmother were so supportive. Grandma watched the press and said, "Why the ruckus?"

VL: What future directions do you envision for VAALA?

YL: I think that art is very important in everyone's life and in every community. Therefore, VAALA is a very important entity in the community. Art speaks to a lot of things that words can't describe. It helps you understand different generations and ethnicities. It helps open dialogues to explore complex issues. It can offer multiple ways to examine a subject. Art is a very important tool for [immigrant] community members to advance after a few decades being here, settling down. There is a void if we don't have art to share through the generations. We are currently the only SoCal organization to support the Vietnamese American arts. I realize that it will take years to have more and more people engage in the arts. We'd need to start building a foundation—a nurturing environment for the arts that would reflect the diversity of our community. If we build it, they will come. I'm optimistic because more people from the Vietnamese American second generation pursue the arts as a career. I would love to have the younger generation involved in learning about the Vietnamese diaspora through the arts. I hope VAALA continues to be a venue to network, to exchange, and to research.

Interview with Prumsodun Ok, Long Beach

An emerging queer-identified dancer, choreographer, filmmaker, and educator, Prumsodun Ok's performance-based work often combines Khmer classical movements and motifs with experimental dance forms to examine sexuality, interracial relations, and traumas such as war, displacement, and HIV/AIDS.

On Saturday, February 18, 2011, I drove to Long Beach to visit the Khmer Arts Academy studio, where Ok is the Associate Artistic Director. On Saturday mornings, he teaches classical Cambodian dance to a new generation of dancers. After his class, he spoke about connecting and embodying in his work, the sacred and profane, male and female, and the "traditional" and the "experimental."

Việt Lê (VL): The first time I saw you perform live was in December 2010 as a special guest performer atop a bar at Blue Chili—a popular local gay bar in Phnom Penh, Cambodia. You stood out from the other standard drag performances (Beyoncé, Pussycat Dolls) because yours crossed gender binaries—beyond drag—as well as the divides between traditional dance and other forms of performance.

As a queer Asian artist, how does sexuality inform your work? For instance, your performance *Of Land and Sky* "mines the landscape of Cambodian myth and pop culture, recasting a tragic history of politically defiant romance into the bodies of gay men." How has work that pushes traditional forms and sexualities been received by different communities?

Prumsodun Ok (PO): In Cambodia, there are lots of queer spaces. Dancers inhabit different personas, different gender identities. In classical dance, women take on the roles of princes, soldiers, and gods. Male dancers also take on various roles, as animals, as humans, as deities; identity isn't rigid or tied to the *rub,* or image or body, of the dancer. Much of Khmer history is primarily oral. Many manuscripts were inscribed on palm leaves, which have been lost due to centuries of war and natural deterioration from the climate. Historically, I don't know if male or female dancers labeled themselves in terms of gender or sexuality.

I know that my work pushes the envelope in Cambodia and in the U.S.; it doesn't fit neatly into "traditional" or "experimental" categories or gendered binaries. I don't see distinctions between high and low, sacred and profane. Many trained dancers in Cambodia respect what I am trying to do.

VL: Your work also politically engages histories of trauma.

PO: As repetitive and as dangerous as the narrative of genocide is, I am only one generation away from it. My parents and teachers, my siblings and friends went through it. I feel it in Cambodia. I have come to understand that this legacy of loss must be a legacy of rebuilding.

Therefore, I am committed to preserving, carrying on, and expanding Khmer classical dance. This means passing on old works and choreographing in the Khmer style. Secondly, teaching, writing, curating, creating interdisciplinary works—tying the tradition to the larger art world and arts ecology it belongs to. After all, we are only one spoke of a large wheel that is the human art tradition.

VL: How do you support your practice, as well as help creatively support the Khmer community in Long Beach? How does the Khmer Arts Academy sustain itself?

PO: I am the Associate Artistic Director of this space, Khmer Arts Academy. I work more than full time, with my artwork and these commitments.

Here at Khmer Arts Academy we are supported through foundation support, and we have some private donors. The Khmer community in the U.S. is not an especially affluent one, and Khmers also rank among the poorer and least educated of Asian populations. There are many reasons for this, including the genocide, which saw the deaths of an estimated eighty to ninety percent of culture-bearers and intellectuals. And, of course, the diasporic population was mostly displaced as a result of a traumatic war, settling into the rough and dangerous neighborhoods without the resources, tools, and network to grow.

For the Khmer classical dance classes at the Khmer Arts Academy, we hope that the younger, more educated, and more affluent generation of Khmer donate, but we don't charge them; parents donate money to provide lunch for our students. Some of our teachers are from the United States, and others are from Cambodia.

VL: With whom do the Khmer teachers train in Cambodia?

PO: Our artists in residence and teachers from Cambodia—they are all Sophiline's dancers from Cambodia and are some of the best classical dancers in the world. [Sophiline Cheam Shapiro is a pioneering dancer, teacher, vocalist, and choreographer as well as the cofounder of Khmer Arts and a leading proponent of Khmer classical dance in Cambodia and overseas.]

VL: Where are your communities?

PO: My communities are global *and* local. I have different meanings in different contexts. I feel appreciated and respected in these different communities. I don't feel all artists with intersecting identities have that privilege. I've had the opportunity to perform at REDCAT in LA; I have friends making work in Cambodia, Thailand, and Indonesia.

In all of these contexts, I am learning, translating ideas and approaches, and rebuilding to push Khmer dance and, on a larger scale, art to new heights.

Conclusion (Loving and Leaving)

Wrestling with the sudden loss of my good friend Boitran Huynh-Beattie, a well- respected and beloved art historian of Vietnamese modern art, I have been thinking, dreaming about community and love.[11] Boitran left so suddenly. Leaving is absence, void. In other instances, departing is also arriving—immigrants leave home to find home again. For us nomads, where and who is home? Do I love her so because she was adopted family, a member of my tribe—a refugee, an art lover, an academic? Or because she loved us so? Jean-Luc Nancy writes, "Love is the extreme movement, beyond the self, of a being reaching completion."[12] Love moves outward, beyond the self. A person's completion, their wholeness, is attained *through* this process. Again, community takes place always *through* others and *for* others. Love is a forward arc—open, extending, engaging. How do we navigate the circumference, sustain the circle, from our innermost selves to society? To love and to be loved is the threshold between self and other.

The artists and organizers in this essay toil tirelessly out of love *for*—and always in love *with*—their craft and their communities. They scale many borders, both real and metaphorical, in a time where borders are increasingly policed—a time of eternal war. Through their labors of love, these artists disrupt what it means to leave, by returning again and again. Through different strategies, these artistic projects embody what it means to be multiply situated in California. California is global *and* local, real and imaginary. California isn't simply the Golden State—it's a state of mind. Love it or leave it.

Notes

1. Jean-Luc Nancy, *The Inoperative Community* (Chicago: University of Minnesota Press, 1991), 15.
2. Moira Roth, "Traveling Companions/Fractured Worlds," *Art Journal* (1999): 82–93.
3. Mariam Beevi Lâm, Fiona Ngô, and Mimi Nguyễn, eds., "Southeast Asian Studies Special Issue: Guest Editors' Introduction," *positions: asia critique* 20:3 (2012): 673.
4. Việt Thanh Nguyện, "Refugee Memories and Asian American Critique," *positions: asia critique* 20:3 (2012): 916.
5. Alice Yang, Jonathan Hay, and Mimi Young, eds., *Why Asia? Contemporary Asian and Asian American Art* (New York: New York University Press, 1998).

6. Joan Kee, "Introduction Contemporary Southeast Asian Art," *Third Text*, 25:4 (2011): 373. See also Nora Taylor and Boreth Ly, eds., *Modern and Contemporary Southeast Asian Art: An Anthology* (Ithaca: Cornell University Press, 2011).
7. Joan Kee, "Introduction Contemporary Southeast Asian Art," 381.
8. Special thanks to Denise Scott and Sayon Syprasoeuth for their invaluable assistance with this essay. Scott, an artist who has exhibited in Korea, is an art consultant to Hancock University (Long Beach), which is an extension facility of Hanseo University in South Korea.
9. A photo printed in *Người Việt* newspaper of UC Davis grad student Huynh Chau's artwork—a foot spa painted with the current Vietnamese flag—caused a community furor. See My-Thuan Tran, "Vietnamese Americans Protest Published Photo," *Los Angeles Times*, May 2, 2012, http://articles.latimes.com/2008/feb/12/local/me-protest12.
10. Assemblyman Van Tran represents the 68th district, which includes Garden Grove, Fountain Valley, Westminster, Costa Mesa, Anaheim, Stanton, and parts of Newport Beach. The letter written by Tran on January 13, 2009, was addressed to Ysa Lê. See Richard Chang, "More Protests Planned; Government Officials Want Images Removed," *The Orange County Register*, February 28 2012, http://artsblog.ocregister.com/2009/02/13/more-protests-planned-government-officals-encourage-censorship/7616/.
11. See Boitran Huynh-Beattie. *Nam Bang!* exhibition catalogue (Casula, New South Wales: Casula Powerhouse, 2009), and Ashley Carruthers and Boitran Huynh-Beattie, "Dark Tourism, Diasporic Memory, and Disappeared History" in *The Chinese/Vietnamese Diaspora: Revisiting the Boat People* (New York: Routledge, 2011).
12. Nancy, *The Inoperative Community*, 89.

CHAPTER 25

Excerpts from *D'FunQT*

D'Lo

D'FunQT IS A ONE-PERSON show that shares hilarious and poignant snapshots of the worlds that shaped who D'Lo is now. Growing up in a strict immigrant family and caught between two overzealous parents, D'Lo did his best to make it all work peacefully while radically and bizarrely challenging entrenched mindsets. His life provides a wealth of material for self-reflective musings, rants, and side-splitting coming out stories. Written and performed Jon Leguizamo–style, the show celebrates the joy of survival in an oft-intolerant world. With a queer/trans lens, D'Lo uses his fluidly morphing form and spot-on timing to bring the fierce with the funny.

As D'Lo states, "This show is my gift to the communities I identify with: Fierce Folks of Color, Queers, QT's and, yes, Islanders. I want to give my people a break. A moment to exhale in peace. To celebrate in laughter. To feel accepted in all your glory amongst other good people."

First Coming Out to Parents (as a theoretical gay)

I didn't even want to come out, but it just happened. I was chillin' with multiple girlfriends who, coincidentally, all kissed real good. I was a senior with two more months until I graduated into further freedom, and I got a phone call . . .

(*Appa is face forward w/Bundy out; D'Lo is to the side*)

Appa: What are you doin?

D'Lo: Chillin. Why? What's up, Appa?

A: Ah, I'm calling to tell you that we found two men for you.

D: Two men for me? What? What for?

A: Well, you don't know what the hell you're going to do after college. You have to get married.

D: You're trying to arrange my marriage, Appa? No way—that's not happening! (*shifts tone*) I mean, that's really nice of you to look out, but I'm okay.

A: What's the problem? They're two doctors from North Carolina!

D: Appa, thank you, but no!

A: What, do you have a boyfriend?

D: NO, APPA, I don't have a boyfriend.

A: Then what's the problem? They're brothers, you can pick.

D: That's really feminist of you. But Appa, really, thanks, but I don't want to get married. I'm fine.

A: What, then? Do you have a girlfriend? (*chuckles*)

D: (*Silence*) Well, what had happened was . . .

A: What—are you telling me that you're gay? You're not gay? Are you gay?

D: I think you're asking a question you don't really want to know the answer to . . .

A: No, you're not gay. I know you're not gay! Don't tell me you're gay! Are you gay?!

D: Yes, Appa, I'm gay.

A: You're not gay! (*Hangs up*)

Two minutes later. It's my Amma.

Amma: Uh, Dillo? Appa said something . . . You know . . . Oh gaaawd . . .

D'Lo: What, Amma?

A: Are you a gay?

D: Yes, Amma, I'm a gay.

A: Oh. How long have you been a gay?

D: Pretty much all my life, Amma.

A: Oh. (*gets scared look on her face*) Who else knows that you're a gay?

D: Pretty much everyone else except you, Amma.

A: How do they know?

D: (*points to self*) I dunno . . .

They couldn't handle it. Needless to say, this wasn't an easy time.

Pager 911 Intro

So I left for NYC for a job. But before I left, I got a New York City pager number.

D'Lo: Amma, when you hear the beep, just punch in your number and press pound. I'll call you when I get to a phone. If it is an emergency, like if you get hurt or anyone dies or is close to dying or you think might be dying, just punch in your number and press 911 at the end. That way I'll know it's an emergency and I'll call back.

But, as I walked away, I remembered that kiss I never gave my sister the last time I saw her on those steps. So I stopped and turned and gave Amma the biggest motherfuckin' hug I had in me.

NYC

New York, boy. It was right when Rudy Giuliani was towards the tail end of his "clean up Manhattan" period. So it still had a beautiful amount of dirt and grime, and the LES (Lower East Side) still held a beautiful amount of shade—the settlement of hipsters and coffee shops only came towards the mid-2000s.

It was the first time I was without my support system, my queer artistic community. And there were no cell phones back then, so keeping in touch was hard.

I was alone navigating the foreign landscapes of opposite-ness that New York and So Cal are: no ocean, but brick buildings for days; no good weather all year long. Instead . . . seasons. Then I understood that if Lancaster was hot as hell, New York was cold as hell. I was all twisted around about the people, too. I thought the Dominicans were Black Mexicans; I thought that Puerto Ricans were South Asians who spoke really fast Spanish; I thought the Jewish People were white.

But at the same time I was missing LA, I was also feeling fresh and free and like I had a brand-new start on life. I was an arts organizer and a youth mentor, spitting at open mics all over the five boroughs. I was trying to save money, biking my ass everywhere, missing Cali, missing traffic, so I started dating women who owned cars.

Jill

I remember one day I was on a date with a beautiful woman named Jill, who had a car, and I brought my Kenyan friend and her cousin. We were going to the Black Lily to see Jaguar Wright and the Jazzy Phatnastees, and we get out of the car and "Pop pop pop!" I'm like "Everybody down!" And I think, "How odd that my first drive-by is in New York . . . and with Africans." I'm like "Jill, you OK?" But she's down on the ground and I see her under the car curled over in pain, so I crawl *(army crawls)* around the car to her and think, "Shit, the woman I love has been shot and if she dies, I don't know what I'll do. Where will I live?" And Jill sees my panic and says to me sweetly, "D'Lo, this is New York. We don't have drive-bys. A fucken hub cap fucken flew into my fucken knee, and it fucken hurts."

I was like, "Phew!" But when her fucken knee got better, she kicked me out of her fucken apartment, and that meant we broke up. And so, I had to find new girlfriend. And this was a steady pattern. Once

I got with a girl, I stayed with her as long as it'd last, aka until she understood that I wasn't ready to commit.

But in between dragging my two suitcases all over Brooklyn. I started to get hella busy around this time, doing hella art shit with other young queer artists.

911 Still?

D'Lo: Yes, Amma. Yes, I'm alive. Yes, I'm still smoking cigarettes. Uh, yes. (*quietly*) Yes, I'm still gay. Look, Amma, I told you just 911 me when it's an emergency . . .

Prachi Mugged

Then in 2001, I was 23 and not living with a girl (*pats himself on the back*). I was living in Crown Heights and like a week or so after 9/11, I got to experience something very VERY New York with my *best* friend Prachi: we got mugged.

And you know, after my sister died, I was like extremely sensitive to people dying. I say OCD sensitive because, like, let's say I hadn't heard back from someone, I would think they might've died. And it doesn't help that a lot of us queers work for the people or the movement or for Black Lives Matter, and so my mind spins to thinking that the FBI or ghosts snatched their ass.

And even more nutty, I would write a list of my friends in my life, and after they were all listed out, I'd go one-by-one and think, How would I feel if this person died?

I would cry if they died.
I would die if they died.
I would be OK about this person.
Oh, this person can totally die.

And for the two years I had been in NYC, Prachi was the first person to see right through my steez, straight to my heart. She was my only family, and I woulda died if she died.

So, being that we were a little drunk coming from a party, when these two dudes ran up on us, I couldn't think straight. And all of a sudden, I saw this dude towering over Prachi and my mind got twisted. So, I tried to fight off my dude but he slipped me into a sweet embrace called a headlock. And I think, "Why did I have that extra shot of Hennessey?" Because I was who I was at that time, I was packing a knife, so I unhooked it, spun it out and stuck him. He threw me off him, I landed on my knees and my knuckles, they take off, and because I rarely get to have the last word, I yelled "Bitches!" as they ran away.

I get up and both me and Prachi run off in the other direction. Next morning, I couldn't walk . . . for two weeks. But, you know, as much as I was in pain from being thrown, I actually felt bad about sticking someone with my knife. Because I'm nonviolent, and I know that I live in a country where it's a privilege to say that. Well, if anything, stabbing him means I left my mark in this world.

911 Dreams

Amma: D'Lo? Yes, this is an emergency. I had a dream. I had a dream you were hurt.

Appa: She always has those dreams.

D'Lo: Oh, hi, Appa.

Amma: Are you hurt?

D: Amma, I'm fine. God is taking care of me.

Appa: Well, that's what we thought about Krishani.

D: That's precisely why I won't die. God wouldn't take both of us out. I'm like collateral. You're stuck with me.

Amma and Appa: (*silence*)

Amma: I dreamt you got in a fight. Have you ever gotten into any fights?

D: No, Amma. I've never gotten into any fights. But other people have gotten into fights with me.

Amma: Who fought you?

D: Interestingly, the two times were with Panjabi men.

Appa: Why are you hanging out with Panjabis? Don't you know they're warriors? They were harvesters, and when they drink, they become volatile—and they carry the swords. They are warriors!

Amma: Why do they worry?

Hustlin/Serial Monogamy

Finally, when I got better, I was back on the hustle n grind, in my warrior state of mind. I still wasn't living with a woman, but since I didn't know I was lonely, I thought I was a mack—getting girls and spending my spare time with 'em, which was usually on the late late night. Same old pattern without the suitcases—"Accidental Serial Monogamy." By the way, this went on for years . . . and I hated it. What was worse was that it was happening even when I DIDN'T want it to happen.

Kate

My homie Leada told me to meet her at our favorite club. It was a club different than the girl bars in Lower Manhattan filled with escapee softball dykes from Ohio—this one was near Port Authority. For those who don't know—mid-town as far west as you can go before you hit the damn bus station. So it was easy for the Jersey and Bronx girls to come and get their swerve on. Club Escuelita.

Walked in, and immediately felt the eyes on me. Studs throwing me shade, femmes whispering to each other. If you wasn't drunk, it was like the worst hazing ritual just walking through the door. If you were drunk, you'd look everyone in the eye, get respect from the studs and flirt with the femmes.

D'Lo: Yo. What up, L? Super fine, but I ain't drunk so it feel like all them femmes throwing shade, doing their "ps-psa" thing to each other.

Leada: Na, man. What they really doing is "who that stud, who that boi, who he, who he, who he." Watch, go n talk to one of them, you'll see . . . look, one right there. Man, fuck you, even if she *is* white, them white girls freaky bitches. I had these two over the other day, one had my dick in her mouth and the other had her mouth on my titties and . . . oh shit, she coming over here. I'm out.

D: She was a cross between a Pin Up Girl and Southern Belle.

Kate: You wanna buy me a drink, sugar?

D: Yo, you white?

K: Yeah, I'm white. Does that mean you not buying me a drink?

D: Naw, I just wanted to know. (*motions for two drinks*)

(*Song comes on*)

"Is this your jam?" By the way she moved, I could tell I didn't get no ordinary white girl. This white girl knew how to hip-hop, salsa, merengue, and bachata. (*D'Lo drinks two drinks, turns into Kate beckoning D, then drops it like it's hot before breaking out for next lines*) I gotta say, I was mesmerized and conflicted. Here's this fine-ass woman who is the sexiest white girl in the whole club—okay, so she was the only white girl in the club!—and this woman is all about me! (*break back*) She start getting real close, and . . .

D: You know what? I gotta get Leada. She hella drunk. Lemme go and check up on her.

K: You trying to leave me all by my lonesome, sugar?

D: Ya—I mean, no. I'll be back to say bye or whatever. What?

K: You know, in this light you look like a statue on a Hindu temple. . . . I'll be at the bar, handsome.

Fuck this exotification . . . What we gonna do, role-play the Mahabaratha?

D: (*to character off-stage*) Mistah, you seen Leada? She left? You sure? Fuck. Naw, that's cool.

. . . maybe I can be OK with being fetishized for one night . . .

D: Hey there. Oh nothing's wrong. Why? Naw naw, I'm good. Quiet? Naw, I'm, uh . . . Can I come home with you tonight? AH SHIT! I know that sounds crazy, but see, my roommate and now Leada gone. And I ain't tryna have sex or nothing. I just need a place to crash. I mean, we don't even know each other. I don't expect you. It's cool. Word? You're saving my life. Yeah, let's go. I'll wait outside for you.

And I'm feeling weird but thankful that this girl letting me stay, and boy, does she make me feel like a God! But the second I step out onto 38th street I hear, "FREAK! WHAT THE FUCK ARE YOU, YOU WEIRD-ASS MUTHA FUCKER?!" (*sound of a bottle crashing at D'Lo's feet*)

I was checking to see if I had been cut when I heard the club door open, and there was White Girl.

K: You OK, sugar?

D: Yeah. Just tell me how beautiful I am again?

And then, just like that, I had a girlfriend again. But this was the last time, I swore. So, by the second month of her having enough of trying to make me love her, she done had enough. And I had too. Plus, she was mostly in love with an image of me I couldn't live up to. So, we broke up.

CHAPTER 26

Of Railroads, Camps, and Strip Malls:

Symbolic Landscapes of the San Gabriel Valley

WENDY CHENG

IN 2008, THE GARDEN OF FLOWING FRAGRANCE (Liu Fang Yuan), a lavish Chinese garden at the Huntington Library and Gardens in the wealthy enclave of San Marino, in Los Angeles's San Gabriel Valley, opened to the public. The irony that this garden, celebrating elite Chinese culture and funded by Asian American and transpacific capital, was situated on the estate of railroad magnate Henry Huntington—whose fortune had been made on the backs of poor Chinese laborers—was not lost on some. "To think at one point we were just poor laborers working on his railroads," mused Angela Wong, a Chinese American, at the garden's plush opening event (Wong's mother, Lily Wong, donated six figures). "I feel proud of the progress we've made."[1]

The Garden of Flowing Fragrance is indicative of the layered histories and complexities of Asian American history and experience in places like contemporary, suburban Los Angeles. The San Gabriel Valley (SGV), where the Huntington estate is located, is an emblematic region in the making of contemporary Asian America. It is a dynamic, semi-suburban area of loosely connected municipalities that is home to the largest concentration of Asian Americans in the United States. The region gained fame in the 1980s and 1990s when the city of Monterey Park, buoyed by an influx of immigrant ethnic Chinese, became the first majority-Asian American city in the mainland United States. Subsequently Monterey Park was dubbed the "first suburban Chinatown."[2] This effect soon spread to its neighboring municipalities. Heated and sometimes xenophobic and racist struggles over space and power ensued, and large numbers of whites fled en masse in reaction to an incoming tide of immigrant ethnic Chinese. However, in the wake of this demographic upheaval, the newcomers and established residents who remained formed dynamic multiracial and multiethnic communities.

These complex social processes are embedded in the landscape. Conversely, the landscape itself also shapes and influences social processes, especially meaning-making. Cultural geographer D. W. Meinig, in a 1979 essay, wrote of the meaning-laden dimensions of landscapes he called "symbolic landscapes," or ideal forms that serve as both "mold and mirror" to the society that creates them. Symbolic landscapes are idealizations of a particular community and expressions of social and cultural values. They are also surfaces of meaning, or fictions, that may obscure a fuller substance or reality.[3] In short, landscapes, in their normative and symbolic capacities, both express and obscure.[4] In the context of Asian American history and experience, we can think of the Chinese Garden at the Huntington, and other such sites, as symbolic landscapes: ciphers for a particular vision and understanding of that history and experience.

In the following pages, we travel to seemingly mundane but nonetheless significant sites in the everyday landscape—suburban tract homes, strip malls, banks, offices, parks—to ask some linked questions: How is contemporary Asian America made, experienced, and expressed in the everyday landscape? How might rendering visible the sites of its making challenge or transform our understanding of this tenuous yet rich category, 'Asian American'?

The Garden

In the late nineteenth century, tens of thousands of Chinese workers were recruited by railroad capitalists to build nearly every single major railroad in the Western United States.[5] They were paid less than two-thirds of what white workers made, and thousands perished in poor and hazardous working conditions.[6] Many were buried in unmarked graves along the tracks or in the mountains, or their bodies transported in the same railway cars whose paths they had laid, for eventual shipment back to China. "Verily the road was built with Chinaman's [sic] bones," noted one Montana newspaper.[7]

Henry Huntington, born in 1850, was the nephew and protégé of Collis Huntington, the founder and president of the Southern Pacific

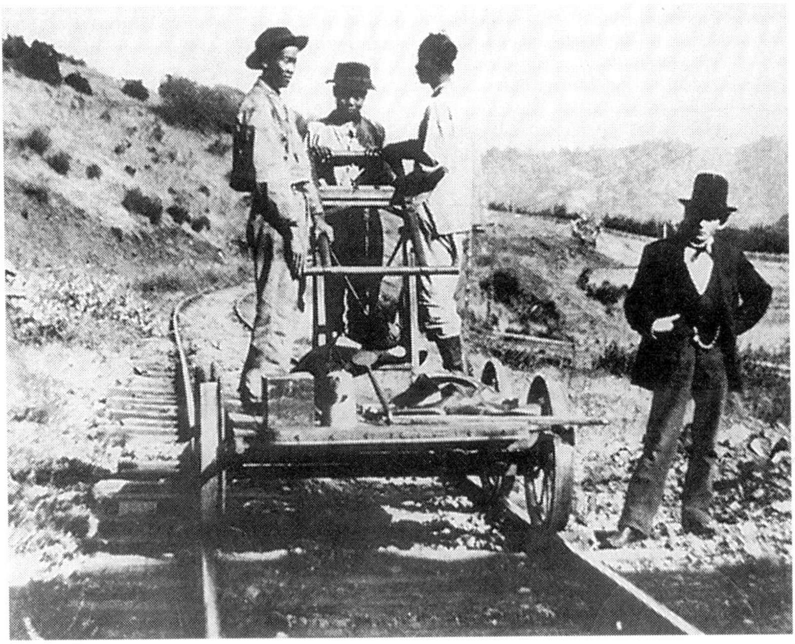

Chinese railroad workers and their boss at Lang Station, 1876. Los Angeles Public Library.

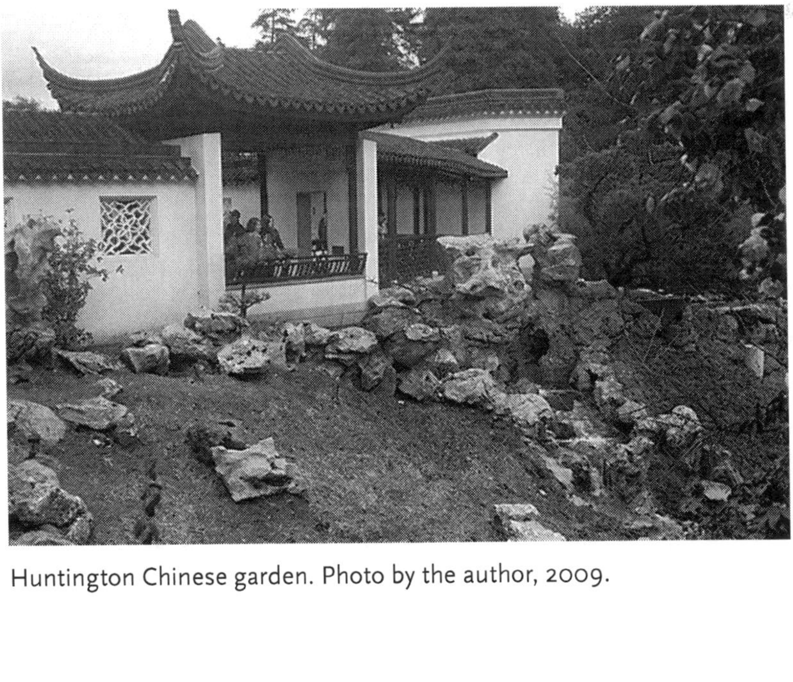

Huntington Chinese garden. Photo by the author, 2009.

Railroad, and one of the instrumental "Big Four" figures in the capitalist development of California. When the elder Huntington died in 1900, his nephew inherited a fortune. Two years later, Henry Huntington purchased the land in San Marino, then a citrus ranch, which would later house his estate and collections, and ultimately become the Huntington Library and Gardens.

A little over a hundred years after Huntington used his railroad fortune to buy the land, more than 50 Chinese artisans and 850 tons of limestone were imported from China to create the Huntington's Chinese Garden. The garden's first phase cost $18.3 million and was substantially funded by the region's affluent Chinese American community, many of whom constituted part of this wealthy (and formerly racially exclusive) enclave's new Asian American majority.[8] Local business leaders like Dominic Ng, the president of East West Bank, participated in fundraising efforts and contributed large sums. A permanent sign at the entrance to the garden, with Chinese characters displayed as prominently as English words, thanked its donors in both English and Chinese. From the institution's perspective, as one official put it, "The garden is a way the Huntington can throw open its doors to an increasingly Chinese neighborhood and an increasingly Chinese world."[9]

Was this progress, as donor Angela Wong would have it? Could one indeed chart an upward trajectory from the Chinese laborers who built Huntington's fortune, to the wealthy ethnic Chinese capitalists who funded the garden and lived in palatial homes just outside the estate's walls? Or were they different stories altogether, linked only tenuously by the presumably shared identity of "Chineseness"? *The road was built with Chinaman's bones.*

The Race Track

Not far east of the Huntington, revelers bet on the races at Santa Anita Park. The race track is perhaps best known as the site of the famous victory by the horse Seabiscuit in 1940. Visitors will likely notice a life-sized iron sculpture of the horse, made and installed not long after its historic victory. Most won't notice a small plaque near the entrance, installed in 2001, describing the incarceration of thousands of Japanese Americans for a period of months there in 1942. Santa Anita Park, like the Pomona Fairgrounds and dozens of other venues, was utilized as an assembly center for tens of thousands of Japanese Americans en route to "internment" in remote Western camps during World War II.

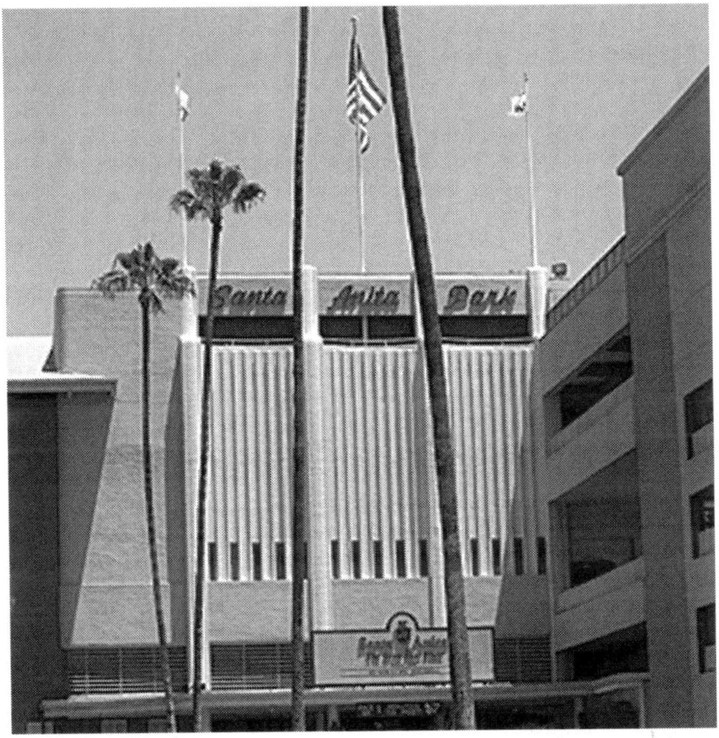

Entrance to Santa Anita Park. Photo by the author.

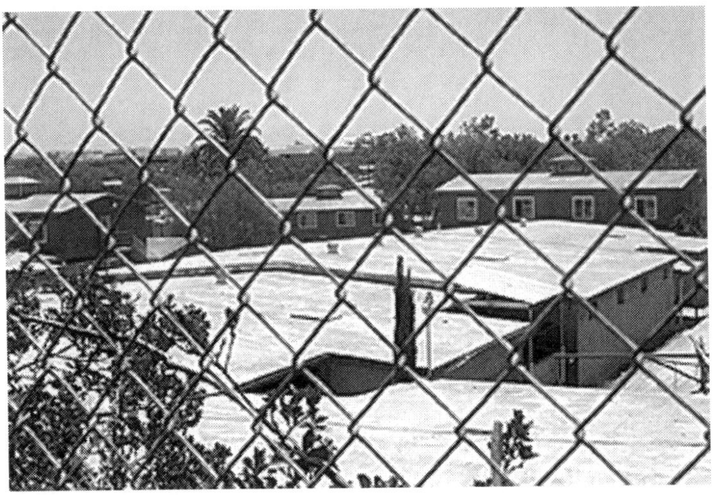

Santa Anita Park, looking over the stables. Photo by the author. 2007.

Santa Anita was the largest and held 19,000 in makeshift barracks and converted horse stables.

On April 6, 1942—just ten days after the track became a detention center—Lily Okuru, a newly married Japanese American woman from Los Angeles, posed for a picture with Seabiscuit's newly cast statue, with a smile and a winsome stance. Okuru and her husband would live at Santa Anita in a horse stable for nine months before applying successfully to be relocated to Omaha, Nebraska.[10]

On the same day Lily Okuru posed with the statue of Seabiscuit, the same photographer made another photograph, of a military police officer patrolling the perimeter fence of Santa Anita. The first photograph, on its own, shows a newlywed young American woman blithely identifying with a symbol of the classic American dream narrative: an underdog overcoming the odds to win a coveted status. The race track figures as an open-ended backdrop of recreation, hopes and dreams,

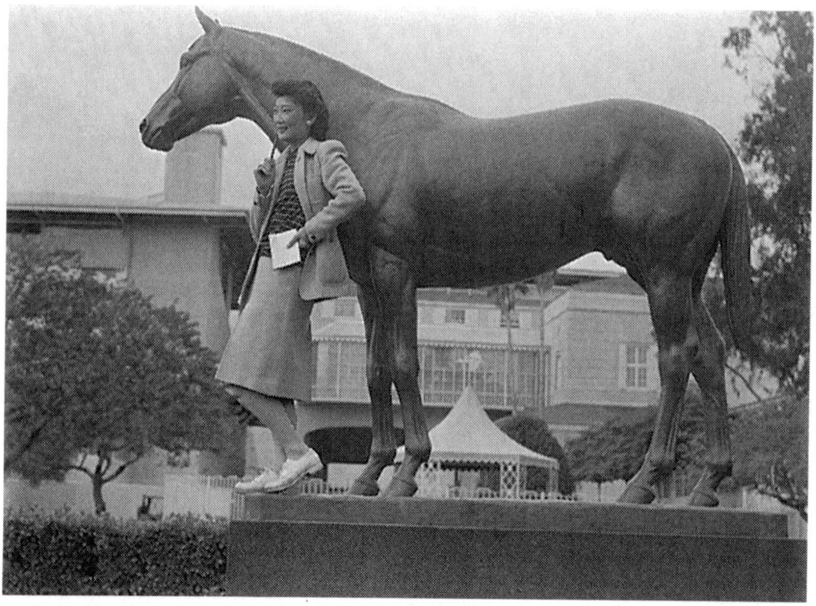

The original WRA caption reads: "Arcadia, California. Mrs. Lily Okuru poses with statue of 'Seabiscuit' in Santa Anita Park, now an assembly center for evacuees of Japanese ancestry." April 6, 1942. Photo by Clem Albers. (Source: http://commons.wikimedia.org/wiki/File:Arcadia,_California._Mrs._Lily_Okuru_poses_with_statue_of_%22Seabiscuit%22_in_Santa_Anita_Park,_now_an_._._._-_NARA_-_537056.jpg.)

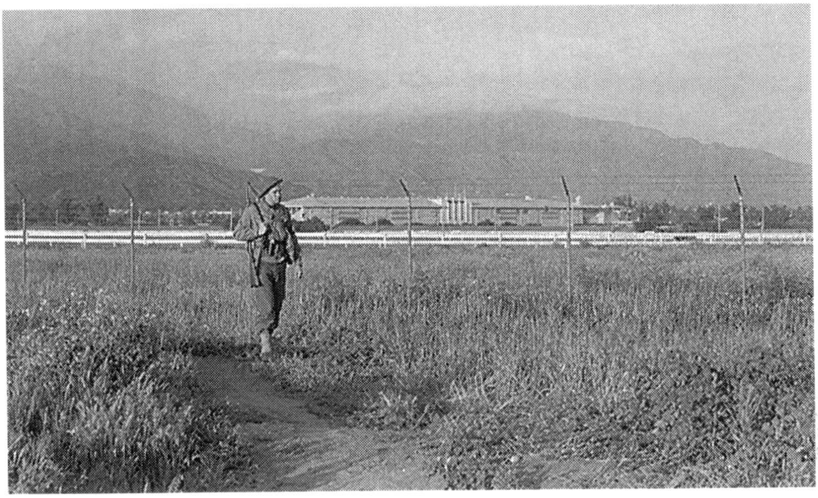

Military police patrolling the perimeter fence, Apr. 6, 1942, Santa Anita Assembly Center, California. Courtesy of the National Archives and Records Administration, Ctrl. #: NWDNS-210-G-B391, NARA ARC #: 537022, WRA. Photo by Clem Albers.

and the opportunity to win big. In the second photograph, the race track is virtually unrecognizable, transformed into an altogether different landscape of incarceration, surveillance, and state-sanctioned violence, ready to be deployed at any moment.

Viewed together, the second photograph reveals the fictions implied in the first.

The Strip Mall

Decades after World War II ended and Japanese Americans were released from the camps, an oversized American flag was installed in front of the Ralphs supermarket at a strip mall in Monterey Park, California. In the 1980s, this shopping center, the Atlantic Square Mall, was the focus of a battle between ethnic Chinese immigrants and established white, Latina/o, and Asian American residents over the right to public and commercial space. The aging mall had been targeted for redevelopment, and established residents and city officials vociferously agitated for "mainstream" stores, English-language signage, and "Mediterranean" architectural style. Ethnic Chinese immigrant–owned

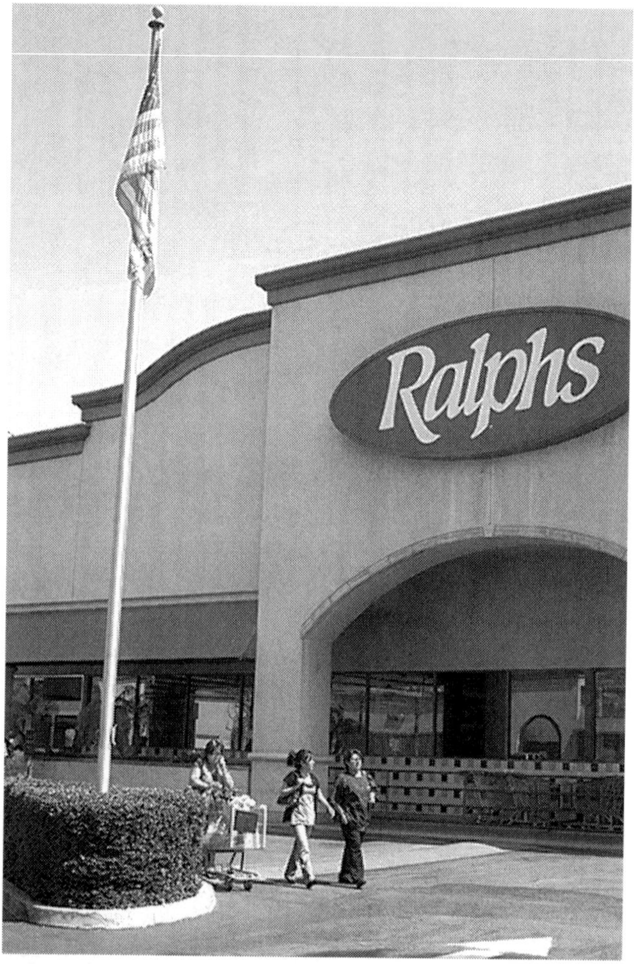

Shoppers at Atlantic Square pass by the American flag posted outside the Ralphs supermarket. Photo by the author.

stores were implicitly and sometimes explicitly excluded from these heavily racialized and nativist priorities. Choices in the vernacular landscape reflected a sense among many established residents of foreign takeover or invasion. "Will the last American to leave Monterey Park please bring the flag?" proclaimed one widely observed sign posted at a gas station during this time.[11]

The nativists won the battle at Atlantic Square, as the conspicuously large flag posted outside the Ralphs grocery store indicates today.

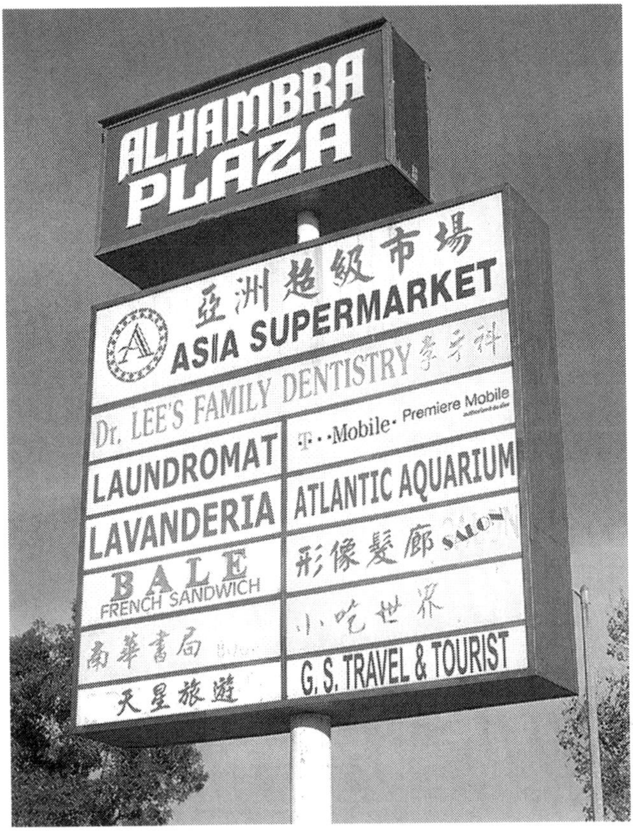

Multilingual strip mall signage in Alhambra, 2012. Photo by the author.

However, in the area as a whole, most of the nativists have indeed taken up their flags and left the area and, in large swaths, ceded the battles over growth and signage. Chinese words and sometimes Vietnamese, or Spanish, play freely over strip mall signs, with English modestly represented or even left out entirely. The strip malls stand as potent symbols of the ways Asian immigration has both occasioned racialized struggles for space, and begun to redefine what counts as "mainstream."

The Faux-Mediterranean Tract Home

The "Mediterranean" architectural style as the style of choice, however, did not lose out. In particular, the faux-Mediterranean tract home as a

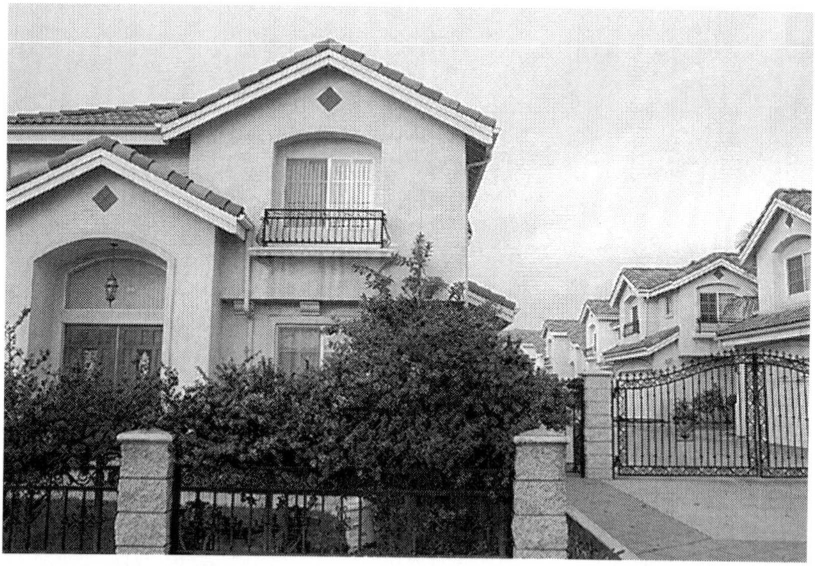

Compact faux-Mediterranean housing development in Monterey Park, 2012. Photo by the author.

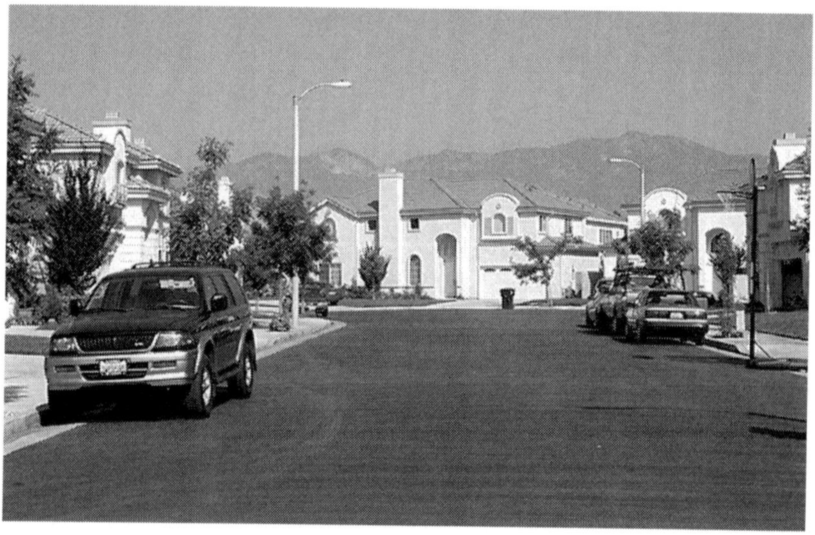

Large faux-Mediterranean tract homes in San Gabriel, 2007. Photo by the author.

coveted form—commonplace among Asian Americans in Southern California—has even leapt westward across the Pacific to China: suburbs such as Orange County, Beijing, built by California developers and patrolled by armed guards, flourish as a potent symbol of the Southern California good life. In the San Gabriel Valley and throughout Southern California, one can find everything from apartment complexes and triplexes to 5,000-square-foot McMansions done up in "faux-Med" style.

Multifamily duplexes, triplexes, and apartment complexes form a mainstay of the housing stock for Asian immigrant families. Flexible and extended-family uses of such spaces, as well as repurposed single-family homes, have been important to the survival and flourishing of poor and immigrant populations. A family might stay at a relative's house for a period of time upon first arriving in the United States, or combine households over the long term in order to save money. A single mother might grow vegetables in the courtyard and sell them to local Asian markets in order to supplement the household income. In Southern California, the pervasiveness of the faux-Mediterranean tract home in Asian immigrant circles illustrates the continuing potency of conventional American suburban ideals, but also the way in which Asian Americans are reshaping the meaning and landscapes of suburbs.

The Ethnic Bank

The ability of large numbers of Asian Americans—especially ethnic Chinese—to purchase homes on a mass scale in the San Gabriel Valley was facilitated in large part by the development of ethnic banks. Asian American banks first developed in Chinatowns due to the exclusion of Asians, along with other nonwhites, from the resources of mainstream American financial institutions. Cathay Bank, in Los Angeles's Chinatown, was heavily community-oriented, developing personal relationships with customers, helping many of their clientele transition from cash-based mentalities, and giving out "character loans" to applicants who would have been denied by mainstream institutions.[12] The bank provided Chinese-speaking tellers and a range of social services such as introductions to immigration lawyers and mediation of intergenerational conflicts. When asked how bank officials knew that the loans would be repaid, one answered, "These were honest and hardworking people. We knew them . . . There was no doubt they would eventually have the money to repay."[13]

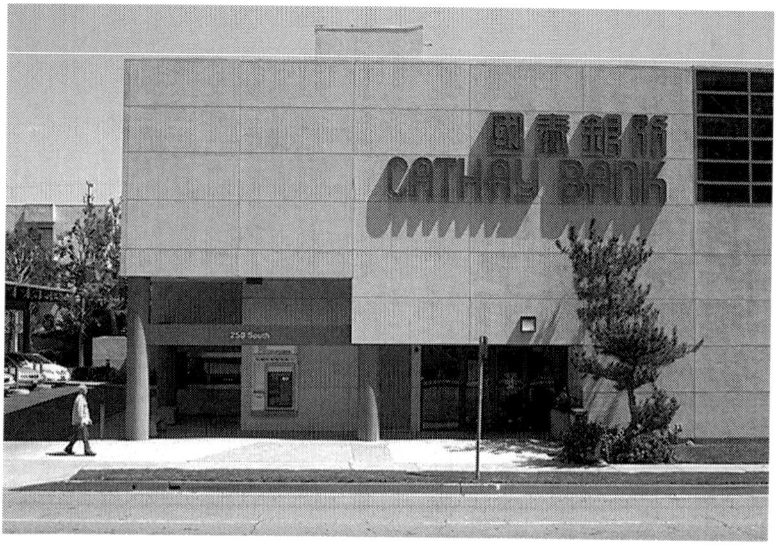

Cathay Bank branch in Monterey Park. Photo by the author.

The first Asian American bank branch in the United States, a branch of Cathay Bank, opened in Monterey Park in the late 1970s. In the decades that followed, the ethnic Chinese banking sector developed and flourished in tandem with the spread of Asian immigrant and Asian American-oriented commercial and residential landscapes in the SGV. The concentration of Chinese American banks on Valley Boulevard in Alhambra was dubbed the "Chinese Wall Street." With the high ratio of bank branches to population, Chinese Americans in Los Angeles County now have much better access to banking resources compared to other ethnic minority groups, and even to the general population. The ethnic Chinese banking infrastructure developed out of both exclusion and opportunity, and the landscapes it has had a central hand in shaping cannot be understood without it.

The Sweatshop

In the San Gabriel Valley as elsewhere, coethnic networks are also used for more sinister purposes. From the late 1980s through 1995, an apartment complex in El Monte was repurposed into an illegal garment factory run by a Chinese Thai family (Suni Manasurangkun, her five sons, two daughters-in-law, and two additional hired workers). Over seventy Thai workers—mostly women—were recruited in Thailand

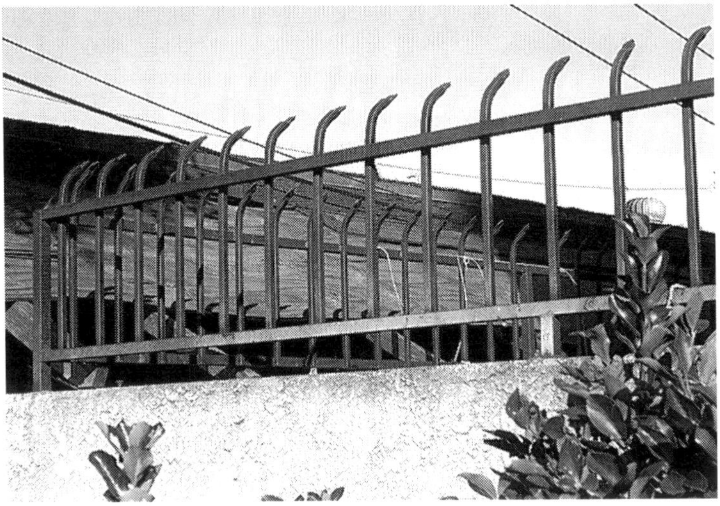

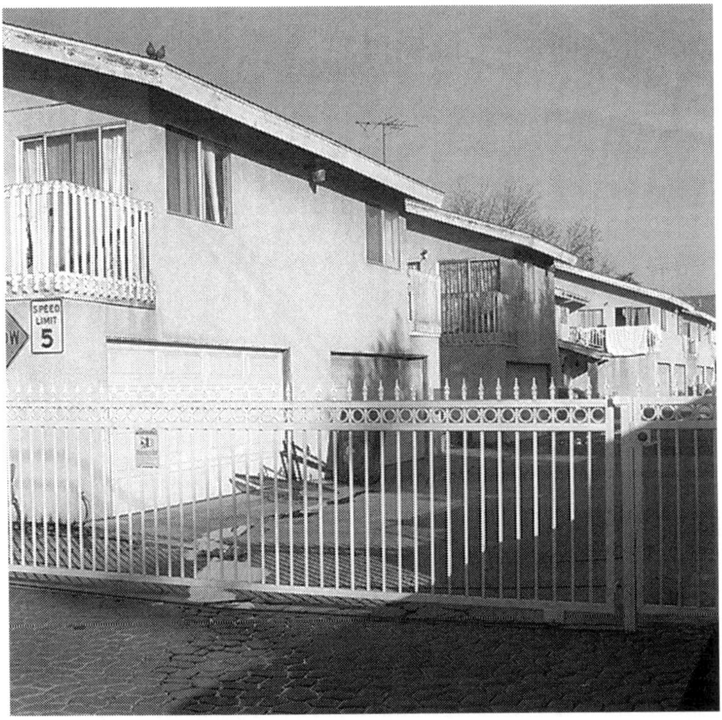

Apartment complex that housed an illegal garment factory and its workers in El Monte. Photos by the author.

with promises of good pay, decent work hours, and weekend trips to Disneyland. Upon arrival, however, they were effectively enslaved for up to four years, working 16 hours a day for what amounted to less than a dollar per hour. The windows were boarded up and the complex enclosed with razor wire and attended by an armed guard. In 1992, one of the male workers, Win Chuai Ngan, managed to escape. In his pocket, he had the address of a local temple from an advertisement he had torn and pocketed from a Thai-language newspaper. He had also torn off the address of the complex where he and the others had been imprisoned. After Ngan, a few others managed to escape as well, eventually leading to a federal raid in 1995. Although the workers, all unauthorized immigrants, were initially set to be deported, public outcry led to them being given amnesty. Most stayed in the United States, and many have since become citizens.

The Manasurangkuns' operation, while extreme, was indicative of the harsh and exploitative conditions in the Los Angeles garment industry as a whole. After the bust, the El Monte workers, with the help of the Asian Pacific American Legal Center, allied with Latina/o workers who had been employed in the Manasurangkuns' front shops downtown, to file suit against corporate retailers who had contracted work with the manufacturer, such as Mervyns. The workers won a landmark, multimillion-dollar settlement, which established that corporations can be legally held responsible for labor exploitation carried out by their subcontractors.[14]

At the apartment complex in El Monte, the workers have gone, but the spiked tips on the fence railings still face inward. They remain as a symbol of the complex intra- and interethnic dynamics of social and labor networks, and how the everyday landscape is implicated in globalized economic systems.

The Park

A stone's throw from the Huntington, San Marino's Lacy Park offers visitors bucolic walks around a vast lawn, in the shade of tall oaks, pines, and lemon eucalyptus trees. Visitors can picnic or play tennis on one of six well-maintained courts. San Marino, incorporated in 1913 by Henry Huntington and wealthy ranchers to protect their extensive land holdings, prides itself on being "the finest, exclusively residential community in the West."[15] Apartment buildings are banned, and property values are three times the county median. Beginning in the

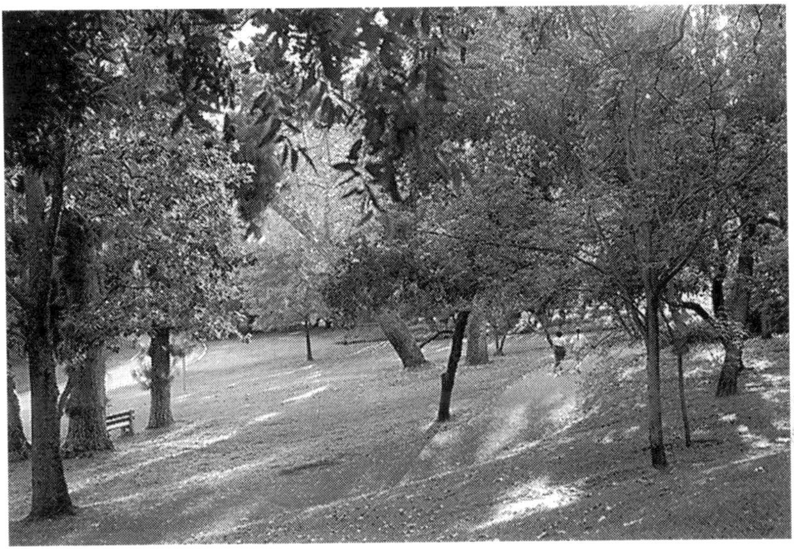

An Asian American couple strolls in Lacy Park during the weekend, 2007. Photo by the author.

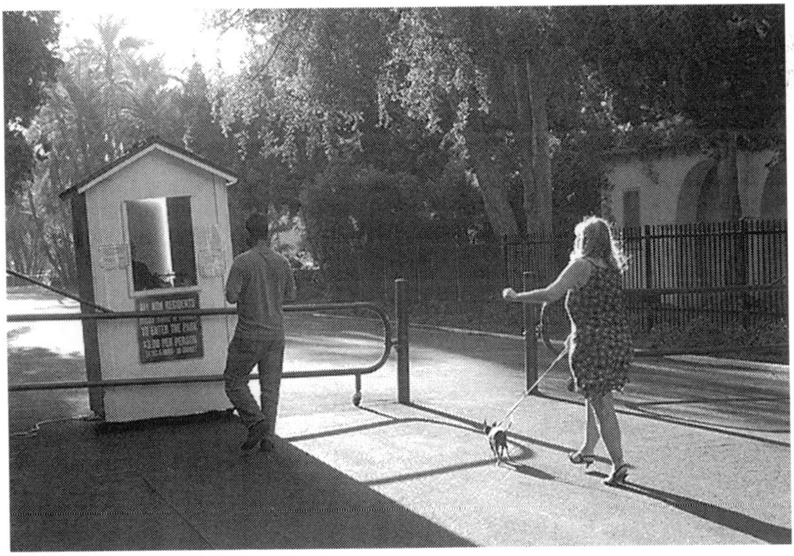

A couple and their dog approach the fee/identification-check booth at the entrance to Lacy Park, 2007. Photo by the author.

1980s, however, the historically all-white community began to change substantially as Asian Americans moved in. In 2010, for the first time, Asians made up the clear majority of San Marino's population. Most of the remaining population remained white.[16] San Marino had its first Asian American mayor in 2001, Taiwanese American orthopedic surgeon and self-made millionaire Matthew Lin, and Asian American representation in city leadership has been consistent since.

In 1988, Lacy Park became the first park in California to charge nonresidents for usage on weekends. Although city officials stated that the fee was necessary due to post–Proposition 13 funding problems, the new policy also coincided with complaints about "outsiders" and "criminal elements." In addition to the $3 (now $4) fee per nonresident, a $50 permit fee was also required for gatherings larger than 15 people. In effect, the new policy made the park less accessible to poorer populations nearby, who are predominantly Latina/o but also Asian, and are unlikely to have comparable park access in their own communities.

In a city in which historically, nonwhites were forbidden to live (with the exception of servants), the rise of a new Asian American majority may *look* significant, but in practice, the conservative and exclusionary tendencies of San Marino—as seen in the racialized and classed effects of the city's management of its "public" park—have remained very much the same.

Back to the Garden

Thinking critically about the "place" of Asian Americans in the twenty-first-century United States serves as a useful starting point for creative and critical engagement for artists and scholars. While no single approach or region can encompass the complexity and heterogeneity of contemporary Asian America, a symbolic landscape approach makes visible a cross-section of important themes and processes in contemporary Asian American life, as instantiated in the everyday landscape. These include the fictions we create in order to live,[17] the racial underpinnings of capitalist labor and development, and the dual mechanisms of exclusion and opportunity.

I feel proud of the progress we've made. Again: was Angela Wong right? Can one trace a line from exploited railroad workers to the graceful sculptures and landscaping of the Huntington's Chinese Garden, and call it progress? If so, what would we call the line leading from a

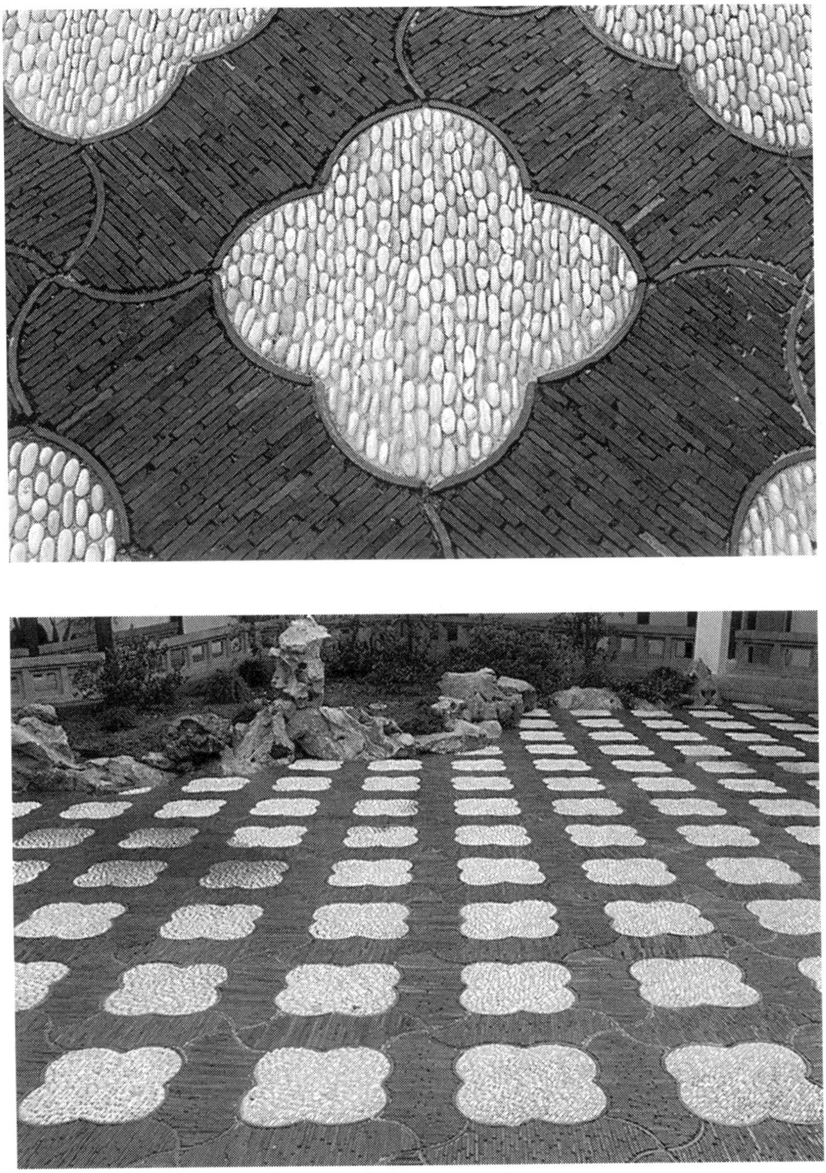

Intricate stone tiles laid by Chinese artisans pave a courtyard in the Huntington Chinese garden, 2009. Photos by author.

race track-turned-detention center to an apartment complex-turned-sweatshop? What would we call the line that connects an ethnic Chinese bank to the large American flag posted in a suburban strip mall? A sustained consideration of the landscape may initially raise more questions than it answers. But it helps us, perhaps, to ask different and new questions.

Notes

1. Teresa Watanabe, "Huntington Library's Newest Garden Celebrates Chinese Culture," *Los Angeles Times*, February 17, 2008, http://latimes.com/news/local/la-me-gardens17feb17,0,3859702.story.
2. Timothy Fong, *The First Suburban Chinatown: The Remaking of Monterey Park, California* (Philadelphia: Temple University Press, 1994).
3. Meining, "Symbolic Landscapes: Some Idealizations of American Communities," in D. W. Meining, ed., *The Interpretation of Ordinary Landscapes* (New York: Oxford University Press, 1979, 164–192), 188.
4. On "normative dimensions of landscape," see Richard Schein, "Normative Dimensions of Landscape" (in Chris Wilson and Paul Groth, eds., *Everyday America: Cultural Landscape Studies after J. B. Jackson* (Berkeley: University of California Press, 2003, 199–218)).
5. Smithsonian Program for Asian American Studies, "On Gold Mountain: A Chinese American Experience," http://apa.si.edu/ongoldmountain/gallery2/gallery2.html.
6. Alexander Saxton, *The Indispensable Enemy: Labor and the Anti-Chinese Movement in California* (Berkeley: University of California Press, 1971), 60–66.
7. Christopher W. Merritt, Gary Weisz, and Kelly J. Dixon, "'Verily the Road Was Built with Chinaman's Bones'; An Archaeology of Chinese Line Camps in Montana," *International Journal of Historical Archaeology* 16:4 (December 2012): 666–695.
8. In 2010, for the first time, Asians made up the clear majority (53.5 percent) of San Marino's population. Most of the remaining population was white (41.3 percent). The city continues to have a strikingly low proportion of Latinas/os compared to surrounding areas (6.5 percent). US Census 2010.
9. Quoted in Teresa Watanabe, "Huntington Library's Newest Garden Celebrates Chinese Culture," *Los Angeles Times*, February 17, 2008, http://latimes.com/news/local/la-me-gardens17feb17,0,3859702.story.
10. Yvonne Shinhoster Lamb, "Public Broadcasting Official Lily Okura, 86; Mental Health Activist (Obituary)," *Washington Post*, July 3, 2005.
11. On the struggle over Atlantic Square Mall, see Leland Saito, *Race and Politics: Asian Americans, Whites, and Latinos in a Los Angeles Suburb*

(Urbana, IL: University of Illinois Press, 1998). On the gas station sign and for general background, see Fong, *The First Suburban Chinatown*. Also see the entry on Atlantic Square Mall in Laura Pulido, Laura Barraclough, and Wendy Cheng, *A People's Guide to Los Angeles* (Berkeley: University of California Press, 2012).

12. All factual information in this entry is from Wei Li, Gary Dymski, Yu Zhou, Maria Chee, and Carolyn Aldana, "Chinese-American Banking and Community Development in Los Angeles County," *Annals of the Association of American Geographers*, Vol. 92 (2002), No. 4, 777–796. Also see entry on Cathay Bank, Pulido, Cheng, and Barraclough, *A People's Guide to Los Angeles*.
13. Li, Dymski, Zhou, Chee, and Aldana, 786.
14. For more information, see entry on El Monte Sweatshop, Pulido, Cheng, and Barraclough, *A People's Guide to Los Angeles*; Daniel E. Bender and Richard A. Greenwald, eds., *Sweatshop USA: The American Sweatshop in Historical and Global Perspective* (New York: Routledge, 2003); Julie A. Su and Chanchanit Martorell, "Exploitation and Abuse in the Garment Industry: The Case of the Thai Slave-Labor Compound in El Monte," *Asian and Latino Immigrants in a Restructuring Economy: The Metamorphosis of Southern California* (Marta López-Garza and David R. Diaz, eds., Stanford, CA: Stanford University Press, 2001); Teresa Watanabe, "Home of the Freed," *Los Angeles Times*, August 14, 2008.
15. Entry on Lacy Park, Pulido, Cheng, and Barraclough, *A People's Guide to Los Angeles*.
16. Asians made up 53.5 percent of San Marino's population, and whites made up 41.3 percent. The city continues to have a strikingly low proportion of Latinas/os compared to surrounding areas (6.5 percent). US Census 2010.
17. Paraphrasing Joan Didion's famous line, "We tell ourselves stories in order to live." *The White Album* (New York: Simon and Schuster, 1979), 11.

Chapter 27

Where You've Been

An Epilogue

Lucy MSP Burns

California Dreaming highlights artistic processes and the circulation of art objects to understand the place of California in the artistic imaginary. The works here present "competing visions/versions of California," as phrased by music scholar Mina Yang.[1] With this collection, we seek to portray a dynamic California, not a single, unified vision. In centering Asian American arts and artistic practices, we consider the aesthetics and politics of contemporary movements of objects and people, embodiment, relations of power, border crossings, and affinity.

In this collection, we grapple with critiques of and in the field that have decentered what Stephen Sumida has coined as "California-dominated paradigm" in early Asian American Studies scholarship. This "California-dominated paradigm" in part privileges critical mass and longevity as categories through which Asian Americans are written into historical existence. Sumida points out that "a Californic paradigm has never been the sole one in the field."[2] *California Dreaming* contributes to anthologies that have brought regional approaches to the field, such as *New England Asian American Studies, Asian Americans in Dixie: Race and Migration in the South,* and *Roots and Reflections: South Asians in the Pacific Northwest.*[3] This turn to regionalism has been an occasion to rethink Asian American Studies by examining how West Coast/California Asian Americans are rethinking themselves.

Our collection does not, however, seek to reestablish a bounded California-centric framework. Two decades ago, I heard Peter Kiang describe the formation of Asian American Studies on the East Coast (where I went to graduate school) as one built on the backs of seasonal, temporary workers.[4] Adjunct professors traveled up and down the East Coast, teaching courses on Asian American Studies in small colleges and universities. Roberta Uno similarly described the labor of Asian American solo performance artists as migratory, calling it "the theatrical cottage industry of the 1980s." Performing stories of Asian American experiences, these artists' work "has become a means to redress stereotyping and misrepresentations and to assert ownership of theatrical production."[5] I cite these two examples of itinerant Asian American labor to speak to the precarious work conditions of lecturers and artists, as contract workers, that build Asian America toward institutional legibility and national recognition.

California Dreaming assembles works that have emerged since the early 2000s, thus representing concerns of the twenty-first century. Portraits of laboring communities and identities do not dominate the preoccupation of the entries in this collection, however. Some pieces are indeed concerned with the early historical presence of Asian migrants. Earlier Asian American artistic works responded to and were inspired by the necessity to capture representations of communities/early migrants.[6] So, what do the works here do now? What are the social conditions that map Asian American art in *California Dreaming?*

Many of the works in this anthology, such as D'Lo's *D'FunQT,* perform an understanding of racial and ethnic identities as intersectional. Ethnocentrism and sentimental envisioning of coalitional relations between racialized communities are tempered. Tensions across racial, ethnic, classed, and gendered boundaries are tackled directly. This is not to say that cross-community solidarity is less of an aspiration nor less desirable; rather, these works remain open to, in the words of Angela Davis, "an experiment in being together," as it attends to inequalities of differences.[7]

The works gathered here portray experiences and encounters of a non-static California and an ever-changing Asian America. They emplace California in Asian America and emplace Asian America in California. To emplace, in the language of computer programming, is to construct and insert a new element into a set or a place, not copy it into a map.

"What Brings You Here?": Emplacing Displaced Peoples

Each contributor formulates differently histories of Asian migration and emplacement in America, in California. *Where are you from? Where have you been? Where are you coming from? How did your people get here? How does a face like yours get a name like that? How did you end up here?* These questions are iterated with varying sentiments in many of the pieces in this anthology. They are invoked to justify, connect, relate, reach out, legitimate, explain, and permit. At times, they are uttered to put someone in their place or make them feel out of place. They convey differences of power and belonging. These are questions or comments that bodies marked as non-belonging are confronted with, bombarded with, and burdened to answer. And yet, I find myself asking those with particular accents I recognize: *Pilipino ho kayo?* (Are you Filipino?) I feel the desire to connect, perhaps most strongly in a place of irreconcilable differences. The work now is to imagine togetherness beyond reconcilability. In this collection, these questions inspire creative responses and engage with the politics and art of emplacement.

Nayan Shah considers the question, "How do diverse people resonate and contend with a particular land and topography?" His essay elaborates on claims to a place and considers one's relationship to landscape. Kevin Fellezs's writing on guitarist Patrick Landeza asks, "How do people bring their histories and cultural practices . . . as they move from one place to another?" Sansan Kwan brings methods of auto-ethnography and movement theory: "The body is made meaningful when emplaced in space and time and in relation to other bodies and objects." She also observes that "[the] multiple migrations and returns that characterize the diasporic body means that these bodies carry layers of somatic experience—of past and current places, homelands and new lands and places in between. These layers are not really settled one on top of another but rather enmeshed at once." Shah, Fellezs, and Kwan all consider what relationship is possible when one is not of or from a place. Each engages and makes clear that the question of one's connection to a place—how to identify or what to call that connection—is a crucial and necessary one. We cannot be both subjects of and subjected to a place.

These works affirm that displaced peoples are not stuck. Having been displaced is not the definitive experience of abjection. It is immobility.[8] By rendering Asian diasporic bodies in their processes and forms of relocation, dislocation, and other forms of movement, Shah, Fellezs, Kwan, and other contributors refuse a portrayal of immigrants as purely abject.

We Are Here Because You Were There

Leilani Chan and Ova Saopeng's performance text excerpt is a vignette from a longer performance, titled the *Refugee Nation,* about Lao refugee experiences. In "Lao Fighters," two men of different generations enact their initiation to manhood in different times, different wars: the Silent War in the mid-twentieth century and the war against immigrants and youths in the early twenty-first century. This scene portrays the parallel lives of a senior Lao fighter and an incarcerated Lao American who grew up in Texas, capturing the effects of war in the formation of Southeast Asian masculinities. They are both initiated into manhood through their participation in wars. War violence forms the kinship structure they come to know and must maintain, what Sri Lankan feminist scholar Neloufer de Mel's phrases as "martial virtue."[9] Chan and Saopeng's *Refugee Nation* thus challenges the neatness with which the refugee trajectory has been mapped out—from arrival to (re)settlement to assimilation, from being refugees to becoming assimilated subjects as citizens. This theater piece ultimately queries how we tell experiences of war and refugee experiences. The work of Chan and Saopeng's *Refugee Nation* is, to paraphrase Lisa Lowe's influential *Immigrant Acts,* to underscore possibilities of irreconcilability against the hegemonic impulse of resolving U.S. national difference.

As the politics of location continue to raise the stakes of power, the compulsion to locate oneself, explain one's actions, and expound on one's perspectives grows forceful. The need to respond to "Where do you come from?" provides explanation, gives legitimacy, and justifies one's actions, one's opinion's, one's point of view. Situating Asian American subjectivities within the ever-changing grounds of racial politics negotiates shifting positions of power and seeks to undo binary positions such as oppressed and oppressor. For example, migrant laborers' subjectivity has been well represented in Asian American histories and cultural imaginary. The paradigm of settler colonialism provides a way to understand dominance and power through challenging representations of migrants as abject. In linking nation- and empire-building with capital accumulation, settler colonialist critiques make more complex immigrant subjectivities, particularly with regard to questions of complicity and relationship to place beyond contributions through labor. Shah's essay on immigrant claims to places, in particular U.S. national parks and Priya Srinivasan's analysis of Indian classical dance at the Srinivasa Temple in Malibu, both address the embattled politics of belonging. Srinivasan examines the performance of Bharata Natyam by Indian American bodies as they lay claim to the Malibu Temple and the land it is built on, originally named as Humaliwo by the Chumash. She opens up the binary by attending to the "messy intersections, the ambivalence of the process of citizenship." Srinivasan concludes that Indian dancing bodies' cultural practices are not pure resistance or pure commodities.

Many questions remain as we circle, pass through, stand at, and get stuck and unstuck at this "messy intersection": What politics can we create and practice as we live the everyday realities of living as occupiers on occupied land? And in turn, how do we continue to make accountable continuing xenophobia and vehement anti-immigrant sentiments enabled by settler colonialism? How do we continue to negotiate varying positions as "immigrants," "natives," "settlers," "sovereigns," "commoners," among other assigned and owned identities? What new identity formations and social relations can we imagine under and beyond conditions of occupation? As unrealized as it may be, the commitment remains in seeing through the tension of being together and not letting our dreams be limited by the realities of rubbing against each other.

Fictive Collisions with the Myth of California

Early anthologies about California, such as *California Uncovered: Stories for the 21st Century, Highway 99: A Literary Journey Through California's Great Central Valley, and Many Californias: Literature from the Golden State,* repeatedly invoke the diversity of the people of this state.[10] What happens when different people, different elements, encounter each other? A common misperception is that diversity or differences lead to harmonious cohabitation, that somehow proximity among different entities/elements will produce virtuous generosity, genuine and long-lasting camaraderie.

We get another glimpse of a "messy intersection" in Jason Perez's "Oh, Angelita Garcia!" set in San Diego's multicultural, multiracial Oceanside elementary school. It tells of a day in the life of young Hasón, who brings his mother, a Filipina nurse once accused of multiple murders by the FBI, to show-and-tell in his third-grade class. Hasón's social life among his Korean, Latino/a, and Black classmates is not quite the paradisic promise of 1980s U.S. multiculturalism, a happy portrait of diversity where hierarchies of difference are erased and all get along.

Perez's story, rather, portrays the process of shifting racial majority away from Hispanic, single-race whites. In his work, the dream of 1980s multicultural ethnic diversity takes the form of unrecognized love and unrealized friendships.

In *Self-Remix,* Robert Karimi mixes sounds of West Asia and Guatemala as they are heard in Union City, CA, to tell the tale of an American child of Iranian and Guatemalan immigrants growing up in California in the 1970s and 1980s in the shadow of the Iranian hostage crisis. Karimi's hip-hop theater is a self-portrait of his mixed cultural heritage (West Asian-Latinx; Muslim and Catholic) peppered with DJ spins of '80s modern rock, slow jam, rap music, and cartoon and television show soundtracks. While the backdrop to Karimi's growing up years is the Iran hostage crisis, the political backdrop to Karimi's *Self-Remix* is the era of Homeland Security and Bush's Axis of Evil. This era, centered on the aggressive hunt for terrorism, brought Union City into focus: here, Arab American and other Asian communities in the south Central Bay Area were under constant police surveillance. Union City was the backdrop for militarized enactments of homeland insecurities, with open and increased racial and religious profiling and gross violations of civil liberties.

The Golden Reel of Dreams: Beyond the Spectacular Persistence of Stereotypes

Gina Osterloh's "Rapture," featuring photographs from her *Somewhere Tropical* series, stages the clichéd California backdrop of palm trees and sunsets over a body of water. "Rapture" localizes Hollywood's role as a dominant image-producing industry. Asian American Studies' critique of mainstream Hollywood's representation of Asian Americans in its imaginary of America and American is well-established, particularly in the form of "stereotype" critiques. Two of the mainstays of such critiques are Deborah Gee's documentary films *Slaying the Dragon* (1988) and Elaine Kim's *Slaying the Dragon Reloaded* (2011).[11] Kim and many other scholars have built a strong criticism of American popular culture, exposing the limits of roles for Asian American actors and the uni-dimensionality of the characters they play. Attentiveness to stereotypes opens up an analysis of the means and control of production against and next to consumer demands.

The study of racist stereotypes can be productive and useful because these images help us understand expressions of uneven relations of power and the dominant racist perceptions of a racialized community. In particular, Asian stereotypes are embodiment of histories of Asian/immigrant exclusion, the "contradictory condition of Asians," as Lisa Lowe phrased it, in the U.S. Just as stereotypes of Native Americans are embodiments of land claims in U.S. history and ongoing colonial occupation, critiques of Asian American stereotypes are more than just cries of sensitivity. They are not simply a call for correct representations. Analysis of stereotypes prompts us to remember exclusionary histories of immigration, territorial occupation, possessions, and discriminatory labor practices. As Edward Said has written, "Representations operate in a specific historical, intellectual, and even economic setting."[12]

Contributors to this anthology redirect and reenergize forms of critique through humor and through artistic production that gives new life to the characters and the story itself. Using humor, Dan McMullin's poem "100 Tiki Notes" confronts the American orientalist fetish for the peoples, objects, and landscape of the Pacific Islands. Prince Golmovilas's playful list calls out Hollywood's habitual erasure of Asian Americans in popular films. In the 1990s, Asian Americans lamented their invisibility in Hollywood, specifically not having their own television sitcoms. In her comedic tele-script "Abstraction 2: Television Sitcom, DentalOptics," Karen Tei Yamashita imagines what an Asian American sitcom would be like, set in the city Gardena, CA, where there is a high percentage of Japanese American residents. Yamashita critically captures the sitcom format: nothing happens; the art of conversation is its content. What does it mean when this "nothing" is enacted by Asian American bodies? Hollywood remains a site of possibility, aspiration, and hope for Asian American cultural production, despite the continuous discourse of non-deliverance.

Asian American Arts Facing East and West

Science fiction writer Ursula Le Guin, in a conversation with fellow science fiction writer Molly Gloss, spoke about East Coast–dominated literary publishing: "Writers writing in the West, or stories set in the West, [are so] unrecognizable to publishers and (by extension) readers from the East Coast–dominated literary publishing that [they] might as well be set on another planet."[13] In a panel on "California Writing" hosted by the Los Angeles Public Library, writer panelists including Lisa See, Hector Tobar, Naomi Hirahara, and Linelle George similarly echo how the East Coast's (specifically New York's) dominance of literary publishing poses a challenge for Californian and other West Coast writers, and comment on the weight of East Coast literary culture against California art forms. Echoing this bicoastal difference, Joyce Lu's conversation with dancer, choreographer, and Kularts artistic director Alleluia Panis details how this dynamic is played out in Asian American cultural institutions in the West. When Panis began her career as a working artist in San Francisco, there was a lack of mentors. She says, "If I was in New York, I could go to an organization and get funding through an organization, you know—whether it's Asia Society or I don't know, La Mama—and be sheltered basically by that institution. So, there's a mentorship that I think is valuable that young artists don't necessarily have here." Lu underscores the ways Panis created the mentorship program she wanted to experience so that many artists now have a solid ground on which they can launch their work.

Kularts's transnational arts programming is an example of how Asian American arts organizations and artists make national and cultural borders porous. Lu's interview with Panis highlights Panis's nearly four decades of linking Filipino Americans and artists from the Philippines through various programming—artist exchanges, tribal arts tours to the Philippines, and collaborative artistic productions that put Filipino artists from different shores on the same stage, with a focus on educating Filipinos in the U.S. and providing opportunities to tribal artists of the Philippines to perform on the international stage. Viet Lê's, Lan Duong's, and Lu's entries in this anthology provide portraits and analysis of how Asian American art and Asian art—visual, filmic, and multimedia performances—circulate across (and beyond) the Pacific. Duong highlights the transnational production of film-making and film distribution practices between Vietnamese American directors in Southern California and Vietnam, tracing the shift from viewing those who left Vietnam as "traitors" to their new roles as "collaborators." The state of Vietnam, he says, now "increasingly incorporates and ingests their [Vietnamese diasporic artists'] labor and talent as part of their efforts to promote Vietnamese culture globally."

Lê's essay features Vietnamese and Cambodian artists and arts organizers, tracing "the overlapping networks of art circulation, consumption, and production." While Lê and Duong discuss the role of the state in developing a Vietnamese diasporic arts economy, Lu states that in the case of Panis's 40-year partnership with various indigenous artists in the Philippines, the Philippine state remains uninvested in the relationship between Filipinx diasporic artists and tribal artists in the Philippines.

Protest art is a well-established oppositional practice among Asian American artists, as life in Asia galvanizes community-organizing among the Asian diaspora. Yong Soon Min's visual essay "Habitual Practices/Making Korean Ridiculous" locates historical incidents influential to Korean diasporic activism: the L.A. riots of 1992 and the Gwangju Uprising of 1980. Min analyzes striking visual images from both events, recalling how streets in Los Angeles and Seoul were lit up by the protests and puts in parallel how both Koreans and Korean Americans keep the flame of agitation against state violence burning.

Reorienting U.S. bicoastal directionality to the trans-Pacific and beyond, Asian American artists uniquely map the transnationalism that has defined Asian American studies, allowing for an approach that has a critical and performative relationship to official national and cultural borders.

"What's in your Baggage?": Everyday Encounters

From slack key guitarist Patrick Landeza's musical practices to the culinary practices of the Mabalon family, contributions in this collection underscore that baggage is not simply objects we carry, but "how people bring their histories and cultural practices, as they move from one place to another," as phrased by Kevin Fellezs. Through his discussion of Landeza's musical practices, Fellezs engages Hawaiian ancestry claims and how they matter to the California-born Landeza. In her essay, Dawn Mabalon remembers her family putting down roots in Stockton, California, through her family's unique recipe for *binangkal*, a Filipino pastry. Mabalon also details the necessary and creative substitutions that her family has had to make, accommodating what is lacking in their new home.

Family traditions can live on in the diaspora despite, or because of, changes and adaptations. Mixed-race Cambodian American artist Tiffany Lytle's personal history of separately training in folk and classical Cambodian dance and contemporary dance insists on the possibilities of fusion forms as methods of expression that can indeed embody mixed-race identity. Artists such as Lytle move forward the project of cultural preservation in the diaspora while exemplifying renewed critical approaches to hybrid artistic practices.

Multimedia artist Philip Huang's home theater festival is a refreshing reminder of how we become attached to the baggage we choose to carry, which may in fact be weighing us down. Whereas Leilani Chan discusses the challenges of producing theater inside buildings and performing plays outdoors, and the challenges faced by her theater-making company, Huang returns us to the basics, reminding us that we sometimes create obstructions to our own creativity, that perhaps our commitment to reforming existing creative institutions may be confused, collapsed, or become synonymous with our art-making.

Everyday encounters consist of varied forms of intimacies, connections, and disconnections. Wendy Cheng's photo essay acknowledges different ways in which Asian Americans are embedded in the everyday urban landscape. By asking, "How is contemporary Asian America made, experienced, and expressed in the everyday landscape?" Cheng broadens how Asian America may be understood, how histories of labor and community formations are dynamically experienced and also disappeared in the mundane. In L.A., where bus riding signals class status, Kristina Wong's insightful wit, humor, and sarcasm explore the rich possibilities of close encounters on the bus routes of Southern California.

Larry Padua's "Reels" frames the largest urban park in the U.S., Los Angeles's Griffith Park, as grounds for queer men in search of sex, intimacy, and other forms of connection. Seeds of intimacy cover Griffith Park, yet, as Padua writes, "time and distance evaporate intimacy." As SanSan Kwan writes, "Our bodies are palimpsests of the numerous kinetic encounters we carry." Next to Padua's "evaporating intimacy," their words make us aware of the effects of temporality on encounters—intimate and otherwise.

Tracy Buenavista and Ray Hernandez's "Dreamers: A Dialogue on Education Rights and the Movement for Undocumented Migrants" discusses the undocumented student movement and its links to militarization. Hernandez grapples with his "artivism," with creating images that have become iconic visual references of the Dreamers. Hernandez's suspended cap and gown imply accomplishment but also the uncertainty of what follows. Underlying Buenavista's and Hernandez's conversation is the question of what is at risk. Beyond the material forms of our dreams, what is fundamentally threatened is the act of dreaming itself. Under the conditions that continue to criminalize being undocumented, dreaming itself is restricted and policed.

While a number of entries in this collection contemplate mobility and globality in city spaces, my entry, along with Mabalon's, Shah's, and Mai Der Vang's, moves away from the urban setting as it maps the rural as a space of global encounters. Our four entries insist on the undeniable place of Central Valley ("the Other California," as Gerald Haslam called it) on the world, specifically in the literary history of Asian Americans. Numerous leading Asian American literary artists hail from Central Valley, including Maxine Hong Kingston, Philip Kan Gotanda, and Janice Mirikitani.[14] In 2016, Mai Der Vang, from Fresno, became the first Hmong-American poet to receive the Walt Whitman Award from the Academy of American Poets. Despite the marginal depiction of Central Valley in popular representations of California, it always seems to be on the verge of discovery, of expansion, and of new invention.

California Dreaming of the World

Abraham Lowenthal writes,

> California has the power as well as the global links and interests of a nation. . . . Californians must understand our state's international connections, stakes, and impact. . . .
>
> California's size, scope, agricultural and industrial output; technological prowess; educational, research and philanthropic institutions; media power; trade-related infrastructure; and extensive international connections make possible a significant potential influence on many global issues. California's advanced telecommunications, computer equipment and software, multimedia, biomedical and environmental technology industries have enormous clout around the world, and affect national and international trends. Cinema, television, music and fashion from California shape values, worldviews and popular culture in a growing number of countries.[15]

California's influence on global imaginaries thus makes it imperative that Asian Americans shape, direct, and participate in how the idea of California circulates in the world. Rather than participate in the continuation of U.S. cultural imperialism, to what extent do Asian American California stories alter or intervene in U.S. cultural domination globally? Do Asian American writers have a responsibility to do so?

Complicating the question is the prediction of a much stronger Asia this century.[16] What role does or can Asian America take in these visions of the future currently being shaped in the present?[17] And what future do artistic expressions and practices assert?

This collection emphasizes the production of place as interactive, performative, and kinetic. The works within the collection do not fetishize the novelty of difference as they remain optimistic about and committed to the possibilities of the unknown through artistic expression and imagination. Twenty years ago, literary anthologies celebrated and marked California's diversity; today we face the question, Where are we now? No longer can we revel in simple declarations of diversity and multiplicity, faced as we are with the challenges of heightened inequality, limited resources, and uneven power relations, in addition to environmental disasters that threaten not only California's food sources but those of the world. We are at a moment of profound possibilities.

My co-editor Christine Balance suggests other analytics inspired by American Studies, postcolonial studies, and transnational media studies, considering what concepts from geoformations such as translocal, archipelago, and islands can bring to Asian American California imaginaries. California's horizon continues to beckon, and those who respond keep potential anew and dreaming alive. Together, the works in this collection explore what conditions of possibility exist that make meaning for Asian American arts today—and pave the way for what is yet to be.

Notes

1. Mina Yang, *California Polyphony: Ethnic Voices, Musical Crossroads* (Urbana-Champaign: University of Illinois Press, 2010).
2. Stephen Sumida, "East of California: Points of Origin in Asian American Studies," *Journal of Asian American Studies* 1:1 (1998), 86.
3. See Monica Chiu, *New England Asian American Studies: Culture and Community* (Durham: New Hampshire Press, 2009); Khyati Y. Joshi and Jigna Desai, eds., *Asian Americans in Dixie: Race and Migration in the South* (Urbana-Champaign: University of Illinois Press, 2013); Amy Bhatt and Nalini Iyer, eds., *Roots and Reflections: South Asians in the Pacific Northwest* (Seattle: University of Washington Press, 2013).
4. Peter Kiang, Lecture delivered at University of Massachusetts at Amherst, 1995.

5. Roberta Uno, "Introduction: Asian American Theater Awake at the Millennium" in *Bold Words,* Rajini Srikanth and Esther Iwanaga, eds. (New Brunswick: Rutgers University Press, 2000), 326–27.
6. Elaine Kim, *Asian American Literature: An Introduction to the Writings and Their Social Context* (Philadelphia: Temple University Press, 1982).
7. Angela Davis, "On Occupy," *Autumn Awakening: Reimagine: Movements Making Media* 18:2 (2011). http://reimaginerpe.org/18–2/davis.
8. Julie Chu, "To Be 'Emplaced': Fuzhounese Migration and the Politics of Destination," *Identities: Global Studies in Culture and Power* 13:3 (2006): 395–425.
9. Neloufer de Mel, *Militarizing Sri Lanka: Popular Culture, Memory, and Narrative in the Armed Conflict* (Los Angeles: Sage Publications, 2007).
10. William E. Justice, James Quay, and Chitra Banerjee Divakaruni, eds., *California Uncovered: Stories for the 21st Century* (Fresno: Heyday Books, 2004); Stan Yogi, *Highway 99: A Literary Journey Through California's Great Central Valley* (Fresno: Heyday Books, 1996); Gerald Haslam, *Many Californias: Literature from the Golden State* (Reno: University of Nevada Press, 1992).
11. Deborah Gee, *Slaying the Dragon* (1988; New York: Women Make Movies) DVD; Elaine Kim, *Slaying the Dragon: Reloaded* (2011; New York: Women Make Movies) DVD.
12. Edward Said, *Orientalism* (New York: Pantheon Books/Random House, 1978), 262.
13. Ursula Le Guin, "A Reading and Conversation with Molly Gloss." (Presentation, Annual Conference of the Association of Writers & Writing Programs, Seattle, WA. March 1, 2014.)
14. Gerald Haslam, *The Other California: The Great Central Valley in Life and Letters* (Reno, NV: University of Nevada Press, 1993).
15. Abraham Lowenthal, *Global California: Rising to the Cosmopolitan Challenge* (Palo Alto, CA: Stanford University Press, 2009), 8.
16. National Intelligence Council, "The Global Trends 2030: Alternative World's report, proclaiming the 21st Century as the rise of a much stronger Asia," last modified December 10, 2012. https://globaltrends2030.files.wordpress.com/2012/11/global-trends-2030-november2012.pdf.
17. Karen Tei Yamashita, "Anime Wong: Fiction, Science, Performance, and the Promises of the Future." (Lecture, UCLA, Los Angeles, CA, April 7, 2014.)

Bibliography

Aizura, Aren. "The Romance of the Amazing Scalpel: 'Race,' Labour and Affect in Thai Gender Reassignment Clinics." In *Queer Bangkok: Twenty-first Century Markets, Media and Rights,* edited by Peter Jackson. Aberdeen, Hong Kong: Hong Kong University Press, 2011.

Aron, Stephen. "The Making of the First American West and the Unmaking of Other Realms." In *A Companion to the American West,* edited by William Deverell. Boston: Blackwell Publishing, 2004.

Assisi, Francis. "The Hinduization of America," *Communalism Combat,* http://communalismcombat.blogspot.com/2005/06/hinduization-of-america-by-francis-c.html.

Bender, Daniel E., and Richard A. Greenwald, eds. *Sweatshop USA: The American Sweatshop in Historical and Global Perspective.* New York: Routledge, 2003.

Bennett, Andy, and Richard A. Peterson, eds. *Music Scenes: Local, Translocal, and Virtual.* Nashville: Vanderbilt University Press, 2004.

Bhatt, Amy, and Nalini Iyer, eds. *Roots and Reflections: South Asians in the Pacific Northwest.* Seattle, WA: University of Washington Press, 2013.

Boudreau, John. "Decades After Fleeing, Vietnamese American Filmmakers Return to a Changed Country." *San Jose Mercury News,* November 24, 2012. https://www.mercurynews.com/2012/11/09/decades-after-fleeing-vietnamese-american-filmmakers-return-to-a-changed-country/.

Boudreau, John, and Nguyen Dieu Tu Uyen, "Gay Weddings Planned as Vietnam Marriage Law Is Repealed." *Bloomberg,* January 7, 2015. https://www.bloomberg.com/news/articles/2015-01-07/gay-weddings-planned-as-vietnam-marriage-law-is-repealed.

Bourdieu, Pierre. *Distinction: A Social Critique of the Judgment of Taste.* Translated by Richard Nice. London: Routledge & Kegan Paul, 1984.

Boym, Svetlana. *The Future of Nostalgia.* New York: Basic Books, 2001.

Bradshaw, Carla. "Beauty and the Beast." In *Racially Mixed People in America,* edited by Maria P. P. Root, 77–88. Thousand Oaks, CA: SAGE Publications, 1992.

Campomanes, Oscar. "New Formations of Asian American Studies and the Question of U.S. Imperialism," *positions: asia critique* 5, no. 2 (1997): 523–550.

Carruthers, Ashley, and Boitran Huynh-Beattie, "Dark Tourism, Diasporic Memory, and Disappeared History." In *The Chinese-Vietnamese Diaspora: Revisiting the Boat People,* edited by Yuk Wah Chan, 332–349. New York: Routledge, 2011.

Choi, Richard. "Saigu: An Oral History." *KoreAm,* April 29, 2012, http://kore.am/april-issue-la-riots-in-our-own-words/.

Choy, Catherine Ceniza. *Empire of Care: Nursing and Migration in Filipino American History.* Durham: Duke University Press, 2003.

Chandler, David. *A History of Cambodia.* Boulder, CO: Westview Press, 1983.

Chang, Jeff. *Who We Be: A Cultural History of Race in Post-Civil Rights America.* New York: St. Martin's Press, 2014.

Chang, Richard. "More Protests Planned; Government Officials Want Images Removed." *The Orange County Register,* February 28, 2012. https://www.ocregister.com/2007/07/21/community-plans-protests-against-magazine-2/.

Chiu, Monica. *New England Asian American Studies: Culture and Community.* Lebanon, NH: New Hampshire Press, 2009.

Chu, Julie. "To Be 'Emplaced': Fuzhounese Migration and the Politics of Destination." *Identities: Global Studies in Culture and Power* 13, no. 3 (2006): 395–425.

Cornell, Daniel, and Mark Dean Johnson, eds. *Asian/American/Modern Art Shifting Currents, 1900–1970.* Berkeley: University of California Press, 2009.

Crouch, David. "Landscape, Land, and Identity: A Performative Consideration," *Spatial Practices* 13 (January 2012): 41–65.

Davis, Angela. "On Occupy." *Autumn Awakening: Reimagine: Movements Making Media* 18, no. 2 (2011): 76–77.

Deleuze, Gilles. *Francis Bacon: The Logic of Sensation.* Translated by Daniel W. Smith. London: Bloomsbury Academic, 1981.

de Mel, Neloufer. *Militarizing Sri Lanka: Popular Culture, Memory, and Narrative in the Armed Conflict.* Los Angeles: SAGE Publications, 2007.

Didion, Joan. *The White Album.* New York: Simon and Schuster, 1979.

Do, Tam Huu. "East Meets West: The Adaptation of Vietnamese International Students to California Community Colleges," *Journal of Southeast Asian American Education and Advancement* 2, no. 1 (2007): 1–29.

Duong, Lan. "Diasporic Returns and the Making of Vietnamese American Ghost Films in Vietnam," *MELUS* 41, no. 3 (2016): 153–170.

España-Maram, Linda. *Creating Masculinity in Los Angeles' Little Manila: Working-Class Filipinos and Popular Culture, 1920s-1950s*. New York: Columbia University Press, 2006.

Fong, Timothy. *The First Suburban Chinatown: The Remaking of Monterey Park, California*. Philadelphia: Temple University Press, 1994.

Foote, Stephanie. *Regional Fictions: Culture & Identity in Nineteenth-Century American Literature*. Madison, WI: University of Wisconsin Press, 2001.

Foucault, Michel. *Discipline and Punish: The Birth of the Prison*. Translated by Alan Sheridan. New York: Vintage Books, 1977.

Friday, Chris. "Where to Draw the Line?: The Pacific, Place, and U.S. West." In *A Companion to the American West*, edited by William Deverell, 271–285. Boston: Blackwell Publishing, 2004.

Florida, Richard. *The Rise of the Creative Class: And How It's Transforming Work, Leisure, and Everyday Life*. New York: Basic Books, 2002.

Fujita-Rony, Dorothy. *American Workers, Colonial Power: Philippine Seattle and the Transpacific West, 1919–1941*. Berkeley: University of California Press, 2003.

Gee, Deborah. *Slaying the Dragon*. Berkeley: Asian Women United, 1988.

Gilroy, Paul. "It Ain't Where You're from, It's Where You're At . . . : The Dialectics of Diasporic Identification," *Third Text* 5, no. 3 (Winter 1990–1991): 3–16.

Glissant, Edouard. *Poetics of Relation*. Ann Arbor, MI: University of Michigan Press, 1997.

Goldman, Danielle. *I Want to Be Ready!: Improvised Dance as a Practice of Freedom*. Ann Arbor, MI: University of Michigan Press, 2010.

Griffiths, Allison. "To the World the World We Show: Early Travelogues as Filmed Ethnography," *Film History* 11, no. 3 (1999): 282–307.

Grosz, Elizabeth. "Bodies-Cities." In *Feminist Theory and the Body: A Reader*, edited by Janet Price and Margrit Shildrick, 381–387. New York: Routledge, 1999.

Gyanendra, Pandey. *Routine Violence: Nations, Fragments, Histories*. Stanford, CA: Stanford University Press, 2005.

Haslam, Gerald. *Many Californias: Literature from the Golden State*. Reno, NV: University of Nevada Press, 1992.

———. *The Other California: The Great Central Valley in Life and Letters*. Reno, NV: University of Nevada Press, 1993.

Huynh-Beattie, Boitran. *Nam Bang!* Exhibition Catalogue. Casula, New South Wales: Casula Powerhouse, 2009.

Jonsson, Hjorleifur R., and Nora A. Taylor, "National Colors: Ethnic Minorities in Vietnamese Public Imagery." In *Re-Orienting Fashion: The*

Globalization of Asian Dress, edited by Sandra Niessen, Ann Marie Leshkowich, and Carla Jones, 159–184. Oxford: Berg, 2003.

Joseph, Miranda. *Against the Romance of Community*. Minneapolis, MN: University of Minnesota Press, 2002.

Joshi, Khyati Y., and Jigna Desai, eds. *Asian Americans in Dixie: Race and Migration in the South*. Urbana: University of Illinois Press, 2013.

Justice, William E., James Quay, and Chitra Banerjee Divakaruni, eds. *California Uncovered: Stories for the 21st Century*. Berkeley: Heyday Books, 2004.

Kauanui, J. Kehaulani. *Hawaiian Blood: Colonialism and the Politics of Sovereignty and Indigeneity*. Durham: Duke University Press, 2008.

Kee, Joan. "Introduction Contemporary Southeast Asian Art," *Third Text*, 25:4 (2011): 371–381.

Kim, Elaine. *Asian American Literature: An Introduction to the Writings and Their Social Context*. Philadelphia: Temple University Press, 1982.

———. "Defining Asian American Realities Through Literature." *Cultural Critique*, no. 6 (Spring 1987): 87–111.

———. "Home is Where the Han Is: a Korean American Perspective on the Los Angeles Upheavals." *Social Justice* 20, no. 1/2 (Summer 1993): 1–21.

Kim, Elaine, dir. *Slaying the Dragon: Reloaded*. Berkeley: Asian Women United, 2011.

Kim, Jay. "L.A. Riots," *Korea Times*, September 30, 2010, http://www.koreatimes.co.kr/www/news/include/print.asp?newsIdx=73767.

Korbin, Jill E. "Hana 'Ino: Child Maltreatment in a Hawaiian-American Community," *Pacific Studies* 3, no. 3 (July 1990): 7–22.

Lâm, Mariam Beevi, Fiona Ngô, and Mimi Nguyễn, eds. "Southeast Asian Studies Special Issue: Guest Editors' Introduction." *positions: asia critique* 20, no. 3 (2012): 671–684.

Lamb, Yvonne Shinhoster. "Public Broadcasting Official Lily Okura, 86; Mental Health Activist (Obituary)." *Washington Post*, July 3, 2005, https://www.washingtonpost.com/archive/local/2005/07/03/public-broadcasting-official-lily-okura-86/b7e46116-050b-4fc3-8801-307c6a478dec/.

Landauer, Susan. "Obata of the Thousand Bays." In *Obata's Yosemite: The Art and Letters of Chiura Obata and His Trip to the High Sierra in 1927*, 18–45. Yosemite: Yosemite Association, 1993.

Landeza, Patrick Kahakauwila Kamaholelani. "How Would You Feel?" YouTube, published on February 28, 2012, http://www.youtube.com/watch?v=R40kRHOJS4I&feature=related.

Lee, Jay. "Saigu: An Oral History," *KoreAm*, April 29, 2012, http://kore.am/april-issue-la-riots-in-our-own-words/.

Lee, Namhee. *The Making of Minjung: Democracy and the Politics of Representation in South Korea*. Ithaca, NY: Cornell University Press, 2007.

Lee, Seung-Ook, Sook-Jin Kim, and Joel Wainwright. "Mad Cow Militancy: Neoliberal Hegemony and Social Resistance in South Korea," *Political Geography* (2010), http://citeseerx.ist.psu.edu/viewdoc/download?doi=10.1.1.461.8977&rep=rep1&type=pdf.

Le Guin, Ursula. "A Reading and Conversation with Molly Gloss." Presentation at the Annual Conference of the Association of Writers & Writing Programs, Seattle, WA. March 1, 2014.

Li, Wei. "Building Ethnoburbia: The Emergence and Manifestation of the Chinese Ethnoburb in Los Angeles' San Gabriel Valley," *Journal of Asian American Studies* 2.1 (1999): 1–28.

Li, Wei, Gary Dymski, Yu Zhou, Maria Chee, and Carolyn Aldana. "Chinese-American Banking and Community Development in Los Angeles County," *Annals of the Association of American Geographers* 92, no. 4 (2002): 777–796.

Lionnet, Françoise, and Shu-Mei Shih, "Introduction: Thinking through the Minor, Transnationally." In *Minor Transnationalism*, edited by Shu-Mei Shih and Francoise Lionnet, 1–24. Durham: Duke University Press, 2005.

Lipsitz, George. *How Racism Takes Place.* Philadelphia: Temple University Press, 2011.

Lowe, Lisa. *Immigrant Acts: On Asian American Cultural Politics.* Durham: Duke University Press, 1996.

Lowenthal, Abraham. *Global California: Rising to the Cosmopolitan Challenge.* Palo Alto, CA: Stanford University Press, 2009.

Mabalon, Dawn Bohulano. *Little Manila Is in the Heart: The Making of the Filipina/o American Community in Stockton.* Durham: Duke University Press, 2014.

Maeda, Daryl. *Chains of Babylon: The Rise of Asian America.* Minneapolis, MN: University of Minnesota Press, 2009.

Manalansan, Martin F. "Diasporic Deviants/Divas: How Filipino Gay Transmigrants 'Play with the World." In *Queer Diasporas*, Cindy Patton and Benigno Sanchez Eppler, 183–203. Durham: Duke University Press, 2000.

———. "The "Stuff" of Archives: Mess, Migration, and Queer Lives." *Radical History Review* 120 (2014): 94–107.

Mankekar, Purnima. *Unsettling India: Affect, Temporality, Transnationality.* Durham: Duke University Press, 2015.

Maresca, Thomas. "Vietnam: Flawed on Human Rights, but a Leader in Gay Rights." *The Atlantic*, April 30, 2013, https://www.theatlantic.com/international/archive/2013/04/vietnam-flawed-on-human-rights-but-a-leader-in-gay-rights/275413/.

McKay, Deirdre. "Translocal Circulation: Place and Subjectivity in an Extended Filipino Community," *The Asia Pacific Journal of Anthropology* 7, no. 3 (2006): 265–278.

Meining, D. W., ed. *The Interpretation of Ordinary Landscapes*. New York: Oxford University Press, 1979.

Merritt, Christopher, Gary Weisz, and Kelly J. Dixon, "'Verily the Road Was Built with Chinaman's Bones'; An Archaeology of Chinese Line Camps in Montana." *International Journal of Historical Archaeology* 16, no. 4 (December 2012): 666–695.

Mirchandani, Kiran. *Phone Clones: Authenticity Work in the Transnational Service Economy*. Ithaca, NY: Cornell University Press, 2012.

Moon, Seungsook. *Militarized Modernity and Gendered Citizenship in South Korea*. Durham: Duke University Press, 2005.

Mootoo, Shani. *A Paddle and Compass*. (DVD). Vancouver, BC: Video Out Distribution, 1992.

———. *The Wild Woman in the Woods*. (DVD). Vancouver, BC: Video Out Distribution, 1993.

Mydans, Seth. "Activists Convicted in Vietnam Crackdown on Dissent." *The New York Times,* January 9, 2013, https://www.nytimes.com/2013/01/10/world/asia/activists-convicted-in-vietnam-crackdown-on-dissent.html.

Nancy, Jean-Luc. *The Inoperative Community*. Chicago: University of Minnesota Press, 1991.

Narayanan, Vasudha. "Hinduism in Southeast Asia," *Encyclopedia of Religion*. https://www.encyclopedia.com/environment/encyclopedias-almanacs-transcripts-and-maps/hinduism-southeast-asia.

Needham, Susan Anne, and Karen I. Quintiliani. *Cambodians in Long Beach*. Charleston, SC: Arcadia Publishing, 2008.

Nguyen, Jennifer. "CSUF Creates First Vietnamese Program," *Daily Titan,* February 26, 2013, https://dailytitan.com/2013/02/new-major/.

Nguyen, Mimi, and Thuy Linh Tu. "Introduction." In *Alien Encounters: Popular Culture in Asian America,* edited by Mimi Nguyen and Thuy Linh Tu, 1–32. Durham: Duke University Press, 2007.

Nguyen, Thu-Huong, and Brian King. "Migrant Communities and Tourism Consumption: The Case of the Vietnamese in Australia." In *Tourism and Migration: New Relationships between Production and Consumption,* edited by Michael Hall, 221–240. Boston: Kluwer Academic Publishers, 2002.

Nguyễn, Việt Thanh. "Refugee Memories and Asian American Critique." *positions: asia critique* 20, no. 3 (2012): 911–942.

Norindr, Panivong. "Enlisting Early Cinema in the Service of 'La Grande France,'" in *Early Cinema and the National,* edited by Richard Abel, Giorgio Bertellini, and Rob King, 109–117. New Barnet, UK: John Libbey Publishing Ltd., 2008.

Obata, Chiura. *Obata's Yosemite: The Art and Letters of Chiura Obata and His Trip to the High Sierra in 1927*. Yosemite: Yosemite Conservancy, 1993.

Ong, Aihwa. *Neoliberalism as Exception: Mutations in Citizenship and Sovereignty*. Durham: Duke University Press, 2006.

Park, Jung-Sun. "Korean American Youth and Transnational Flows of Popular Culture Across the Pacific." In *Transpop: Korea Vietnam Remix*, edited by Viet Le and Yong Soon Min, 109–117. Seoul: Arko Arts Center/Arts Council Korea, 2008.

Perry, Charles, and Linda Burum. "Real Fireworks." *Los Angeles Times*, January 26, 2005, https://www.latimes.com/archives/la-xpm-2005-jan-26-fo-dimsum26-story.html.

Pugh, Jonathan. "Island Movements: Thinking with the Archipelago," *Island Studies Journal* 8, no. 1 (2013): 9–24.

Pulido, Laura, Laura Barraclough, and Wendy Cheng. *A People's Guide to Los Angeles*. Berkeley: University of California Press, 2012.

Roberts, Brian Russell, and Michelle Ann Stephens, eds. *Archipelagic American Studies*. Durham: Duke University Press, 2017.

Roediger, David. *Working Toward Whiteness: How America's Immigrants Became White: The Strange Journey from Ellis Island to the Suburbs*. New York: Basic Books, 2003.

Rohrer, Judy. *Haoles in Hawai'i*. Honolulu: University of Hawai'i Press, 2010.

Romero, Dennis. "See a Map of Korean Businesses Targeted During L.A. Riots 20 Years Ago." *L.A. Weekly*, April 24, 2012, https://www.laweekly.com/news/see-a-map-of-korean-businesses-targeted-during-la-riots-20-years-ago-2386976.

Roth, Moira. "Traveling Companions/Fractured Worlds," *Art Journal* (1999): 82–93.

Said, Edward. *Orientalism*. New York: Pantheon Books/Random House, 1978.

Saito, Leland. *Race and Politics: Asian Americans, Whites, and Latinos in a Los Angeles Suburb*. Urbana: University of Illinois Press, 1998.

Sampson, Mike. "Humaliwo: Where the Surf Sounds Loudly." *California Department of Parks and Recreation*, accessed May 2012, https://www.parks.ca.gov/?page_id=24435.

Saxton, Alexander. *The Indispensable Enemy: Labor and the Anti-Chinese Movement in California*. Berkeley: University of California Press, 1971.

Schein, Richard. "Normative Dimensions of Landscape." In *Everyday America: Cultural Landscape Studies after J. B. Jackson*, edited by Chris Wilson and Paul Groth, 189–218. Berkeley: University of California Press, 2003.

Sedgwick, Eve. "Paranoid Reading and Reparative Reading: Or, You're So Paranoid You Probably Think This Essay's About You." In *Touching Feeling: Affect, Pedagogy, Performativity*, 123–151. Durham: Duke University Press, 2003.

Sennett, Richard. *Flesh and Stone: The Body and the City in Western Civilization.* New York: W. W. Norton & Company, 1996.

Sheller, Mimi, and John Urry. "The New Mobilities Paradigm." Special issue, *Environment and Planning A* 38, no. 2 (2006): 207–226.

Shilpa, Dave, Leilani Nishime, and Tasha Oren, eds. *Global Asian American Popular Cultures.* New York: NYU Press, 2016.

Sidel, Mark. *Vietnamese-American Diaspora Philanthropy to Vietnam.* Report, Harvard University, 2007.

Smithsonian Program for Asian American Studies, "On Gold Mountain: A Chinese American Experience," http://apa.si.edu/ongoldmountain/gallery2/gallery2.html.

Sohn, Stephen. "These Desert Places: Tourism, the American West, and the Afterlife of Regionalism in Julie Otsuka's When the Emperor Was Divine," *MFS: Modern Fiction Studies* 55, no. 1 (March 2009): 163–188.

Solnit, Rebecca. "California as an Island," *BOOM: A Journal of California Studies* 14, no. 1 (Spring 2014), accessed July 20, 2018, https://boomcalifornia.com/2014/03/25/california-as-an-island/.

Song, Jason. "USC Has Second Most Foreign Students in the Nation, Again," *Los Angeles Times,* November 16, 2015, https://www.latimes.com/local/lanow/la-me-ln-usc-second-most-foreign-students-20151116-story.html.

Song, Min Hyoung. *Strange Future: Pessimism and the 1992 Los Angeles Riots.* Durham: Duke University Press, 2005.

Staeheli, Lynn A., and Don Mitchell. "USA's Destiny? Regulating Space and Creating Community in American Shopping Malls," *Urban Studies* 43, no. 5–6 (May 2006): 977–992.

Su, Julie A., and Chanchanit Martorell. "Exploitation and Abuse in the Garment Industry: The Case of the Thai Slave-Labor Compound in El Monte." In *Asian and Latino Immigrants in a Restructuring Economy: The Metamorphosis of Southern California,* edited by Marta López-Garza and David R. Diaz, 21–45. Stanford: Stanford University Press, 2001.

Sudden Rush. *Ku'e!!* Way Out West, 1997.

Sumida, Stephen. "East of California: Points of Origin in Asian American Studies," *Journal of Asian American Studies* 1, no. 1 (1998): 83–100.

Tachiki, Amy, Eddie Wong, Franklin Odo, and Buck Wong, eds. *Roots: an Asian American Reader.* Los Angeles: UCLA Asian American Studies Center, 1971.

Tatar, Elizabeth. "Slack Key Guitar." In *Hawaiian Music and Musicians: An Illustrated History,* edited by George S. Kanahele, 350–360. Honolulu: University of Hawai'i Press, 1979.

Taylor, Nora, and Boreth Ly, eds. *Modern and Contemporary Southeast Asian Art: An Anthology.* Ithaca, NY: Cornell University Press, 2011.

Taylor, Philip. "Introduction: An Overture to New Ethnographic Research on Connection and Disconnection in Vietnam." In *Connected and Disconnected in Viet Nam: Remaking Social Relations in a Post-Socialist Nation,* edited by Philip Taylor, 1–40. Acton: The Australian National University, 2016.

Tran, My-Thuan. "Vietnamese Americans Protest Published Photo." *Los Angeles Times,* May 2, 2012, https://www.latimes.com/archives/la-xpm-2008-feb-12-me-protest12-story.html.

Trask, Hauanani-Kay. "Coalition-Building Between Natives and Non-Natives." *Stanford Law Review* 43, no. 6 (July 1991): 1197–1213.

Uno, Roberta. "Introduction: Asian American Theater Awake at the Millennium." in *Bold Words,* edited by Rajini Srikanth and Esther Iwanaga, 323–332. New Brunswick, NJ: Rutgers University Press, 2000.

Urry, John, and Jonas Larsen. *The Tourist Gaze 3.0.* London: Sage, 2011.

Vazquez, Alexandra. "Salon Philosophers: Ivy Queen and Surprise Guests Take Reggaeton Aside." In *Reggaeton,* edited by Deborah Pacini-Hernandez, Wayne Marshall, and Raquel Z. Rivera, 300–311. Durham: Duke University Press, 2009.

Watanabe, Teresa. "Huntington Library's Newest Garden Celebrates Chinese Culture." *Los Angeles Times,* February 17, 2008, https://www.latimes.com/local/la-me-gardens17feb17-story.html.

Wei, William. *The Asian American Movement.* Philadelphia, PA: Temple University Press, 1993.

Wong, Julia Carrie. "The Complicity Cost of Racial Inclusion." *Al Jazeera.com,* August 24, 2014, http://america.aljazeera.com/opinions/2014/8/asian-americans-racecomplicitymodelminority.html?utm_content=opinion&utm_campaign=ajam&utm_source=twitter&utm_medium=SocialFlow.

Xia, Rosanna. "Number of International Students in U.S. Colleges at an All-Time High, and California is their Top Destination," *Los Angeles Times,* November 25, 2016, https://www.latimes.com/local/lanow/la-me-study-abroad-students-20161124-story.html.

Yamashita, Karen. "Anime Wong: Fiction, Science, Performance, and the Promises of the Future." Lecture, University of California at Los Angeles, April 7, 2014.

Yang, Alice, Jonathan Hay, and Mimi Young, eds. *Why Asia? Contemporary Asian and Asian American Art.* New York: New York University Press, 1998.

Yang, Mina. *California Polyphony: Ethnic Voices, Musical Crossroads.* Urbana: University of Illinois Press, 2010.

Yogi, Stan. *Highway 99: A Literary Journey through California's Great Central Valley.* Berkeley: Heyday Books, 1996.

Contributors

Christine Bacareza Balance is associate professor of Asian American Studies at Cornell University and author of the award-winning *Tropical Renditions: Making Musical Scenes in Filipino America.*

Tracy Lachica Buenavista is professor of Asian American Studies and a core faculty member in the Educational Leadership doctoral program at California State University, Northridge.

Lucy Mae San Pablo Burns is associate professor of Asian American Studies at the University of California, Los Angeles, and the author of *Puro Arte: Filipinos on the Stages of Empire.*

Leilani Chan is founding artistic director of TeAda Productions, a nomadic theater of color. Devised ensemble plays include *Masters of the Currents, Global Taxi Driver,* and *Refugee Nation.*

Wendy Cheng is associate professor of American Studies at Scripps College. She is author of *The Changs Next Door to the Díazes: Remapping Race in Suburban California.*

D'Lo is a queer, transgender Tamil-Sri Lankan-American actor/writer/comedian whose writing range includes short story, poetry, plays, solo theater, and stand-up comedy. His solo shows have toured internationally. His website is dlocokid.com.

Lan Duong is associate professor in cinema and media studies at the University of Southern California and author of *Treacherous Subjects: Gender, Culture, and Trans-Vietnamese Feminism.*

Kevin Fellezs is associate professor of music and African-American and African diaspora studies at Columbia University and the author of *Birds of Fire: Jazz, Rock, Funk and the Creation of Fusion.*

Prince Gomolvilas's plays include *Big Hunk o' Burnin' Love, The Theory of Everything,* and *The Brothers Paranormal.* He won the PEN Center USA Literary Award for Drama. His website is www.princegomolvilas.com.

Raymundo M. Hernandez-Lopez is an artist and cofounder of the Im: Arte collective. Hernandez-Lopez seeks to create awareness of social justice, empower communities, and devise a new methodology of political action with his art-making.

Philip Huang founded Dana Street Theater, a queer performance space based out of his bedroom, and The (International) Home Theater Festival, which encourages artists to put on shows in their own homes. He is the author of *A Pornography of Grief.*

Robert Farid Karimi created *Self (the Remix), Farid Mercury,* and the film *Lumpia Campesina.* Karimi's *The People's Cook* is a culinary cultural engagement project using comedy, culture, and food to make healthy messaging delicious.

SanSan Kwan is associate professor in dance and performance studies at the University of California, Berkeley and author of *Kinesthetic City: Dance and Movement in Chinese Urban Spaces* and *Love Dances: Loss and Mourning in Intercultural Collaboration* (forthcoming).

Việt Lê is associate professor in visual studies at California College of the Arts. Lê's writings have appeared in *positions, American Quarterly, Amerasia Journal, Strange Cargo,* and *Modern and Contemporary Southeast Asian Art.*

Joyce Lu is associate professor in the department of theater and dance at Pomona College. She performs, writes, and directs, and is currently starting a Playback Theater Company in Los Angeles.

Tiffany Lytle is a singer/songwriter and performing artist. Her *Cambodian Child* (EP) was released in 2017. She is currently a doctoral student in the department of theater and dance studies at UC Santa Barbara.

Dawn Bohulano Mabalon (1972–2018) was born and raised in Stockton, California. She was associate professor of history at San Francisco State University and author of *Little Manila Is in the Heart: The Making of the Filipina/o American Community in Stockton, California.*

Dan Taulapapa McMullin is author of *Coconut Milk,* a book of poetry included on the American Library Association Rainbow List's Top Ten Books of the Year. He is coeditor of *Samoan Queer Lives* with Yuki Kihara.

Yong Soon Min is professor emerita of art at UC Irvine. Notable exhibitions include the 7th Gwangju Biennale, 3rd Guangzhou Triennial, 10th Havana Biennale, and her archive in the Art Culture Center in Gwangju, Korea.

Gina Osterloh is assistant professor of art at Ohio State University. Her work is represented by Silverlens (Manila), Higher Pictures (New York), and Ghebaly Gallery (Los Angeles).

Laurence Angeleo Padua works in public health. Writings include "The Lord/The Cat" (with Mena Kamel) in *A Night at the Opera with Hosni Mubarak, Hosted by Dave Eggers.*

Jason Magabo Perez is assistant professor of English and creative writing at California State University, San Bernardino and the author of *Phenomenology of Superhero* and *This is for the mostless.*

Nayan Shah is professor of American studies and ethnicity and history at USC and author of *Contagious Divides* (2001) and *Stranger Intimacy* (2012).

Ova Saopeng performs and teaches for and is associate artistic director of TeAda Productions. Her recent social justice–driven theater project *Masters of the Currents* explores climate refugees from Micronesia.

Priya Srinivasan is a Melbourne-based scholar/artist exploring feminist decolonizing practices through live art, visual art, and interactive multimedia. She is the author of *Sweating Saris: Indian Dance as Transnational Labor.*

Mai Der Vang is assistant professor of English in creative writing at California State University Fresno, and the author of *Afterland* (Graywolf Press, 2017). She was the recipient of the 2016 Walt Whitman Award.

Kristina Wong is a performance artist, comedian, and writer, as well as the elected representative of Wilshire Center Koreatown Sub-district 5 Neighborhood Council. Appearances include American Public Media's *Marketplace,* PBS, *VICE,* Jezebel, *Playgirl Magazine,* Huffington Post, and CNN.

Karen Tei Yamashita is a writer. Her books include *Tropic of Orange, Circle K Cycles, I Hotel, Anime Wong: Fictions of Performance,* and *Letters to Memory.*

INTERSECTIONS

Asian and Pacific American Transcultural Studies

RUSSELL C. LEONG AND DAVID K. YOO
Series Editors

Bulletproof Buddhists and Other Essays
FRANK CHIN

A Ricepaper Airplane
GARY PAK

New Spiritual Homes: Religion and Asian Americans
DAVID K. YOO, ED.

Words Matter: Conversations with Asian American Writers
KING-KOK CHEUNG, ED.

Music through the Dark: A Tale of Survival in Cambodia
BREE LAFRENIERE

Blues and Greens: A Produce Worker's Journal
ALAN CHONG LAU

Tomorrow's Memories: A Diary, 1924–1928
ANGELES MONRAYO
RIZALINE R. RAYMUNDO, ED.

Fighting Tradition: A Marine's Journey to Justice
CAPTAIN BRUCE I. YAMASHITA, USMCR

The 1.5 Generation: Becoming Korean American in Hawai'i
MARY YU DANICO

This Isn't a Picture I'm Holding: Kuan Yin
KATHY J. PHILLIPS
JOSEPH SINGER, PHOTOGRAPHER

Sparrows, Bedbugs, and Body Shadows: A Memoir
SHELDON LOU

Entrys
PETER BACHO

What Is Asian American Biblical Hermeneutics?: Reading the New Testament
TAT-SIONG BENNY LIEW

The New Sun
TARO YASHIMA

Hakka Soul: Memories, Migrations, Meals
CHIN WOON PING

A Japanese Robinson Crusoe
JENICHIRO OYABE

Rosebud and Other Stories
WAKAKO YAMAUCHI
LILLIAN HOWAN, ED.

The Dance of Identities: Korean Adoptees and Their Journey toward Empowerment
JOHN D. PALMER

From Okinawa to the Americas: Hana Yamagawa and Her Reminiscences of a Century
AKIKO YAMAGAWA HIBBETT, ED.

Transforming the Ivory Tower: Challenging Racism, Sexism, and Homophobia in the Academy
BRETT C. STOCKDILL AND MARY YU DANICO, EDS.

Ancestry of Experience: A Journey into Hawaiian Ways of Knowing
LEILANI HOLMES

Scrutinized!: Surveillance in Asian North American Literature
MONICA CHIU

Encountering Modernity: Christianity in East Asia and Asian America
ALBERT L. PARK AND DAVID K. YOO, EDS.

Transpacific Studies: Framing an Emerging Field
JANET HOSKINS AND VIET THANH NGUYEN, EDS.

Out of the Dust: New and Selected Poems
JANICE MIRIKITANI

Romancing Human Rights: Gender, Intimacy, and Power between Burma and the West
TAMARA C. HO

The Blind Writer: Stories and a Novella
SAMEER PANDYA

Ship of Fate: Memoir of a Vietnamese Repatriate
TRẦN ĐÌNH TRỤ
BAC HOAI TRAN AND JANA K. LIPMAN, TRANS.

Freedom without Justice: The Prison Memoirs of Chol Soo Lee
CHOL SOO LEE
RICHARD S. KIM, ED.

Tadaima! *I Am Home: A Transnational Family History*
TOM COFFMAN